EDGE
BOOKS™

THE KIDS' GUIDE TO

the Constellations

by Christopher Forest

Consultant:
Karen Vanlandingham
Department of Geology & Astronomy
Associate Professor, West Chester University
West Chester, Pennsylvania

CAPSTONE PRESS
a capstone imprint

Edge Books are published by Capstone Press,
1710 Roe Crest Drive, North Mankato, Minnesota 56003.
www.capstonepub.com

 Books published by Capstone Press are manufactured with paper
containing at least 10 percent post-consumer waste.

Library of Congress Cataloging-in-Publication Data
Forest, Christopher.
   The kids' guide to the constellations / by Christopher Forest.
   p. cm. — (Edge. Kids' guides)
   Includes bibliographical references and index.
   Summary: "Describes various constellations, including the myths surrounding
them and how to locate them in the night sky"—Provided by publisher.
   ISBN 978-1-4296-6007-5 (library binding)
1. Constellations—Juvenile literature. I. Title. II. Series.
QB802.F67 2012
523.8—dc22   2011002487

Editorial Credits
Mandy Robbins, editor; Kyle Grenz, designer; Wanda Winch, media researcher;
   Eric Manske, production specialist

Photo Credits
Constellation images from Firmamentum Sobiescianum sive Uranographia by
Johannes Hevelius, courtesy of the United State Naval Observatory and the
Space Telescope Science Institute's Office of Public Outreach, 10 (top), 11 (middle
drawing), 12 (top), 13 (middle drawing), 14 (top), 15 (middle drawing), 16 (top),
17 (middle drawing), 18 (top), 19 (bottom drawing), 20 (top), 21 (middle drawing),
22 (top), 23 (bottom drawing), 26 (top), 27 (bottom drawing); Dreamstime: Igor
Sokalski, 6 (bottom), 7 (bottom starfield), 8 (bottom), 9 (middle starfield), 10
(bottom), 11 (middle starfield), 12 (bottom), 13 (middle starfield), 14 (bottom),
15 (middle starfield), 16 (bottom), 17 (middle starfield), 18 (bottom), 19 (bottom
starfield), 20 (bottom), 21 (middle starfield), 22 (bottom), 23 (bottom starfield),
24 (bottom), 25 (bottom starfield), 26 (bottom), 27 (bottom starfield), Photohare,
cover (telescope); iStockphoto: Brett Lamb, cover (Orion constellation), Clifford
Mueller, 4, David Bukach, 28, 29, Sertii Tsololo, cover (nebula); NASA: JPL-
Caltech/UCLA, 11 (bottom), Nova Development Corp., telescope design;
Shutterstock: Albert Barr, 15 (bottom), alin b., space design used as background,
Chyrko Olena, 9 (bottom), LilKar, cover background, Mike Norton, 13 (bottom),
More Similar Images, 24 (top left), 25 (middle drawing), Thomas M. Perkins, 21
(bottom), Verbanika, 17 (bottom); Wikipedia: Scott Foresman Pearson, 6 (top),
7 (bottom drawing), 8 (top), 9 (middle drawing); www.pixheaven.net: Laurent
Laveder, 5

Printed in the United States of America in North Mankato, Minnesota.
052012   006767R

Table of Contents

A Brilliant Display

The night sky is filled with amazing sights. The appearance of the moon changes every 29.5 days. **Comets** and **meteors** race across the sky. And stars light up the night with brilliance.

For as long as humans have lived, the night sky has fascinated them. But thousands of years ago, stars were a mystery. Without scientific knowledge, people didn't know what stars were. They would never have believed these small twinkling lights were really giant balls of burning gas.

comet—a ball of rock and ice that circles the Sun

meteor—a piece of rock or dust that enters Earth's atmosphere, causing a streak of light in the sky

In ancient times, many people thought stars represented gods and goddesses. They made up stories about the star patterns, or constellations. People also noticed that the patterns moved throughout the year.

Stars are no longer a mystery. By 1930 scientists had identified all 88 constellations. With practice, you can find constellations in no time.

The Big Dipper

The Big Dipper is a group of seven stars in the northern sky. Knowing its location can help stargazers locate other stars.

The Big Dipper is not a true constellation. It is an **asterism**. The Big Dipper is part of a larger constellation called Ursa Major. Ursa Major means "the Great Bear."

GAZING GUIDE

Look in the northern sky for seven stars. The first three stars look like a spoon handle. The other four stars form a square dipper.

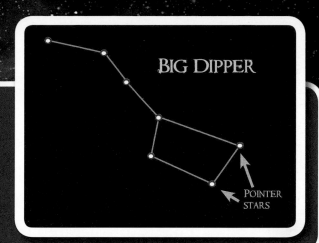

BIG DIPPER

POINTER STARS

Stellar Fact

The two stars at the edge of the dipper are called pointer stars. Star gazers use them to find other constellations.

According to Greek **mythology**, this big bear had once been a woman named Callisto. The Greek god Zeus fell in love with Callisto. But Zeus had a problem. He was already married to Hera. Jealous, Hera turned Callisto into a bear. Then Zeus placed her body in the night sky.

asterism—a group of stars that form a separate shape that is part of a larger constellation

mythology—a collection of myths

The Little Dipper

The Little Dipper is also made of seven stars. The star at the end of the dipper is Polaris, or the **North Star**. The Little Dipper seems to **revolve** around the North Star throughout the year.

The Little Dipper is also an asterism. It is part of Ursa Minor, which means "Little Bear." According to Greek mythology, the little bear was Callisto's son. He was turned into a bear and placed into the sky to be with his mother.

North Star—the star in the northern sky located directly over the North Pole

revolve—to move in a circle around another object

GAZING GUIDE

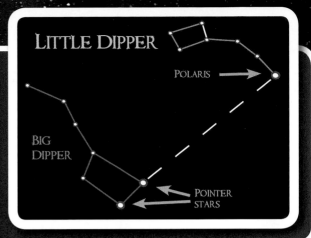

First locate the pointer stars of the Big Dipper. Follow the line of the stars to the next bright star. This is Polaris. Start there and follow down the handle to see the rest of the Little Dipper.

LITTLE DIPPER

POLARIS →

BIG DIPPER

POINTER STARS

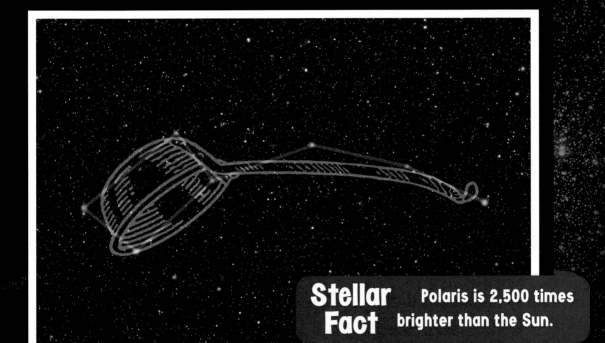

Stellar Fact Polaris is 2,500 times brighter than the Sun.

A Map of the Stars

Hundreds of years ago, sailors used the stars to help guide them across the ocean. They looked for the North Star to help them find which direction was north. They used the position of constellations to figure out where to sail. They also learned that the Big Dipper traveled around the North Pole once every 24 hours. Sailors used the Big Dipper to tell time.

Cassiopeia

Cassiopeia is named for a queen in Greek mythology. She bragged about her beauty and angered Poseidon, the god of the seas. When Cassiopeia died, Poseidon flung her into the sky.

Cassiopeia can be seen in the northern sky. The constellation has five main stars that form a tilted "W." It is said to show Cassiopeia sitting on her throne.

Follow the pointer stars in the Big Dipper past Polaris. Look for a tilted "W." The direction of the tilt will depend on the time of year.

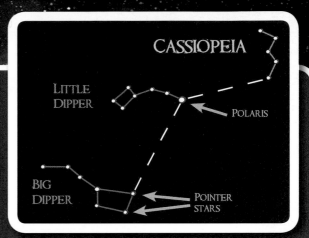

CASSIOPEIA

LITTLE DIPPER

POLARIS

BIG DIPPER

POINTER STARS

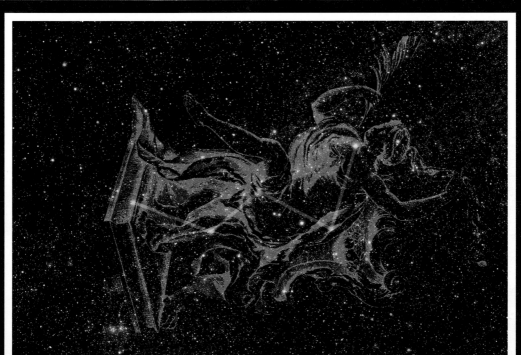

The Bright Lights of Cassiopeia

In 1572 and 1680, **novas** appeared close to Cassiopeia. The nova in 1572 became brighter than the planet Venus in the night sky. Scientists believe both novas actually occurred 9,700 years before they were seen. It took that long for the light from the novas to reach Earth.

nova—a star that becomes suddenly brighter

Cepheus

Cepheus is a constellation in the northern sky. According to Greek mythology, Cepheus was the king of Ethiopia. He was married to Cassiopeia.

The constellation Cepheus is made up of many stars. But only five are easy to see. These five stars create a constellation that looks like a square house with a triangular roof.

Look about one-third of the way between Polaris and Cassiopeia. The top star of Cepheus, named Errai, is located there. It marks the peak of the triangle shape.

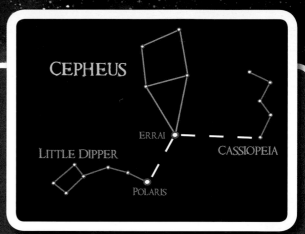

CEPHEUS

LITTLE DIPPER

ERRAI

CASSIOPEIA

POLARIS

Pointing North

Over time, the Earth wobbles as it spins. Because of this wobble, the North Star changes every few thousand years. Right now Polaris is the North Star. In the next 5,000 years, Errai will become the North Star.

Andromeda

Andromeda was a princess in Greek mythology. Her mother, Cassiopeia, angered the Greek god Poseidon. To punish Cassiopeia, Poseidon chained Andromeda to a rock along a shore. A brave warrior named Perseus rescued her before she was devoured by a sea monster.

Andromeda is a small V–shaped constellation in the northern sky. It is made up of seven main stars. The bright star at the point of the "V" is Alpheratz. It represents Andromeda's head.

GAZING GUIDE

First, find Cassiopeia. Locate the bottom of her throne. Follow an arc from the back star at the bottom of the throne to a V-shaped constellation. This is Andromeda.

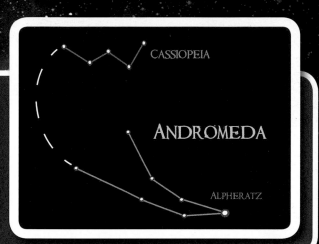

CASSIOPEIA

ANDROMEDA

ALPHERATZ

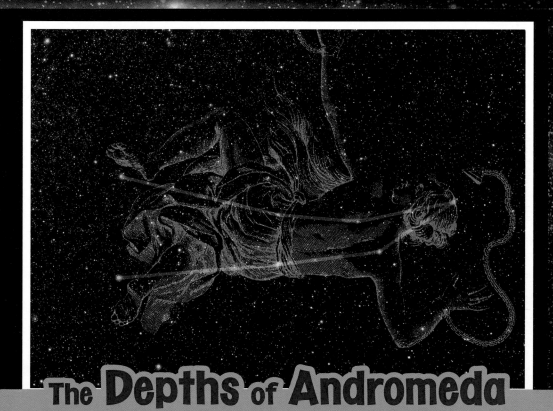

The Depths of Andromeda

Look at the region between Andromeda and Cassiopeia. You will see a small cluster of stars. This tiny cluster is another **galaxy**. The Andromeda Galaxy is twice as big as our own galaxy, the Milky Way.

galaxy—a large group of stars, plantets, dust, and gas

Orion

The constellation Orion is named for a Greek hero. According to a myth, he was a hunter who was killed by a scorpion. The gods later hung his body in the sky.

Stellar Fact The star Betelgeuse represents Orion's shoulder. *Betelgeuse* is an Arabic word meaning "Armpit of the Giant."

Orion is one of the most recognized constellations in the sky. It can be seen in both the northern and southern skies. Orion's three brightest stars form his belt. To the left, above the belt, is Betelgeuse. Other stars form his shield. Orion has a sword hanging from his belt. The sword is represented by the Orion **nebula**.

nebula—a cloud of dust or gas in space

Look south if you're in the northern **hemisphere** or north if you're in the southern hemisphere. Spot three bright stars in a row. This is Orion's belt. From there you can spot the rest of the constellation.

ORION

BETELGEUSE

ORION'S BELT

THE ORION NEBULA

Are all stars white?

Stars look white from Earth, but they are actually different colors. A star's color depends on its temperature. Blue stars are the hottest. Their surfaces can be 18,000 degrees Fahrenheit (9,982 degrees Celsius). Red stars are the coolest. Their surfaces can be about 5,500°F (3,038°C). The Sun is a yellow star. Its surface is about 10,000°F (5,538°C).

hemisphere—one half of Earth

Canis Major

Canis Major was an important constellation to the ancient Egyptians. They used the stars as a type of calendar. The Egyptians lived near the Nile River, which flooded each year. Canis Major appeared high in the sky at the same time of year as the flooding. By watching the constellation, the Egyptians could prepare for a flood.

Canis Major appears close to the Orion constellation. Its name is Latin for "Big Dog." It represents Orion's dog. In mythology, Canis Major helped Orion hunt.

GAZING GUIDE

Locate the Orion constellation. The stars in Orion's belt point to Sirius. From there, you can spot the rest of Canis Major.

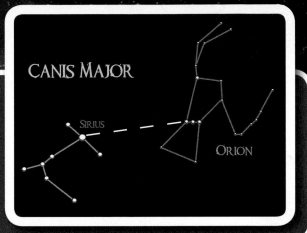

CANIS MAJOR

SIRIUS

ORION

Canis Major can be seen in both the northern and southern skies. Canis Major consists of eight main stars. The brightest star, Sirius, marks the nose of the dog. It is called the Dog Star.

Leo

The constellation Leo is represented by a lion. This constellation was probably named by the ancient Egyptians. The sun rose in the sky through Leo when the Nile River flooded. At the same time, lions appeared more often in the Nile River Valley.

Leo is a well-known **zodiac** sign seen in the northern sky. The stars in Leo form two recognizable shapes—a **sickle** and a triangle. The sickle represents the head of Leo. The triangle is the hind legs and tail.

zodiac—a belt in the sky that includes the path of the Sun, Moon, and planets; 13 constellations make up the zodiac

sickle—an arc-shaped blade used to cut grass or crops

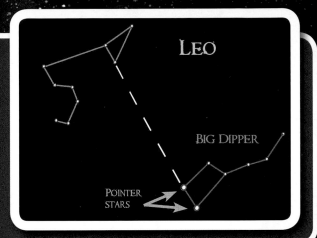

Locate the pointer stars of the Big Dipper. Follow them in the opposite direction of the North Star. You will find a group of stars that look like a triangle. The sickle is on the other end of the constellation.

LEO

BIG DIPPER

POINTER STARS

The Zodiac

The Sun seems to travel across the zodiac throughout the year. During different times of the year, people can see different zodiac constellations. The 13 zodiac constellations are Aries, Taurus, Gemini, Cancer, Leo, Virgo, Libra, Scorpio, Ophiuchus, Sagittarius, Capricornus, Aquarius, and Pisces.

21

Taurus

Taurus is a Y-shaped zodiac sign in the northern sky. It represents a bull. In the top left section of Taurus is a star called Aldebaran. It is a double star. A double star consists of two stars that are so close together that they appear as one without a telescope.

On the right side of the "Y" is a star cluster that makes up the bull's shoulder. This cluster is called the Pleiades. According to Greek mythology, they represent seven sisters. There are hundreds of stars in the Pleiades, but they are too far away to see with the naked eye. However, a good pair of binoculars will allow you to see several dozen of them.

GAZING GUIDE

Locate Orion. Orion's belt points to Aldebaran. Look to one side of Aldebaran to find the bull's horns, and look to the other side to spot its body.

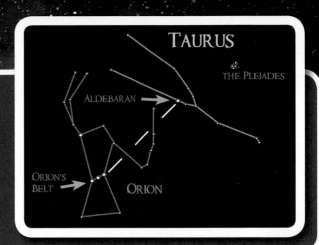

TAURUS

THE PLEIADES

ALDEBARAN

ORION'S BELT

ORION

The ancient Greeks thought Taurus represented the god Zeus. According to Greek mythology, Zeus turned himself into a bull. Orion hunted Taurus as the stars moved across the sky.

The Southern Cross

The Southern Cross is the smallest constellation, but it is the most well-known one in the southern sky. The Southern Cross is made up of five main stars.

Early explorers had plenty of constellations to guide them in the northern hemisphere. But in the southern oceans they needed a way to locate south. Sailors spotted a small cross-shaped group of stars located over the South Pole. Early explorers named it the Southern Cross.

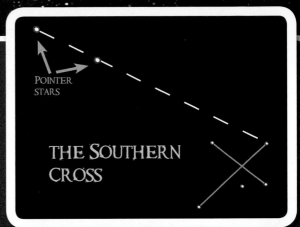

POINTER STARS

THE SOUTHERN CROSS

First of all, you must be in the southern hemisphere. Look south. The Southern Cross forms a "t" with another star beside it. To the left of the cross there are two very bright stars. The stars form a line that points to the Southern Cross.

The native people of Australia thought the Southern Cross looked like an eagle's footprint. Today this constellation is represented on Australia's national flag.

Pegasus

The constellation Pegasus is named for a winged horse in Greek mythology. According to the story, the warrior Perseus cut off the monster Medusa's head. Drops of her blood fell into the water and formed a flying horse named Pegasus.

Pegasus is seen in both the northern and southern skies. The ancient Greeks thought the stars in Pegasus looked like a horse. The body looks like a giant square made of four stars. The remaining stars form Pegasus' front legs, neck, and head.

GAZING GUIDE

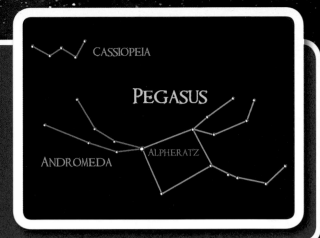

CASSIOPEIA

PEGASUS

ANDROMEDA
ALPHERATZ

Follow a line through the bottom throne region of Cassiopeia. Find four bright stars that form a square. This is Pegasus' body. Pegasus shares the star Alpheratz with Andromeda.

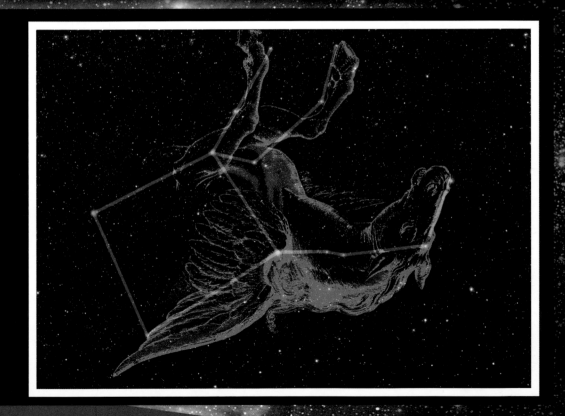

Stellar Fact

People in the Middle East had a different name for Pegasus. They called it the water bucket.

A Sky Full of Wonder

For thousands of years, people have gazed in wonder at the night sky. The patterns of the stars have been the subject of amazing stories.

Northern Sky

The stars have also served practical purposes. They have helped guide explorers, helped people tell time, and even served as yearly calendars.

Southern Sky

You've learned how to find 11 common constellations. But don't stop now! Keep star gazing, and one day you'll be able to locate all 88.

Glossary

asterism (ASS-tur-iz-uhm)—a group of stars that form a shape but are part of a larger constellation

comet (KOM-uht)—a ball of rock and ice that circles the Sun

galaxy (GAL-uhk-see)—a large group of stars, dust, and gas

hemisphere (HEM-uhss-fihr)—one half of Earth

meteor (MEE-tee-ur)—a piece of rock or dust from space that enters the Earth's atmosphere

mythology (mi-THOL-uh-jee)—a collection of myths

nebula (NEB-yuh-luh)—a cloud of gas and dust in space

North Star (NORTH STAR)—the star in the northern sky located directly over the North Pole

nova (NO-vuh)—a star that suddenly becomes brighter and then fades back to normal

revolve (RIH-volv)—to move in a circle around another object

sickle (SIK-uhl)—a long, curved blade with a handle

zodiac (ZOH-dee-ak)—a circular, imaginary belt in the sky; 13 constellations are part of the zodiac

Read More

Gendell, Megan. *Shoot for the Stars: Everything You Wanted to Know About Astronomy, Stars, and Constellations.* New York: Scholastic, 2008.

Rey, H. A. *Find the Constellations.* Boston: Houghton Mifflin Harcourt, 2008.

Snedden, Robert. *Exploring Space.* Sci-Hi: Earth and Space Science. Chicago: Raintree, 2010.

Internet Sites

FactHound offers a safe, fun way to find Internet sites related to this book. All of the sites on FactHound have been researched by our staff.

Here's all you do:

Visit *www.facthound.com*

Type in this code: 9781429660075

Index

Books by **AL BARKOW**

Gettin' to the Dance Floor 1986
The Master of Putting (with George Low) 1983
The Venturi System (with Ken Venturi) 1983
The Venturi Analysis (with Ken Venturi) 1981
The Good Sense of Golf (with Billy Casper) 1980
Golf's Golden Grind: The History of the Tour 1974

Gettin' to the Dance Floor

Gettin' to the Dance Floor

An Oral History of American Golf

AL BARKOW

NEW YORK   *Atheneum*   1986

Library of Congress Cataloging-in-Publication Data

Barkow, Al.
  Gettin' to the dance floor.

  1. Golf—United States—History.   2. Golfers—United
States—Biography.   I. Title.
GV981.B37   1985   796.352′0973   85-47660
ISBN 0-689-11517-2

FIRST EDITION

FOREWORD

The idea of golf is to get the ball in the hole. Since the green is where the hole is, that's the place where emotion is ultimately released, or expressed. When a player holes a crucial short putt, or rolls one in from sixty feet, it is on the green—on the "dance floor," as golfers like to say—where he punches the air and does a little jig of celebration.

But the metaphor of the green as a "dance floor" has other connotations.

The green is a wonderfully smooth and uncluttered place compared to the rest of the golf course. There are no trees or sand traps, no shin-high grass, no ponds or streams to impede the journey to the place where the hole is. Once on the green, the golfer is out of harm's way, more or less, for while putting, which is the business done on the green, has its own set of perils, they are much more subtle than all the others he faces in getting there. While making his way to the green the golfer is melded with, if not swallowed up by, the trees and sand traps, ponds and streams. He is but part of a rather "busy" landscape—and one of the smaller parts at that. But when he steps onto that broad, clean expanse of tightly mown grass that is the green, he is out of the clutter and stands out in sharp relief.

Every golfer knows the sensation of singularity that

v

comes from walking onto the "dance floor." It has something to do with ego. And the feeling is magnified for competitive golfers on the big-time tournament circuits. When they walk through the gallery onto the green, they might be likened to ballroom dandies out to waltz a pretty lady while those who are perhaps less brave—or lucky—watch from the balcony.

There are other dimensions to the allegorical dance floor that pertain especially to the generation of people telling of their life in golf on the following pages. They all came into the game during the first quarter of this century. Golf was still relatively new to the United States then, and had a rather narrow social and economic base. It was played and administered largely by those of means and "status." For those not so favored who wanted to be in golf in a substantial or significant way, in particular as professionals, it meant starting at the bottom. They started as caddies, and scrounged around for the time and place, and equipment, to play themselves. If they showed an aptitude for playing the game—for, above all, it was (and still is) the ability to play golf well that captured the eye of those who could be of help—they were moved up to pro-shop assistants. They learned the golf craft, which in their day was club repair and clubmaking. Eventually they became full-fledged professionals—either as tournament players or as teachers, or both, and perhaps also as administrators of the game. They worked their way up to a "dance floor" that was much more than the place where the hole was; it was where their life would be.

For some of those who started at the bottom, the passage to the dance floor had a further obstacle. They ran into golf's national and ethnic traditions. It seems that when one tribe comes first to something special—or, as in the case of golf, "invents" it—the inclination is to look coolly on outsiders who want in. The tendency can be intensified when the "inventors" are of a homogeneous tribal strain shaped in the isolation of an island nation. In short, golf was still a fairly fresh export from Great Britain back in 1910–20, and while those out of America's melting pot who were not of English or Scottish lineage and sought a place in the game were not entirely thwarted, they did have to weather a certain "attitude" toward them by the "ins." Gene Sarazen and George Fazio allude to this in

these pages. The black American's experience in this regard
was at least doubly difficult, and actually of a different order,
as we shall see through the stories of Chink Stewart and Bill
Spiller.

The "right" tribal background aside, more than a few of
the people in this book had to deal with the objections of their
parents to their golfing aspirations. The parents were generally from the "working class," and often immigrants to the
country. Golf, to them, was a rich man's game, a frivolity for
the upper class that offered their offspring no perceptible
financial future. And they were surely right at that time. Golf
was a hard living. What's more, golf professionals were
reputed to be heavy drinkers, and often gamblers. Thus, to
Italian immigrant parents and Scotch-English Fundamentalists
alike, the "dance floor" was a dance *hall*, a haven for idlers.
Nowadays, the situation has about-faced. The children of the
suburban middle class are encouraged by their parents to get
into golf and either play the rich and glamorous pro circuit or
use the game as an entree to excellent business connections.
The people in this book did so much to shape today's attitude
toward the game, and the opportunities it presents.

But whether the entry into golf was difficult, and for
whatever reasons, everyone once "in" was—and is—subject to
The Game itself, and in the same way. Golf knows nothing of
social or economic factors or of feelings. It captivates— cap-
tures—one and all with its insouciant, inscrutable mystery.
Therefore, although this was not meant to be, and is not, a golf
instruction book—a "how to" on the grip, stance, and all the
rest—there is in it a great deal of discussion about golf-swing
technique. This is what many of the people wanted to talk
about as much as, if not more than, anything else. They
seemed driven to do so. It couldn't be because they had nothing else on their minds concerning their days in the golfing
sun. Golfers are travelers—it goes with the territory—and
almost everyone recalled well what it was like on the road
before Interstate highways, 8-cylinder automobiles, jet aircraft. Yet the attitude as I perceived it was that driving the
crowded little Ford coupé over pocky asphalt roads and one-
way bridges, and staying in roadside rooms with "Kleenex-thin
walls," was an experience of no lasting consequence. The com-

ing of bigger, faster, more comfortable cars and more convenient motels was to these people simply a matter of natural evolution, and in that sense unremarkable.

Ah, but finding the solution to the golf swing! Now, that's something for the ages. Which is not to say that everyone I spoke with is still in the throes of search and discovery. After all, you would hope that after someone has reached his eighties, and spent most of that time experimenting with and contemplating the golf swing, he would end up with some sort of positive conclusions. Indeed, Henry Picard, whose first fifteen years in golf had been a golfer's odyssey in search of The Method, appears now to be in no quandary at all about the best way to hit a golf ball. In his crisp New England manner, he sounds absolutely convinced he has found The Way. Bill Mehlhorn is equally positive *he* has it. Frank Walsh, a kind of frustrated romantic, regrets he did not know sooner what he now knows, and rues that when at last the revelation hit him he could not get it across to enough of his students.

Not only are they convinced, they are convincing in their convincedness. When I left Mehlhorn, I said to myself that I had just been to The Mount. But no sooner was I in the presence of Walsh than Mehlhorn was forgotten and I was in another thrall. Then came Picard, and the other two were demolished . . . until I listened again to Fazio and Burke. I'll say this: if you are a golf-swing-theory buff, my kind of work can be dangerous.

So, for many the route to the dance floor is through a knowledge of, or understanding of, or informed guess about the mechanics of the golf swing. It is a devious but totally fascinating passage. No quarter would be given to Magellan for his trip around the world. What the hell, he had the stars to guide him. Which is to say that for readers who enjoy delving into the seemingly endless discussion—some would say morass—of swing theory, this book should be a rich source of material. Be advised, however, that you will get no complete theories, and will come upon many seeming contradictions. For example, when Gene Sarazen found a way to keep his left hand turned more to the right in his grip, he was on his way to being a finished golfer. However, Ben Hogan, according to Henry Picard, had to turn his left hand more to the *left* in order to become a great champion.

Foreword

It is interesting to note, by the way, that no one in this book expresses much interest in the business of the dance floor itself: putting. Just about everyone complained that he would have been better, or better still, if he could have putted decently. Yet no one expounded a theory of putting, elaborate or otherwise. This is not unusual among golfers, past or present, even though putting represents almost half the strokes taken in a round by a good player, and even though everyone admits that you can't be a winner in golf without good putting. Some people explain this peculiar lack of interest by saying that putting is simply unfathomable; that there is no solution to it; that there can be no universal way to do it when you consider how totally different are the putting styles of such masters of the art as Jack Nicklaus and Bobby Locke.

There may be something to all that, but my feeling is that putting is just not as interesting as hitting full golf shots. Putting is not as complex an action, for one thing, but mainly there is the factor that the best-stroked putt in a lifetime does not bring the esthetic satisfaction of a perfectly hit wood or iron shot. There is nothing to match the whoosh and soar, the almost magical flight of a beautifully hit drive or five-iron. To go through all those movements of the body and get that result even once in a while is more thrilling than a hundred ten-foot putts that drop to the bottom of the cup.

It is the *gettin'* to the dance floor that is the most fun.

Each "chapter" of this book is the story of a particular man or woman who spent a lifetime in American golf. Each tells of how he came into the game in the first place, then quickly moves on to how his career developed and what he learned about himself and the game he chose for a life's work, and in many cases about some of the people he met along the way. Each is a personal story, of course, and on a surface level of perception they may all ring similar—after all, everyone in this book is very much "in" golf. But by gathering together in one volume a fair cross-section of people in terms of regional birthplace, gender, economic background, and tribal descent, just below the surface you will find distinctive variations on the same theme. For example, Sam Snead, from the mountains of West Virginia, had a far different initiation into golf, and outlook on the game, than the big-city country-club player Sam

Parks, Jr. The cumulative effect of such variations produces a sense of what it was like to be in American golf before the game was relatively streamlined and homogenized by the mass production of equipment, clothes, grasses, young players, and the public-relations demands that seem inherent to the entertainment business.

Thus, this collection of thoughts and reminiscences does not have the kind of historical precision people may expect when they see the word "history." Of course, I have corrected dates and the like that were misquoted in the spur-of-the-moment recall of events that occurred decades earlier. But dates are not what this book is about. It is the *feel* of the times that is meant to be projected.

However, the people in this book have been chosen in some part because they did (or do) represent certain important aspects of American golf history. For instance, Jim Ferrier personifies the Australian "invasion" of American golf. He was one of the first of many who have since come here from Down Under and made successful careers. Willie Turnesa speaks for the amateur side of the game, Betsy Rawls and Patty Berg for the women, Joe Dey and Leo Fraser for the administrative end, and so on. There is also some cross-referencing. Golfworld is something of a neighborhood. A lot of people know each other, or at least came in touch with each other. To mind are Sam Snead and Johnny Bulla, who have been close friends since their salad days in golf. They refer to each other, and to certain incidents they shared even though they were not interviewed together.

A good many of the people in this book have had celebrated careers in golf, and are quite well known by the general golfing public, such as Byron Nelson and Sam Snead. Or they have been involved in at least one great historic moment in American golf—Sam Parks, Jr., the surprise winner of the U.S. Open, for instance, and Chandler Harper, victim of Lew Worsham's magnificent wedge shot for an eagle two to win the Tam O'Shanter "World" championship and a then sensational $25,000 first prize.

Others are perhaps not at all known by the golfing public. Lee Trevino said on one of his golf telecasts, when a player's approach got on to a green but 100 feet from the hole, "He's on the dance floor, but too far away to hear the music." That might be said of Errie Ball or Harold Sanderson, if you think of a life in golf only in terms of a successful career on the pro tournament circuit. They didn't have that, either because they didn't quite have the stuff or simply because they didn't want the life-style. But that does not diminish their contribution to the game and its history. Indeed, as dedicated teachers—professors—of golf, they have in ways been closest to the heart of the game. Besides, those who do not become champion players often have the most articulate and insightful views on the game.

In a word, the people who comprise this book were chosen for something more than their ability to play golf at the highest competitive level. Golf history is far more than the sum of its championships.

Each of the "chapters" in the book is in the form of a monologue. But it should be understood that what appears in these pages are actually distillations of what the individuals said, distillations made by me. It was my job to draw out from those who were interviewed what I thought was pertinent or interesting, and then to make it as concise and pointed as possible. So, in this respect, the monologue is in fact a two-sided conversation.

I want to express my sincerest gratitude to all those who appear in this book. They were especially gracious, and generous with their time and thoughts. The same gratitude goes out to those who were interviewed but, for one reason or another, do not appear in this volume. I thank everyone for his or her contribution, and hope Golfworld does, too.

Al Barkow

CONTENTS

Contents

Contents

Gettin' to the Dance Floor

WILLIAM "WILD BILL" MEHLHORN

Photograph by Al Barkow

"I was the world's worst putter."

My father came from Germany when he was sixteen, a year before he was supposed to enlist in the army for four years. Everybody had to enlist in Kaiser Wilhelm's army, so he left. He was a bricklayer, and I did some of that. My father finally played golf when he was older—played cross-handed— but I was the only golfer in the family. I was born in Elgin, Illinois, in 1898, then moved to Glencoe. They were suburbs of Chicago just as they are now, except they weren't built up as much.

I got into golf because some kids talked about caddying and I went out to Skokie Country Club when I was ten and got thirty cents for my first eighteen holes. Three dimes. It was like a million dollars. Well, the game intrigued me and I developed in it very fast. I had a knack for it. But my golf might be different than anybody else's, because baseball was my first love and everything I teach in golf is the same as hitting a baseball. I made a golfer out of Sam Byrd. He played for the New York Yankees, then played on the pro golf tour. There wasn't one shot in golf that I didn't talk to Sam about how he could do it the same as if it was in baseball. Like throwing underhanded across the body, or sidearmed, which is the way you swing a golf club.

3

I worked it all out as a caddie. When I was eleven I caddied for two old men who broke all the theories of the game of golf. They were ex-baseball players, both of them were in their seventies and couldn't hit the ball over 150 yards, but they were never off the fairway. They broke every theory regarding keeping your head still, don't sway, stuff like that. They didn't even have golf grips. They kept their old baseball grips. And they hit the ball flush every time. So I said, where the heck did they come up with all these theories of the golf swing? It's like . . . well, put it down this way. Ten people see an accident, do you get two people who describe it the same way? Someone says, "Oh, that happened very quickly." I say the golf swing is very quick, too. Everybody has a little different feel.

I believe there is only one thing that helps everybody play golf, and they can use it in every solitary thing that takes movement. Muscles and joints at ease in their movements, that's the secret to the golf game. There should not be any intention of hardening any muscle or joint. And the elbow joint is the most important we have. I defy you to eat, unless you want to eat like an animal, without the use of your elbow. There's no way you can get your hand to your mouth. And every doctor will tell you that the harder you make your muscles, the less you can move. So why should there be any intentional hardening of the muscles, which is promoted by the word "firm"? I contradict the use of that word in golf, completely.

Another thing I contradict in golf theories is one-piece action. There's too many pieces moving. A smart person will say that the pieces move independently but in unison. Another thing I'm against is full extension. Full extension is stretching. You're retarding something when you stretch it. Take a stone at the end of a three foot string and swing it around. If you swing that stone on a string ten feet long, it will go slower. It has full extension, too, but has to go slower. So you can move something faster in a smaller space than you can in a wider one.

Everybody is looking to hit the golf ball 300 yards. How do you do it? You need speed, and some weight behind it. If you can swing a heavy object as fast as you can swing a lighter one, you've got to hit the ball farther. They talk now about lightweight clubs. But you can't move the ball with them. You must have some mass. It's according to the laws of physics. It was proven. A manufacturer put a seven-ounce head on a shaft and put the club on a machine. It hit the ball 200 yards. He took that same shaft with a 7.5-ounce head, the club moving at the same speed, and the ball went five to ten yards farther. You need mass with speed. In my younger days I experimented with every solitary thing you could in hitting a golf ball, including a women's club. It felt so much better than a man's club. I even played with it for a month, but I couldn't hit the ball far enough. I got shorter.

Out of that I built a different kind of golf club—iron. I changed the shape of it. The heads on irons were too thin and long, so I cut a quarter-inch off the end and soldered it on the back to make it heavy enough. I took it to Forgan, the clubmaker in Scotland, because one of the cleekmakers there had caddied for me. I asked him if he could make a set of clubs like it. He said sure. It took him a week to hammer them out. Instead of names, I put numbers on them, because it was easier. No one had done that before. But the main thing was I had an iron with a shorter, more compact head, and with the weight behind the blow.

Another thing I did, experimenting with the game, I played golf left-handed for a month because I read the same thing everyone else read and it said golf was a left-handed game, that it took a strong left hand. Well, I found out, playing left-handed, that I felt everything in my left elbow and forearm, and the forefinger and thumb of my left hand. I found out I had to get my right arm out of the way. I also found out I had to let go of the club with my right hand, because of this big pull of the club away from you as you swing it. So I said to myself, what the hell am I doing on this side of the ball? Why don't I get back where I belong? If the left arm did everything playing left-handed, then it's the arm behind the ball that counts more than the arm in front of it. Now, I've got a good right arm. I can throw a baseball far, so I ought to be able to hit a golf ball farther playing right-handed. The arm behind the ball and the hand closest to the clubhead count twice as much as the others. The weak can never teach the strong. The

5

useless can never control the useful. If you're right-handed, that's the one that should be in control of the golf swing. Like when you work an ax or sledgehammer, the hand lowest on the handle is moving up and down the shaft and doing all the work.

I went one year and one week to high school, and the only reason I quit was I threw my arm out pitching baseball. We won the Cook County Championship—I went to New Trier High School—and I pitched three days in a row. The athletic director tried to stop me, but I insisted I pitch because we had to win the championship. I struck out seventeen men in seven innings. Later on in life I ran into Babe Ruth and bet him I could throw a golf ball farther than he could. Now, mind you, he had been a pitcher. I threw the ball forty-two feet farther than he did. When I had my golf school in Chicago, I bet a bunch of baseball pitchers I could hit a golf ball with a full swing more accurately than they could throw it. And you talk about pitchers cutting corners with their pitches. They said I was crazy. One of the pitchers was Charley Root, of the Cubs. I had a canvas with a six-inch hole and I used a three-iron. I didn't care if they only tossed it, not threw hard. Three different times I hit seven out of ten through the hole, and each one of the pitchers did it only once. They said it was unbelievable, and I said I used the golf club the same way you use a fungo bat.

I say you must swing a golf club at approximately a forty-five-degree angle to the ground. It varies slightly according to the length of the shaft—the shorter the club, the more vertical you swing it—but it is basically a sideways move. I don't call it flat, I call it a sideways move. One guy said Mehlhorn was trying to change all the language, but, goddamn it, a wall is flat. Where are you swinging a golf club flat to that? A wall is flat, but a golf swing isn't.

All my life I did everything in a hurry, but I swing my club slower than my natural tempo. Tommy Armour said to me that every time he played with me he got mad because I hit it so far so easy. What does that imply to you? It goes right along with what I've been preaching. Muscles and joints have to be at ease in their performance. Joints are there to be used, not to be kept stationary. Go look up the word "stationary" for yourself and you'll never use it again in golf. It says "immobile, fixed." That's why I believe in bending your left elbow in the backswing. If you keep the arm straight, you don't use it, you lock that joint. Harry Vardon bent his left elbow almost at right angles. That's what I learned from him. I started out as a hooker of the ball, but after playing with Vardon in 1921 I changed. I worked thirteen months at it, to hit the ball from left to right. But not only that, to hit it easier.

The one thing Vardon said to me was to never use more than two thirds of my effort, except on rare occasions, and be sure those are near the end of the round, because if you do it earlier you may lose your timing and play a poor round. When you use all your effort, how consistent can you be? You've got to be within yourself. In anything. Suppose you had to cut down a lot of trees, that was your job. How much effort do you use in every blow? You don't even use seventy-five percent, because you couldn't last. So that's what I came to.

Who were the great players of this century? To start with, Harry Vardon. Next is Bob MacDonald. I copied them more than anyone else, because they looked so easy doing it. They never had to be contortionists to do it. I say that if you do everything absolutely natural according to your physique, there's no way you can hurt your back. Now the greatest player today, Jack Nicklaus, has hurt his back. In my day in the '20s no one ever hurt their back hitting a golf ball. No one ever had a pinched nerve in his neck or hip. Just think of how many guys in the last twenty years have hurt their back or had pinched nerves. If you do things naturally, you can't hurt yourself. Someone says, "It's natural for me to do it this way, why shouldn't I keep doing it?" I say you can keep on doing it, but it's unnatural if you hurt yourself. It's a *habit*, not natural. It's the same as the guy who learns to drink a lot. He's a drunkard. It's a habit. He smokes a lot; it's a habit. Or go to the guy who eats a lot. That's not natural, that's a habit. Well, muscle habit is even more so.

So how did Nicklaus win so much? Because he could finish a hole better than anybody else. As a player he's the greatest of all time, but as a golfer I can't even put him in the first fifty. Hogan had the greatest swing—not Snead—because Hogan had a more sideways movement.

7

William "Wild Bill" Mehlhorn

I quit high school at sixteen when Walter Fovarque, the pro at Skokie Country Club, called me one day and said he wanted me to work for him as his assistant. I started at $30 a month and it went to $55 by the end of the year. That was my apprenticeship. Then I went to work at Calumet Country Club for Fovarque's brother, down on the south side of Chicago by the Illinois Central Railroad, American Brake and Foundry, and the Pullman works. I worked there a year, then said I wouldn't come back on account of the conditions there—smoke on three sides. Then I was in Miami one winter and got a call from George Simpson regarding the assistant's job at Oak Park Country Club. I asked him what he was offering, then I told him I wanted all the money from my lessons—no sharing what I got for them. I would make clubs for him, get $150 a month and my room and board. And when I said board, I meant just like the members, I eat in the clubhouse. Six hours later he called back and said I was hired. This was in 1918.

My first head-pro job was at the Tulsa Country Club in 1920. Chick Evans recommended me for the job. But they went and rebuilt the whole golf course and there wasn't any business. All I could do was hit balls and give a few lessons. There wasn't any golf at all. I got $100 a month salary.

But I also made a living playing bridge. I learned that game all by myself, watching them play on the train going down into Chicago from the suburbs. Two cars of bridge players, a big game in every four seats. You paid the conductor a dollar for the cards. One time they needed a player and asked me in. I said I'd never played before, but knew a little about it from watching. Well, I took their money away from them the first time I sat down, because I saw things they didn't. Because I had an analytical mind of my own.

I went to Miami every winter when I was in Chicago. One year, 1919, I paid my way giving golf clinics and selling subscriptions to *Golf Illustrated* magazine. Tim Hartnett was the publisher, in Chicago. I stopped in towns on the way down and walked into the center of town with my golf bag, luggage, and a big trophy. There was no such thing as a taxi to take you in. I'd go into the lobby of the main hotel and let the word out that I was a golf pro and was giving lessons at $2 an hour and would give a clinic or an exhibition if they could raise the money.

When the people came, I also tried to get them to sell subscriptions to *Golf Illustrated* at $4 each. If they sold fifty of them, they got a trophy like the one I was carrying, which they could use as a prize in a tournament. It was a beautiful-looking trophy, three feet high. I wasn't out to sell it, I used it as a sample, but I'd take an order if someone wanted to buy one. I left Chicago with $70 in my pocket, and when I got to Miami I had $700. And I had to pay all my own expenses.

In Miami I'd stay at the Martinique Hotel for $3 a day, which was a special rate for golf professionals. There was a tournament at the Miami Country Club, about two miles from the hotel, one up in Palm Beach, some others up north on the east coast, and there was one over on the west coast just outside of Fort Myers. Know how I got to that one from Miami? Now you can drive straight across in an hour and a half, but back then I had to take a train up to Jacksonville, another across to Tampa, then one down to Fort Myers. The Atlantic Coast Railroad. It took about three days, at three cents a rail mile.

I think the reason I was on the first American golf team that was sent abroad was because I worked for *Golf Illustrated*. See, Tim Hartnett got that team up, paid all the expenses, and gave everybody $1,000. Everybody said, "What's Mehlhorn doing on this team? His record doesn't show anything." Well, I wasn't the worst player on the team, that's for sure, because I finished third among the ten guys that went over, which was in 1921. It was before the Ryder Cup matches were started. Jock Hutchison went, Freddie McLeod, Tommy Kerrigan, names most people never hear of now. The idea was for us to go over and play a match against the British pros at Gleneagles, play in the British Open, then come home. We all got slaughtered at Gleneagles. I'll never forget Jock Hutchison. He was four up with five to go and ended up losing the match. He wouldn't stay over with the rest of the guys. He wanted to go to St. Andrews and he got hold of me and said, "Let's go, we'll get a cab." I said I didn't have any money for that, but he said he'd pay. So we went over and played thirty-six holes in three hours, believe it or not, with about 500 spectators. It wasn't an exhibition, the people just came out to see Jock and an American by the name of Mehlhorn. We played so

9

fast they were running. I broke 80 for both rounds. Jock Hutchison won the British Open that year. It was the first time the cup came to the United States. Tom Kerrigan finished third, and I was seventh. So I beat everybody but two guys from our team.

St. Andrews never impressed me at all. I wondered how the devil it got such a reputation. The only reason could be on account of its age. Everything was flat, except for the little rolls in the fairways, so all the shots were blind shots. You had to shoot at a steeple five miles away.

My nickname, Wild Bill, has nothing to do with my having any kind of temper, as a lot of people have thought. I'll tell you, Leo Diegel and I were buddies. We did a lot of things together; we were the same size, wore the same hat, shoes, gloves, same everything. He gave me the name Oklahoma Bill when I went to Tulsa. It stands to reason. Then we had a cyclone and he changed it to Cyclone Bill. Next year we're down to play the Southern Open at his course, New Orleans Country Club, and Diegel and I are paired with Gene Sarazen and Cyril Walker. This is an exhibition match, but we never got paid. They were something like three or four up at noontime and Diegel says I better get going or we'll never hear the end of it. Well, in the afternoon on the first five holes I'm one under threes and I three-putted one green. I broke the course record by four shots. Now, Diegel is writing for the New Orleans newspaper at the time, and he writes that Bill Mehlhorn went wild. I tried to stop that wild stuff, because I thought it hurt my image, but that's what made it stick, trying to fight it. Then in the 1927 U.S. Open it comes over the ticker tape that Wild Bill Goes Wild. Because I went out in 32 the last round when nobody else broke 40. So every time I burned things up they said I was Wild Bill.

It had nothing to do with temperament, but with my shooting some impossible scores. Like in the 1930 Western Open I shot 65 the last round. I wasn't anywhere near the prize money starting that round, but ended up in third and took in as much money as Sarazen did for winning, because I got $100 for low score in the tournament and $100 for setting the course record. People couldn't figure out how I shot such a low score on such a tough course—Indian Wood, in Detroit. I said nothing but false courage did it, because I had really retired at the end of fifty-four holes. But they said I had to play the last round because I was paired with Clarence Gamber, the local boy and a long hitter. In the meantime I had gotten drunk with Jock Hutchison and Bob MacDonald in the locker room between the third and fourth rounds. And I mean *drunk*. I even fell down when I teed up the first ball. I had the caddie tee the ball up for me the rest of the round. And get this—I shot 33 on the front nine, two under par, with three three-putt greens, and came home in 32, five under par, and I missed an eighteen-inch putt on the seventeenth hole and drove out of bounds on the eighteenth. I had 65 with three bogeys and an out of bounds; made eight birdies and an eagle.

Why didn't I win more? I was the world's worst putter. If I had thought on the putting green the way I did for the rest of the game, none of these guys would have won a tournament. Everybody tried to help me, even some of my enemies. They felt sorry for me. Some of the guys would say they didn't know how Mehlhorn could go out and play the next day after the way he putted. Listen to this. I was playing in a pro-pro event right here in Miami, at the Biltmore. Earl Holland was my partner. There was a gale of wind blowing, and I went out in 34 on my own ball. I started back birdie, birdie, par and put it ten feet from the cup on the next hole, and I told Earl to pick up his ball, I wouldn't need him. Then I took six putts. And I never hit a careless one, except the sixth. After the first putt I was never over eighteen inches from the cup. I walked off the green twice. The sixth putt I just hit with the back of the putter. The only careless putt I hit went in.

In a tournament in Dallas one time I was on the thirteenth hole and had about a three-footer to tie for the lead. Craig Wood was standing in back of the green and had to get out of the way of my ball. I pitched it past him. I had the yips, and it wasn't just in tournaments—practice rounds, too. I'm just like everybody else, I used an alibi. Mine was that I didn't have the touch because my dad had to put in a basement in one of his buildings and we had to cut down all of these trees with an ax and dig out all the roots, and there were no machines for the job. So I said that because of doing all that heavy work when I was thirteen, I never had the touch for putting. But, of course, it wasn't that at all. I'll tell you. I've always believed that what your mind believes your body achieves. Mind over matter. That's the way I played golf, but I couldn't use it on the putting green. For example, I went out to play golf a year ago and told Bob Shave I wasn't going to three-putt another green. And I didn't; sixty-, seventy-footers, two slopes in them, I laid them all dead. Mind over matter.

Now, you might say great ball-strikers tend not to be very good putters because putting's not as interesting, not as satisfying as hitting a fine five-iron shot. Well, I'll grant there's something to that, and it may have been my problem. It's true I had to make *some* putts, since I won over forty tournaments in a ten-year period, but listen to these two stories. At El Paso one year I played the last six holes seven under par and holed one putt about three feet long. We were putting on cottonseed-hull greens, by the way. Then at Skokie Country Club, in 1922, on five straight par-four holes my ball finished one inch behind the cup four times in a row, and on the fifth I holed out with a two-iron. What I did was hit the ball as close to the hole as I could so I didn't have to do much putting. But that's hard to do regularly.

I think my being called Wild Bill had to do with an incident that is always brought up about me—that I climbed a tree and tried to upset Bobby Cruickshank from beating me in a tournament. It was in San Antonio, the Texas Open. The last hole and Cruickshank has two putts to win. He four-putts. I had run out from the clubhouse to watch him finish, and got up in a tree so I could see over the gallery. Well, there's a delivery truck right across from the green delivering groceries to the clubhouse. So I hear Jack O'Brien say to the truckdriver not to start his motor, to wait until they finished the hole. I said to O'Brien—he was running the tournament—"What the hell do you know about machinery?" Well, the newspapers wrote it up that I said that to upset Cruickshank, because Bobby pointed to me up in the tree when he came off the green. But he was fifty yards away from me when I made that remark to O'Brien. All the newspapers around the country had it: "Mehlhorn Causes Cruickshank to Blow Tournament!"

William "Wild Bill" Mehlhorn

The very next year I happened to be playing with Cruickshank in the last two rounds of that same tournament. We're one-two leading, and I refuse to go off in the last round if the gallery doesn't turn around and become just as favored of Bobby, because they were booing his shots and applauding mine because of what happened the year before. Bill Forland, who was running the tournament this time, made the announcement that I would walk off the course if it kept up. Cruickshank managed to beat me by one shot, but I wasn't going to win by the gallery being unruly. I won the tournament the next two years.

Why did I make that remark to Jack O'Brien in the first place? Oh, just to have something to say.

Many of Bill Mehlhorn's contemporaries—and even Ben Hogan, who came a little after Bill's best years—say to this day that he was one of the finest strikers of the golf ball they have ever seen. Bill won the 1924 Western Open, his most prestigious victory. In U.S. Open play between 1922 and 1931, Mehlhorn finished third three times, fourth twice, and was in the top fifteen on three other occasions. He was also, by all accounts, a world-class bridge player.

Bill lives in Miami, and spends a lot of his time at the Fountainebleau Golf Course, where he gives instruction to players on the Florida International University golf team. Bobby Shave, the FIU golf coach, helped Bill write a book that was recently published, Golf Secrets Exposed, *which is a compilation of Bill Mehlhorn's golf-swing theories and reminiscences of his long life in the game.*

GENE SARAZEN

Photograph by Al Barkow

" . . . Yes, I had a reputation for being tough.
You had to be when you were Italian."

I sometimes think I was born a pro. I was a caddie when I was ten. Ed Sullivan and myself were caddie mates at Apawamis [Golf Club, Rye, New York]. Ed became a newspaper columnist and was on television. He was number 98, I was 99. We stayed up on the hill until we were needed, then the caddie master, George Hoose, would yell up, "Nuuumber ninety-eight, nuuumber ninety-nine."

I always remember a time with Sullivan. You know, we went by the bag. If a guy had a new bag and a new set of clubs, you figured he had the dough, he's going to give a good tip. So, one time, up come these two bags. One had a brand-new set of irons and woods, and the other one was a little Sunday bag with rusty clubs. The caddie master called out, "Next twooo!" Sullivan could run like Nurmi in those days, and he outran me to get the good bag. When the players came up, one of them was a very attractive fellow—he had on white flannels and was wearing a gold key chain—and the other guy was a big, fat palooka. He was the police commissioner of New York, Enright; he had the new bag and clubs. I got hooked with this little Sunday bag and I said, "I'll get no tip here." Well, that bag belonged to Grantland Rice, and he and I became very intimate friends from that day until he died. Oh yes, he gave me a substantial tip that day.

Gene Sarazen

You could say my caddie days were fun. I had great experiences, because the people you caddied for in those days were entirely different than today. You didn't hear the language you hear today. They were very high-class people. All college graduates. I learned a lot from them, from listening to them. I learned a lot about life. And I learned my golf in the caddie yard. We walked from Harrison to Rye to caddie, and had nine holes between which we made ourselves in empty lots along the way. There was nothing but big open fields then, between Harrison and Rye. But nobody gave me lessons. I used to watch the players. I'd go miles and miles to watch players in tournaments. My favorite golfer was Walter Hagen. I used to admire his ways, his technique, the way he would slash at the ball. And the way he dressed. He was my hero. He was still a great star when I began my playing career, and, yes, it was a great kick when I beat him in matches and tournaments.

In 1922, after I won the Open championship, the PGA championship came along and Hagen wouldn't play in it because he was up in Buffalo playing an exhibition. I won that PGA, but Hagen hadn't been there, so somebody started up the World Championship Match between us. We played seventy-two holes, Hagen and I. He was five up on me at one time, but I managed to beat him three and two. We played Oakmont thirty-six holes, and Westchester-Biltmore thirty-six holes. That was the most grueling seventy-two holes I ever played in my life, because I had appendicitis and I took it for just a pain in the stomach. Well, when I got through playing at Westchester-Biltmore the pain got worse. I went up to my room and threw up, and I called one of these Park Avenue doctors and he said, "Oh, that's just nervous indigestion." So, finally, about three o'clock in the morning it got very serious and I called my friend Dr. Frank Landolfi, from Portchester, to come and see me. He examined me and first thing you know I'm on my way to the hospital in Yonkers. They got Joe Kirkwood, who was living at the Westchester-Biltmore, to help carry me down. When I got to the hospital Frank got a surgeon to operate on me right away. The appendix hadn't burst, but it was on the verge. That was a very dangerous event. In those days a lot of people died from appendicitis, because they thought it was an upset stomach and would take a physic and that would burst it. Nobody knew then. So I won the World

Championship by beating Hagen, but I couldn't play any exhibitions because I was recuperating. I couldn't take advantage of it.

But I had a more serious illness when I was younger. In 1916, when I was fourteen, I had empyema. That's pus in the pleural cavity—in your lungs. It was during the war, when I was working at Remington Arms in Bridgeport [Connecticut]. I was the first case recorded where they sawed the rib, put in a tube, and blew a gallon of water in there to push that stuff out. Every morning. It was cleaned out, and then it started to heal. But it didn't look like I was going to make it at first. I was on the deathbed for four or five days. There was no such thing as sulfa drugs or anything then. I remember lying in the Bridgeport Hospital and these priests would come in and pull the curtain around. They figured I was going to go. That was in 1916, and in 1920 I could hardly break 80.

Two years later I won the U.S. Open and the PGA championship. How do I account for that? Well, I was young and could get my strength back quickly. Otherwise, I think it was because I had a lot of spirit and fight in me. I was fearless. It might have been because I had been so close to death as a boy. What could scare me on a golf course? Nothing. I'll never forget playing the last hole at Skokie in the '22 Open. I hit a good drive, and for my second there was water to the left and out of bounds on the right. My caddie wanted me to play safe, but I heard somebody say Jones and Mehlhorn were right back of me and I said, "Oh hell, give me that brassie." I shot right for the green and put it about twelve feet from the hole. On the seventeenth Jones hit it out of bounds, and I won by a stroke.

Of course, I was a great chipper and putter at that time. That helped. I was a bold putter, and when I practiced putting I hit just three-footers, not ten- or twelve-footers, because I didn't expect to hole them. But I was not a great hitter of the ball. I had a bad grip. My right hand was way underneath, and once or twice in every seventy-two holes I would hook one out of bounds. That's why after I won those two championships I sort of went to pieces. I had that bad grip, and it caught up with me.

Well, I decided I had to do something about the right hand. Instead of having it underneath, I had to put it up like Jones and Hagen had it. One day I was playing golf with Ty

Cobb, and I asked him what he did to exercise his hands and arms. He said he had a heavy bat loaded with lead that he kept in his room and would swing. He gave me an idea. I took a golf club and made it into twenty-two ounces, and took it up to my farm in Germantown [New York]. I would swing that club all the time. Finally, one day, I found myself playing in a tournament with the same grip Hagen and Jones had. You see, I couldn't hold on to that heavy club the other way, because my hand would twist when I swung it. But when I put the hand up on top it didn't move. I swung that heavy club religiously. I had a half-dozen of them made at Wilson's, and I would put them all over the farm and pick one up and swing it thirty or forty times, back and forth.

Another problem I had was the shot out of the bunker. That was one of my weakest shots. I lost several Opens because of it. So when I invented the sand iron I licked the sand, and I had licked the hook. In 1932 I knew I had it all. I was ready, and that year I won the U.S. and British Opens.

The idea for the sand iron came when I was taking flying lessons while I was living in Florida. I used to pal around with Howard Hughes, we played a lot of golf together. Hughes was a good golfer, by the way, about a three handicapper. Anyway, when I took off in the plane I pulled the stick back and the tail went down and the nose of the plane went up. Something flashed in my mind, that my niblick should be lowered in the back. So I had Wilson send me seven or eight niblicks. I went downtown in New Port Richey and bought all the solder I could get my hands on and put it on the clubs. What I did was put a flange on the back of the club and angled it so the flange hit the sand first, not the front edge, which was now raised. It was just like the airplane when it took off. Now I could hit behind the ball and explode it out. See, in those days we played out of the sand with a regular niblick, which didn't have a flange, and you had to chip the ball. You couldn't explode it, because the front edge of the club was sharp and would dig too much. Hagen was a terrible exploder. So was Jones . . . and Sarazen. Everybody was. When I first tried my new club I said, "My God . . . "

I spent hundreds of hours practicing that shot and getting the flange just right, and it got so I would bet even money I could go down in two out of the sand. When I went to the British Open in 1932 I practiced and played with the club and then put it under my coat and took it back to my room at night, because if the British had seen it before the tournament they would have barred it. Oh yes. In the tournament I went down in two from most of the bunkers.

There was a sand iron before mine, one with a concave face. That's the one Bob Jones used when he made his Grand Slam, won those four big tournaments in 1930. But in 1931 it was barred. At that time Horton Smith was connected with the Hagen company, which made the club, and before you could get one of them you had to buy a whole set of Hagen irons. That's the demand it was in. When they found out you hit the ball twice with it, because of the concave face, they barred it. But I didn't get my idea from that club. Oh no. I couldn't hit the damn thing. It had a rounded back. In 1931 I invented the real sand iron. They couldn't bar it, because they'd have to bar all the irons. You see, everybody then came out with irons with a flange on all the irons, not just the sand iron. So they didn't do anything about it.

I learned to work on golf clubs in the first place at the Brooklawn Country Club, in Bridgeport, Connecticut. I was a boy in the shop. There were a couple of people at that club, the Wheeler brothers, and they took a fancy to me. When they came over in the spring of the year looking at clubs, they'd always pick out the ones I worked on. "Oh, I like that one there, George," they'd say, and George, the pro, would say, "Ahh no." George wasn't for the Italian boys.

Yes, it was tough for a little Italian. The Scots and the English pros didn't much like us. I remember in 1922, at Skokie, Francis Ouimet asked me to join him, Chick Evans, and Jim Barnes for a practice round. Barnes said he didn't want to play with me—"that little guy," as he put it. Well, after I won that Open, there was a special match arranged to be played in New Jersey between the current Open champion, me, and the previous one, which was Barnes. The night before the match Barnes asked me if I wanted to split the purse, and I told him no, it's winner take all. I beat him six and five.

Yes, I had a reputation for being tough when I was young. You had to be when you were Italian. When I was about sixteen years old I used to look at my name—Saraceni—and it sounded and looked like it should be on a violin, not a golf club. So I changed it around a few different ways and came up with Sarazen. Then I looked in the phone book and there was no Sarazen, and I said, "Geez, that's good." There's nobody in the world by the name S A R A Z E N. If there is, now he copied it from me. Yeah, Saraceni was a violin player.

My father was a carpenter. He became a contractor in this country, but went broke two or three times because he got caught by the First World War, then the Depression. He saw me play golf once, when we lived in Pelham, New York, and the PGA championship was being played there. I bought a house for my parents there. He took a trolley car to the golf club and stayed outside the fence at the tenth hole, which was near the road. He didn't come onto the course, because he felt Italians weren't welcome and he would be uncomfortable. I was playing a fellow named Willie Campbell, and had a forty-foot putt that I missed by about six inches. My father said, "Can you imagine him being paid for missing things like that?" He wanted me to be a carpenter. He kept all his old tools so they'd be ready for me to take over. Like we do now with our grandchildren, we save our golf clubs for them and they don't want them. But I was a carpenter during the war, in 1914. I was building barracks in Yaphank, Long Island. The carpenters didn't like hammering nails, so they'd put the boards in place and say to me, "Hammer that, kid."

My first head-professional job was in Titusville, Pennsylvania. I was nineteen years old, and it was really my first time away from home. I remember I lived in the clubhouse and there was nobody there at night—just me—and when there was a thunder-and-lightning storm it was a scary place. There were two women there that cooked for the club, and they would cook all my meals. I have very, very pleasant memories of that place. But what happened, I used to go down to Pittsburgh and play in some of the tournaments, and I met a man by the name of Emil Loeffler. He was the greenskeeper and pro at Oakmont Country Club. He thought I was a comer, and was instrumental in getting me a job at the Highland Country Club in Pittsburgh. So I left Titusville to go there. Well, my course wasn't ready, so they let me play Oakmont and one day I played with Bill Fownes, who owned the course. This is in

1922, early in the year. After we played he said to Emil, "I want you to take this boy out to Skokie [Country Club] and let him practice." This was a month before the U.S. Open was going to be played there.

So we got to Chicago on a Saturday night and Sunday we went out to play, but the pro wouldn't allow us. Emil was very disturbed and called Mr. Fownes, who told him to stand by, he'd call right back. So Mr. Fownes called up Bob Gardner, who was a U.S. Amateur champion and a businessman in Chicago, and said to him, "See that this kid plays that course just once." So it was arranged. Oh, the pro was sore as hell. We went out, I looked the course over, and I knew what I had to do. I went back to Pittsburgh and wrote a card to Tom Kerrigan, the pro at Siwanoy, who was a good friend, saying that the course is built right around my game.

So I went to Skokie. I was staying out at the Edgewater Apartments. Bob Jones and Stewart Maiden were there, too, and I was rooming with Leo Diegel. Well, after shooting two good rounds I went down into Chicago and had dinner with a guy by the name of Pietzcker. He was a photographer. He kept me out until twelve o'clock at night. I didn't even know how to find this apartment, going back at night. Finally I got back and Diegel says, "You idiot, here you are almost in striking distance of the Open, and you're staying out this late." So I go to bed, get up the next morning and take a good shower, and go out and shoot a 75. And I was lucky to be 75. Then the next round, that afternoon, I shot 68. So 145 and 143 made it 288, and I won.

I guess the sand iron would have to be one of the most important contributions I've made to golf. That was a big one. I think the club saves everybody six shots a round. But I also think the reminder grip was a great contribution, although it wasn't my idea. In 1931 I had trouble with my left hand, keeping it in the same position all the time. My grip would change, and my thumb would go straight down the center of the shaft. So one day I was in Mr. Icely's office at the Wilson company and I saw this plug. I asked him what it was, and he said some fellow from Canada wanted Wilson to put it on their clubs. It was a wooden plug with a flat side that hit you on the pad of the left hand. It put the hand in the correct position, turned to

21

the right. You couldn't hold it any other way. I said it looked like a pretty good thing, and asked Mr. Icely if he would make me up a couple of sets with it. He was the president of the company. He did, and at first it was uncomfortable and I said it would never go. Then I began to see the fruit ripen. The ball would draw the same way every time. That meant my left hand was in the same position every time. By 1932 I had it perfected and they came out with it and, oh, it went wild. I remember after it was out for a while I was up in Canada and a fellow pulls up in a Rolls Royce and comes over to me and says, in an English accent, "Sarazen, I want to buy you a drink. You made me rich. I invented the reminder grip. I got a penny a grip."

Mind you, I didn't get a cent out of it, no more that I did with the sand iron, because in fine print in my contract with Wilson it said it all belonged to the company. I got nothing for the grip, and I popularized it. They had to stop making it, because of the labor costs. This was a tailor-made thing. You can't make it by machine. See, they had to stick it in the steel, line it up just right, and put a rivet through it. If it didn't line up right, it was bad.

My most satisfying achievement as a player? Winning all four of the modern major championships—the Masters, the U.S. Open, the PGA, and the British Open. I was the first one to do that. Ben Hogan was next to do it, when he won the British Open in 1953. I won my only British Open in 1932, and I almost didn't get there. See, I was wiped out by the stock-market crash, like a lot of people were. So, no matter how much I made during the '20s, I was absolutely flat in 1930, '31. All my securities were worthless. That's why I had to work so hard on my game. I remember I had my eye on the British Open in 1932 and Mary, my wife, said I had my game just right and I ought to go over. I said, "How could I? We don't have any money to spend, a thousand dollars." She said, "You're going to go. You've improved your sand shot and your grip. You should win." So she got me the tickets and I went over and won the championship. First prize was only £100, but it was the title that meant something. Then in 1935 I won the Masters to complete the four victories. That's when I made the double eagle. Which was just a lucky shot. It had to be luck.

Gene Sarazen

Gene Sarazen almost won the 1940 U.S. Open, at age thirty-eight, when he finished in a tie with Lawson Little. Had he won, he would have been the oldest winner of the championship, just as he is the youngest ever to have won it. However, he lost in the playoff with Little. After World War II Gene went into eclipse as a public figure, but made a comeback in the 1960s as host of "Shell's Wonderful World of Golf," perhaps the most popular golf program ever produced for television.

Gene lives most of the year now in Marco Island, Florida, and is a public-relations representative for a number of major corporations. In recent years he has been one of the two honorary golfers to start play at the Masters Tournament. His short, compact swing rarely fails him to this day.

HENRY PICARD

Photograph by Al Barkow

"I loved it when that gong rang."

When I was a young boy I went up to the Plymouth Country Club to caddie, got interested in the game, and eventually they asked me to take over the stewardship at the little clubhouse they had there. A stewardship was just keeping the place clean, getting people drinks. And I'd serve at parties, nights. Well, they had a big vacant field out there, so the first thing I know I can hit balls during the day, and I had the privilege of the course to play after work. One day I shot 73 with nine threes, and Donald Binton, the pro, thought that was pretty good. Then I got to hitting them a little better, and when I was seventeen years old Binton asked me if I would like to go south with him for the winter. He had the winter job here at the Charleston Country Club. I talked to my dad about it and he said, "Yes, but I'm going to give you a little advice. You'll always be rated by the people you choose as friends." That's all he said, and the more I look at it, the more that statement has meant everything to me.

So I passed my eighteenth birthday in Charleston. This is 1925. Eventually, Binton asked me if I would run the shop in Charleston during the summer. I said fine, so I did that for five straight years. After that, Binton decided to retire, so I took over as head professional summer and winter. If you're at the right place at the right time, everything works out.

Henry Picard

I don't know that I had any special gift for golf. I was twenty-seven when I first won anything important, the North and South. Oh, I won sectional tournaments, but I don't call that anything. I came to Charleston when I was seventeen, so it took me ten years to learn how to play; that is, play exceptionally well. I hit quite a few golf balls. I loved it, and loved the tournaments. I loved it when that gong rang.

Who were my models as players, who inspired me? Well, one day in 1930 I went over to the Savannah Country Club and saw Bobby Jones play. I was playing just ahead of Jones, and on the ninth hole I noticed he had hit a very long drive. I was putting on the green and this ball lands and bounces through my legs. It was Jones' second shot. Now, the next hole parallels the ninth. In fact, the next four or five holes run parallel to each other, and at every one Jones came over and apologized for hitting into me on the ninth. I finally said to him, "Mr. Jones, what time do you start tomorrow? I want to see you play, because I didn't think anyone could hit a ball as far as you did there on nine." I've been back there quite a few times just to see if I could put the ball on that green with two drivers, which I never could. The hole is 540 yards long.

So the next day I met him on the second hole. I'd put a driver on this green, which I thought was pretty good—it was a par-four hole—and I noticed Jones was just moving his ball around on the ground, trying to find a tuft of grass. Finally he got it on a little knob, took a three-wood, and popped it on that green as pretty as anything you ever saw. I started studying his swing, and the more I looked at it, I could see it was big and long. So I made up my mind that I would have a long swing, too.

Why I selected a four-wood to start my new swing with I'll never know, but I broke four of them from hitting the ball on the heel all the time. I couldn't time that swing. Well, I was playing almost every day and getting shellacked. Every day I played it cost me about $12 or $14. My partners would always be working me over, saying why don't I go back to my old swing, we're losing, and so on, but I'd tell them they'd probably be playing against me tomorrow and they'd get even because I'd pay again. I went that way for about two or three weeks straight. Then one day as I was going out to play with

26

Frank Forde, a member of the club and a very fine player, he asked me how I was going and I said I couldn't play a lick. He said, "But, boy, does that swing look good. You're going to be good now." I said, "Well, I'll use it one more day." See, I was about to give it up. So I played and, of course, lost again. Then in July of that year, on the fourth of July, I played with Frank Forde all day and beat him in the morning and afternoon. I shot two 67s and he said, "At last you beat me." See, because of that one statement he made to me, I never gave up. I just kept doing it.

Then I had a man here at the club named McCabe, and another one named Dana Osgood, and each of them thought they could make a player out of me. Osgood bet me on par rounds. If I shot under, he paid me $2; if I shot over, I paid him $1. And every putt had to go to the bottom of the hole. No gimmes. We had a rule that if you knocked my ball away, even if it was an inch from the hole, you had to charge yourself a stroke and put my ball back.

Then McCabe came to me and said, "We're going to play stroke-play tournaments every weekend all summer for you." We played eighteen holes on Saturday afternoon and fifty-four on Sunday. Walking! We played for quite a lot of money, more than I could afford, but I never bet more than I could pay off. And if I lost sometimes, he'd play me five extra holes, $50 a hole, to let me get some of it back. All that went on for four years, then one day we're walking to the fifteenth tee and McCabe turns to me and says, "We've trained you well, dollar nassau from hereafter." He said I was well trained, and I was. Putting the ball in from a foot or two didn't mean anything to me, I'd done it for so long. I can't seem to get people to do that today. Golf has slipped a lot in that respect.

Why did they do all that for me? I guess they were interested in me. I look back and realize I didn't appreciate it as much then as I do now. After that we just played a dollar nassau. But, no, I wasn't a finished player yet. I went to Pinehurst in 1934 to play in the North and South Open, and I got some information from Al Watrous. I thought that what he told me was pretty good. He said I was a little too upright. I couldn't change it right away, but I guess I made the plane a little flatter because I won the tournament. Then in '35 I made the winter tour, representing the Hershey Country Club in Pennsylvania. I had gone there earlier to play in the Hershey Open, and they were trying to hire Ky Laffoon. Ky wasn't interested, but he said, "Why don't you hire Picard? He just shot a sixty-seven. He can play." So, sure enough, we signed a contract. It wasn't much money as money goes today, but then it was a lot. I got $5,000 from Hershey, and I was getting $3,500 from the Spalding company, so it wasn't bad.

That winter, at the Los Angeles Country Club, I got my first inkling of how good I was. They had these small greens and I could toss it on them almost every time. I looked at the other guys and said, "They're pretty good, big names, but I can hit the ball better than they can, I know that." I played fair in Los Angeles, then I went to Agua Caliente and won there, and that made me. Then I knew I could play out there. At the end of the winter I was the high money winner. I won seven tournaments.

But in the summer of 1935 I'm playing just fair, and I meet Alex Morrison in New York. I'm there to play in the Metropolitan Open. A few days before, I was putting on an exhibition at a club and the pro there knew Alex well and wanted me to meet him. We go to his house and Alex asks me if I've read his book [*A New Way to Better Golf*]. I said no, but I'd read a lot of others and I wasn't playing too well and wanted to have a little information off him. He said he would give me some information if I would talk on the radio with him after I won the tournament that week. I said, "You think I'm pretty good?" He said, "We'll see."

So he came out to watch me. I hit about twenty-five balls and I said to him, "I've hit all these balls, and you haven't made a remark yet." He said, "It's difficult to put my finger on exactly what will make you win this tournament." He finally suggested that I hold my head longer after impact—hold it steadier. And, sure enough, I win the tournament. When I got through talking with him on the radio, I told him I wanted to hire him for a week at Hershey. I wanted to get all he knew. So he came down. Now, this is a funny story.

I have a caddie teeing up the balls, and two chasing them. We go pretty good for about an hour, Alex telling me this and that, and me going back at him. Then he looked at me and said, "I'll tell you what, if you speak to me again without me asking you to, I'll get in that car and leave you." I said fine, but can I talk to that caddie? Yes. So he says my first job was to hit sixteen or seventeen balls off a tee without moving it. It took me forty-three hours to do that, with a seven-iron. Then he said I could take a five-iron. It took me two hours to accomplish it with that club. The idea was to get good posture. See, when you're out of plane . . . You know how when a wagon is out of plane it ducks? Well, that's what I was doing. I had the ducks. When I stood up, the swing got into the correct plane and I could clip the ball right off the tee. That's how fine he wanted it. He was right. He proved it to me.

I was hitting balls seven hours a day for him. I was all taped up. He had a bucket of water and he made the ground wet, I'll say that. But I was rolling my ankles the way he wanted, and I still got blood blisters on each foot. He didn't know that. And he took pictures. The film was developed by a druggist I knew while we were eating lunch, so I could see right away the advancements I was making. He could somehow mark it on the film when each swing was made, on what day and so on. So finally he told me to hit my spoon and I hit it and my right foot came way up. I was mad and said to him, "Don't you open your mouth." I had the caddie tee up another ball and I whipped that thing, and a doctor friend of mine who was there said, "Boy, did you hit that," and I said, "That's got whip, yes, that's gone." I asked the caddie if it went straight, and he said like a bullet. So that settled it, and Alex said, "Now go play golf."

I go down to the Cascades to play in a tournament, and everything is going fine until I get to the sixteenth hole. I push a drive to the right and play the wrong ball. I make a nine on the hole. On the next hole I push it again and it's sticking up in a bush. I try to chip it out, get under it, and the damn ball drops into an unplayable lie. I make seven. The next hole I hit a nice two-iron that is just short and ends in the bunker. I leave the first sand shot in the bunker. I make five. Nine, seven, five, and I finish with 84 blows. What kind of a wire do you think I get from Alex? He said, "The worst is over." How do you like that for a wire?

Well, I felt I could really play golf again. I played in the Ryder Cup matches and against Ernie Whitcombe put every shot against the pin on the par threes. I was hitting my irons

29

pretty good, and Jim Barnes walked over and said to me, "You think you're hitting those irons pretty good, don't you, son?" I said yes and he said, "Well, you couldn't caddie for Hagen in his day," and I said, "Then Hagen must have holed a hell of a lot of shots, get away from me." That's all I said. Then I started back on the tour. I won second at Columbus, second at Augusta, second at the Los Angeles Open, and Alex called me and asked how I was practicing. I said I was too lame to practice, because I was standing in front of a mirror trying to get this plane he was talking about, and the roll of the feet, and getting the hips just right. He said, "Well, you're doing pretty good," and I said I'll do all right, don't worry about that. As a matter of fact, he tried to hire me for $70,000 for ten years. Everything I won he would get. But I told him no. I told him that what he did is good, there's no system in the world that compares with it, but I don't want to put a burden on myself. He said he'd insure my health, and everything. I think he would have gotten it back through endorsements, articles in magazines, on radio. He had other income opportunities that I didn't have, and he would have made those into a big thing. I finally wound up a pretty fair player, and he could have done very well with it.

What Morrison was saying was this. The coordination of the arms and body as a unit, and how you get this organized is critical. And footwork, the rolling of the ankles. But in a nutshell—posture, balance, and the plane of the swing. Most people are out of plane, most people swing too short going back and never get wrist action. A number of years later I was in Detroit watching Hogan play in the Open and Al Watrous comes over and says he's teaching the Morrison way, too, because Alex knows it all. I said, "Thank you," then I said to Al, "What you gave me at the North and South that year was part of it, wasn't it? Morrison." He said that was right, but now he was going all the way. The more people get to thinking about how to swing, they all come up to the same genius. Now Nicklaus has come up with it, and I give him credit, after all his success, to make that change.

If the club is not in plane, you can quit talking about what you're doing down at the ball. And everyone has the same plane. It doesn't relate to size or physique. Nooo, that's what

Morrison said, and he's correct. It doesn't make an iota of difference how you're built. All you've got to do is learn it. I had already won on the tour before I met Morrison, but I knew my plane wasn't right. He told me where it belonged. He made it, finished it. Now, in 1937 I went to the British Open and hurt my thumb. I was in agony and couldn't play. I finally went to a doctor in Philadelphia and he said, "Go to the interlocking grip and it'll never hurt again." That meant, take my thumb off the club. It was the grip Morrison taught; the doctor had been to Morrison, too. I didn't get into it when I spent all that time with Morrison because we were working on so many other things. So I took that grip and won the PGA and the Masters. I've used the grip ever since, and recommend it to all my pupils, especially older players. It's basically a fist with the left hand, and the little finger of the right hand interlocks with the index finger of the left hand. Gene Sarazen gripped it that way. I could play the other way, but now I could get my swing longer and looser. You get a lot of wrist action.

Sam Snead tells the story of getting a driver from me out in Los Angeles, and how it helped his game so much, which is true. But I also told him how to work his feet. Then Hogan came along, and I was after him, too. Finally he came to me and asked, "Why don't I win?" I said he hadn't told me what he was doing wrong. He said he was a hooker, and I said I could change that in five minutes. So I did. This was back in the '30s. Of course, he had a great golf swing to start with. He brought the club far back in the early years, way past parallel, but that was what made him hit it so far. He was another one of those superhuman beings. Like Bobby Jones. I saw Jones once at Augusta on the first hole, which is now the tenth. You know how steep that hill drops down in the middle of the fairway? Well, he had a ball on it and he hits a four-wood and gets it way up in the air and the ball came down on the green so softly. From that kind of lie, that was just fantastic. He could turn his body to do it. I asked him how, and he said it was just a gift. Same with Hogan. He could bend around, and he had great posture, footwork, everything. Why did he hook so badly? Well, that's one of those things that will cause a big argument. In teaching golf you come to know how much coun-

31

terclockwise motion with their left hand and arm each individual produces in the downswing. That tells you where the left hand belongs on the club. Quite a statement, huh? Everybody can do it, but they've got to find out how, and how much, which is why there is no set left-hand grip. I will say that openly to anyone. Everyone can turn their hand counterclockwise just so much and they have to know their limit and adjust to it. You grip the club in such a way to make it work. Hogan had too much counterclockwise because of his flexibility, so I just told him to move his left hand to the left; weaken his grip, as we say. That's all there was to it. I said if he could hook it then, I'd eat the golf ball. He said later, "I can't hook," and I said, "That settles it."

I don't know if that's why Ben dedicated his first book of golf instruction to me. I just helped him when he was just coming out. Hogan was sort of a funny coincidence. One night while on the way to the coast I stopped at the Blackstone Hotel with Jack Grout to have dinner. In Fort Worth, I guess. Well, I look over at a corner of the dining room and Hogan was over there with his wife and they were arguing. I didn't know Hogan real well then, but I walk over and say, "What are you arguing about?" She said she wanted Ben to go to the coast, but they both couldn't afford to go. I looked at him and said, "I'm not the richest man in the world, but if you need money, I've got it. You go to the coast with her." And I walked away. He never used a dime of my money, but he had that security.

Now, a few months later we needed someone to fill the field in my match-play tournament at Hershey, and I told them to let Hogan in. All of my officials were giving me a pretty good workout about this. They didn't think Hogan was good enough. I remember Mr. Hershey coming to me and saying, "You think Mr. Hogan is pretty good?" I said I'd never played with him, but that he was very, very good. I'd seen him hit balls. How could I recommend him so highly? I don't know. This is how your brain works when you start studying under Morrison. You're educated to what you're looking for. Now you can see things about a golfer you couldn't before. So Hogan comes to Hershey and I ask him to play with me. We played and I looked at him and said, "Ben, you have the swing I've always desired. You can beat the world." Those are the exact words I told him. I said, "You've got it. You'll play well here." And he went out and won the tournament, with Vic Ghezzi.

But it was another two years before he won on his own. Then, in the Miami Open we both had 70, 70, 70, and he made that remark about he'll never win a tournament. I told him if he went out and shot a 68 or 69 he would be in there. So I shot 68 and finished third or fourth, he shot 69 and was fifth, something like that. Then he asked me about his hook and I told him what to do, and to go to Pinehurst and practice for a couple of weeks.

I play in a couple of tournaments, win one, get in a playoff for another, and by the time I get to Pinehurst I'm exhausted. Well, Hogan knew where I always parked my car there and he's waiting for me. "We're going to play, you promised," he says. Okay. On the first hole I tell him to turn it loose. He hits it down the fairway 290. Like a bullet. On the second hole we had to wait. I'm laying on the ground and I said, "Ben, if you return that thing [club] at full capacity to the ball, the club-head will true itself up at impact." He said, "Up to that statement I thought you were smart, but now you're the most ignorant man I ever saw." I told him if I wasn't so tired I'd hit him in the head with my club. Then I told him, "On the left is the railroad tracks. You've been over there a lot, haven't you?" Yes. "On the right is a lot of shrubbery. You better pin it! Wheel it as hard as you can."

Well, he went out and won that tournament, and I would say a lot of it was the result of the grip change. Now we come to the next tournament, at Asheville. I finished the last round before he did and I meet him on the tenth hole, and he makes a six or five and goes behind two shots. Lawson Little was leading, I think. I said, "Do as I tell you and you'll beat this guy to pieces." I tell him to drive to the left on the next hole, and he does. Then he chips up and gets a three. Next hole is out of bounds to the right, all this junk on the left. God, it's awful, and I say to Ben, "You better wheel it here. Turn it loose." He says, "If I slice, it'll be out of bounds; if I pull-hook, it's unplayable." He wheels it. I had played the hole with a four-iron for my second shot; he's got a seven-iron and he knocks it against the hole. Another three. On the next hole I tell him to play short of a fairway bunker, because it's full of holes. He makes another three. The next hole is another one with out of bounds right, bushes on the left—hard driving hole. "Let it go again," I tell him. He does, and makes another three. The next is a par-five, and he wheels it down there and has a four-iron to the green. I hit two woods on the green and thought that was pretty good. I said, "You're leading by two strokes, you don't have to hole that putt." He two-putts for a birdie, pars the last hole, and wins by three shots. So he went from there to Greensboro and won that and I told him he didn't need me anymore, he was all right now.

What I was saying to him was: if you have a true swing, the harder you hit, the better you'll hit it. He knew all about counterclockwise, and once I told him about the grip, well, you only tell a person once, and if he's not smart enough to do it after that . . .

I played the tour for about seven years straight—the winter tours. I had a club job in the summer like most of us did, and only played in spots then. I didn't want to play much longer than that. It's why I turned down Alex Morrison's offer. I had a family, and in 1934 I had started putting a boy through medical college, a boy that worked for me, not my son. My wife agreed with it, she was a trained nurse. Then I had four children of my own. I thought golf was a great thing, but if I stayed on the tour seven or eight years, that would be enough. I never regretted not playing more. I won twenty-seven tournaments. No, I thought there were other things in life besides golf. And I still think the same way.

Henry Picard

Henry Picard is retired now as a club professional, and lives in Charleston, South Carolina. He is an honored member of the Charleston Country Club, where his career really began. He plays fairly regularly, and well, and gives a few lessons more or less informally to friends.

It needs mention here that when Henry talks about the "correct" swing plane he means it is what most of us would call "flat." Henry does not like to use that term. He says only "correct."

As for Ben Hogan's grip change, Henry told him to turn his left hand more to the left into what is known as the "weak" position.

"LIGHTHORSE HARRY" COOPER

Photograph by Al Barkow

"First you've got to be good, but then you've got to be lucky."

I got into golf very early in my life, because my father, Sid, was a golf pro. Dad served his apprenticeship under Old Tom Morris at St. Andrews in Scotland. I suppose that sounds incredible, Old Tom Morris seems so far back, but Dad lived to be eighty-six. Of course, I never met Old Tom.

I was born in England, in the town of Leatherhead in Surrey, but the only place I've ever played in the British Isles, to this day, is in Wales. And that was when I was very young. I began playing golf when I was three. The first year of my life we lived in Slough, which is near Windsor Castle. Then we moved to the Aberdovey Golf Club in Wales. I remember that the sheep mowed the fairways there, but they put little fences about thigh high around the greens to keep them from being trampled. There was no chipping there. You had to pitch over the fences to get on the greens. My dad was the professional and manager of the club there for eight years. He was also the private pro to Lord Herbert Tempest, and the bugler of his troops. Then Dad came over here.

The first time I came over was in 1912, to Canada. My dad took a job at the Hamilton Country Club. We followed the *Titanic* over, and went through the same ice floe it ran into.

37

We saw tugloads of bodies coming in covered with sheets. My mother, my sister, and myself went back to England in 1913, then my mother and I came back here that same year. We were supposed to land in New York, but the German U-boats were after us and drove us into Halifax. We had to wait for a British warship to escort us into New York. They were quite dramatic crossings. Anyway, I've never been back since, although those crossings had nothing to do with that.

My father taught me how to play at first, the fundamentals. He was a good player. The only tournament he ever played in in the United States, he won. The Indiana Open, in 1915. But I wound up giving him lessons. I was playing very well by the time I was fourteen, but it wasn't until then that I could beat my mother. She was a professional, too. Alice Cooper. When I say professional, she helped Dad out in the shop and running the club, and she did some teaching.

My dad was a friend of Arthur Tillinghast, the golf architect, and it was he who got my dad his first job in the United States. That was in Peru, Indiana, in 1915. There was a golf club there, believe it or not. It was pretty primitive by today's standards, but they had grass greens. It wasn't until we went to Texas that we were on sand greens. I played on those for quite a while, although we were on Bermuda grass greens, too, at Cedar Crest in Dallas. Playing on sand greens was good. They were actually truer putting than grass. Absolutely. It was a combination of sand and oil, and you'd scrape them smooth for your putt. Most sand greens had a clay base, then the sand on top. You could usually hit approach shots right up to the hole and the ball would stop dead. It all depended on how high your ball came in, and how deep they put the sand. If the ball went down and hit the clay and that was hard, the ball came up pretty fast.

Dad was at Cedar Crest for quite a long time. Tillinghast laid the course out, and Dad finished building it. A PGA championship was played there once. I could never understand how my father could take a piece of property and do the drainage and everything else without any formal education as far as engineering is concerned. He built around twenty-five courses in Texas, a lot of them in the oil fields. So, yes, I'm really a

Texas-bred golfer and professional. It was in Texas where I really learned how to play golf. That's where I won my first professional tournament, the Texas PGA, in 1923. At the Galveston Country Club. My mother and I drove down there from Dallas, and it took two days. God knows how many tires we went through.

But I was born in England, and that led to one of my biggest disappointments. You see, all the years I played on the tour I qualified for the U.S. Ryder Cup team, but I wasn't eligible because I was not a native-born American. Same thing with Tommy Armour. He certainly should have been on the Ryder Cup team. And Bobby Cruickshank. Neither of them was eligible, either, which was a very unfair thing, except they learned their golf in the old country and I learned mine over here. They were fully grown when they came over, but I was only ten, which is a little different situation. The rule has since been changed, but I couldn't play and it was very disappointing. Ryder Cup players have a big thing going for them all their lives. They qualify for this, that, and the other thing— get a lot of perks, as they say now.

And I would have played in the British Open a lot of times. I never did, because it wasn't economically feasible. It took a week to go over on the boat, a week to come back, and a week to play. Well, on any weekend here I could make $500 playing an exhibition, so there wasn't any point in going over there. Besides, even if you won, you couldn't even make expenses. I was with the Spalding company at the time, but they didn't pay for me or anyone to go over for the British Open. And a lot of boys wouldn't have gone over if they hadn't been on the Ryder Cup team, because they had all their expenses paid when the matches were over there, and they just stayed to play in the British Open.

My nickname? Lighthorse? Damon Runyon put that on me in 1926 at the Los Angeles Open, when I won the first $10,000 Open. George Von Elm and I played the last round in two hours and a half with 5,000 people following us. I was always a fast walker, fast player . . . and fast swinger. George had seven birdies in the first nine holes, but he didn't pick up a shot on me. I had two on a par-three while he was taking a six, and I had a two on another par-three while he was taking a four. I won $3,500 that time, and won the tournament again eleven years later in 1937 and got $1,000 less. Of course, that was during the Depression and we were lucky just to have a tournament to play.

I played a lot of tournaments, but I wouldn't say I was always a touring pro. In the winters, yes, but I held a club job every summer. And there was an eighteen-month period when I disappeared from the tournament scene. I had my hand in a cast for five weeks, and then had to work from my long swing to a shorter swing. I came out with a great big long swing, and had to go to a shorter backswing. Just like that. It took me a year and a half of really hard work to get it where I felt confident of it. But for the next ten years I had the best record in the game. And then I was a member of the famous Spalding tour. I was on full-time salary with Spalding in 1937, '38, and part of '39 when I made that exhibition tour with Jimmy Thomson, Lawson Little, and Horton Smith. The idea was to promote Spalding equipment, and interest in the game. It was quite a grind. We spent as many as thirty straight nights on sleeper cars. We'd give a forty-five-minute shotmaking demonstration, then play eighteen holes and be off to the next town. We played in every state in the Union, and in Canada and Mexico. But the worst of that tour was, in the clinics some of the instruction we were giving was against my own playing principles. I was the last to join the tour, and the clinic had already been worked out by Bobby Jones and Horton Smith. It was a lot of Jones' theories, and some of it finally crept into my game. Nonetheless, I had very good years in competition during that stretch, I must admit. In fact, 1937 was my big year. I won seven tournaments by myself, and two with Horton Smith as my partner. I won a total of $14,138. Total. Everyone laughs at those figures now, but the truth is that it was a lot of money at the time. I mean, you could live well with that much. I also had royalties from my golf clubs. In 1937 I did $10,000 in royalties, which was a lot of money then. No taxes, remember.

What really hangs over me about my career is that I never won a major title, despite all my success otherwise. And it was simply a matter of luck. First, you've got to be good, but then you've got to be lucky. At Baltusrol in '36, for example. The U.S. Open record at the time was 286. It had been that for about thirty years. I shot 284, and it lasted for thirty minutes. I don't know whether this had anything to do with it or not, but on the fifteenth hole of the last round Johnny Bulla came up to me and said, "Harry, all you've got to do to win is be standing up when you finish. You can't lose. It makes no difference what you do from here in."

Well, I was above the hole on the fifteenth, which is a slopy green, and had a left-to-right putt. I was always a weak left-to-right putter on fast greens, so I three-putt for a bogey. Now, on the next hole, a par-three, there's a grass pathway leading to the green with bunkers on each side. All right. The gallery had started coming from all over when they heard I was winning, but there were no gallery ropes and nobody there to handle the crowd. People were standing in the pathway and wouldn't get out of the way. Of course, I should have waited until they moved out, but I said to hell with it and hit. Whether Bulla saying what he did to me had anything to do with it or not, I don't know. Anyway, my ball hits somebody and bounces back in a trap. I'd have been on the green, otherwise. Well, I couldn't go for the pin because the hole was cut right in front, so all I could do was go for the green itself, which I did, and made a four. I parred the next hole with a five, then hit two nice shots on the eighteenth and am on the green. But I have to stand on that green for eight solid minutes before I could putt, waiting for my playing partner. He's back there trying to find his purse. Somebody had picked his pocket. Les Madison was his name. He had worked for my father. Of course, I was a little nervous and wanted to go. I stood there for a long while, and apparently it affected me, and I three-putted the damn green. So now Manero comes up with a 67 the last round, out of nowhere. He was playing with Sarazen, and afterwards the newspapermen came in and raised a formal complaint—they did, I didn't—that Sarazen was clubbing Manero and otherwise helping him all the way around. The USGA held a meeting for over an hour, and finally did nothing about it. So that was that.

Then, go back to '27. The U.S. Open at Oakmont. If I knew what was going on, I couldn't have lost it. I had about a ten-footer going downhill on the seventeenth in the last round and I went for it. I thought I needed it and hit it firm and three-putted the damn green. Then Tommy Armour knocks in a twenty-footer on the last hole to tie me. In the playoff, at the tenth hole he hit a one-iron that was going like a bat out of hell over the green, but a spectator kicks it back. That would have made a difference. I was leading by two shots at the time. Then on the sixteenth, the par-three, Armour hit his ball over the green. I hit what I thought was a perfect shot right on the flag, but it hit just below the rise. If it hit another foot up, it would have been on the green, but it rolled back in the bunker. Well, in those days they were the furrowed traps of Oakmont, and we didn't have sand wedges then. The ball was down in one of those furrows and there was no way I could reach the green. I hit it halfway up the hill in the long grass and make a five. Now, Tommy's ball is on the path going to the seventeenth tee. There were traps on either side and he could have been in the same fix I was, so there's the luck of the draw. On the seventeenth I knock the ball up a couple of feet from the hole, Tommy skulls his and it runs up inside mine. That was it.

Yes, naturally you get a few good breaks, too. There's no question about it. But I had four opportunities to win the U.S. Open and in every one of them something happened. And not particularly because of me. Same thing with the Canadian Open. I won it twice, but should have won it three times. I come up to the last hole and there is a big crowd all on the right side, because the out-of-bounds fence is close on the left. Now, I seldom hit a ball out of bounds—they used to call me Pipeline—but as I get all set to hit my ball, a galleryite started crossing the fairway. I had to stop and start all over again. Then the fellow ran out a second time—same guy. Next time I went up, I was blank and I knock it out of bounds and take a seven on the hole.

Now Snead comes up and hears what I did, so he knocks his ball way to the right, over the gallery and a little creek and a dry ditch. There's no way in God's good heaven he can get home from there, and he knocks it up 100 yards short of the green. I'm standing on top of the Paramount sound truck, watching. The pin is stuck in the front of the green and there's no way Sam or any other man can land the ball on the green and hold it. He has to play a pitch and run, but the whole approach up to the green, for fifty yards, is nothing but worm casts. The ball could do anything on that. So he played the shot and the ball ran up about three feet from the hole. He made the putt for the tie.

That was on Saturday. In Canada in those days, '38, they couldn't charge a gallery fee on Sunday, so we couldn't play off until Monday. In the meantime we had an exhibition scheduled for Sunday about seventy-five miles north of Toronto. Horton Smith had arranged it. This was when we were making the Spalding tour full-time. I told Horton I would like to skip the exhibition to be ready for the playoff, but he said, "Well, you won it last year, you know, and you're tied for it this year"— meaning the Canadian Open—"and the people up there will be awfully disappointed if you don't come up." So I let him talk me into it. We drove up, seventy-five miles, in the rain, and it rained all day. We did a forty-five-minute shotmaking demonstration, played eighteen holes, and had to drive back because I had to be on the first tee at ten o'clock Monday.

This is the time when Sam hit into the gallery five times, and every time it saved him. It started off right on the first hole. There's a man standing directly behind the pin on the back edge of the green. If you roll over that green, it's unplayable. There's nothing but woods back there. So Snead was carrying the green with his second shot, but the ball hits the guy back there in the chest and bounces back on the green. He saved himself one or two shots there. Anyway, we come to the eighteenth still tied and both on the green in two about the same distance and same line. He putts first, so I get to see the line and get the distance. He two-putts, then I hit an absolutely perfect putt. Never hit a better one in my life. Everybody started screaming "It's in, it's in!" It went right in, came out, and stopped half in, half out. It wouldn't drop. So we had to go another nine and I was pooped by that time because of that exhibition the day before, and Snead won.

"Lighthorse Harry" Cooper

When you ask if I learned anything about golf from these events, if there's something I know now that I wish I knew earlier in my career, it would be that I wish I hadn't been in such a hurry to play, had learned to wait, to be more patient. But that wasn't my nature.

"Lighthorse Harry" Cooper

Not only did Harry Cooper win twenty-seven tournaments on the pro tour, he was runner-up twenty-eight times. He also won twelve State Open and PGA championships. He has received the Metropolitan Golf Association Distinguished Service Award, and the Metropolitan PGA Sam Snead Award for distinguished lifetime contributions to the game of golf. Harry is a member of the National PGA Hall of Fame. He continues to maintain a full teaching schedule. His home is in Hartsdale, New York, and during the summer he teaches at the Westchester Country Club in Rye. For the past few winter seasons he has taught at the PGA National Golf Club in Palm Beach Gardens, Florida.

PAUL RUNYAN

Paul Runyan watching his drive, along with Ben Hogan, in a match during a PGA Championship in the late 1930s.

Photograph by Steve Szurlej/Golf Digest

"I had to work for it. I was not a natural."

I started out in golf as a caddie at the Hot Springs Golf and Country Club in Arkansas. My father was a dairy farmer right across the road, practically, but I discovered I could make more money at the golf club than I ever could as a farmer, and I would have more fun, too. My father whipped my fanny several times for going over there to the club, and when he whipped, it wasn't ordinary. He didn't object because I didn't want to become a farmer, but because he saw it as frivolity. Golf wasn't work, and he couldn't see it. But I finally looked him in the eye and said, "Dad, you can whip me if you want, but it won't do you any good, because I'm going over to the golf course, and I'm going to become a golf professional." He was no fool. He recognized I was bringing home $45 a week to my mother and had more money to spend than any kid in Hot Springs. But I still regret the fact that he would never come to watch me play. He never saw me play one hole. My mother came out a couple of times, but I never played well either time. Her impression? She never understood the game, but she was proud of the recognition I got, and enjoyed the money I was able to give them.

Jimmy Norton was the professional at Hot Springs and he took a liking to me and gave me chances that most of the kids couldn't get then. Caddies weren't allowed to play the course,

47

not even in the summer, which was the off-season. If you were caught, you were fired. But I was made an apprentice to Jimmy Norton and got to play four holes on the way to school and five on the way back. Me and my brother got a couple of extra years of schooling we might not have had otherwise, because the headmaster would give us our afternoon lessons at the morning recess and during lunch hour so we could get to work at the club.

I wasn't a good player right from the start. I had to work for it. I was not a natural. All the kids in the caddie pen beat me, until I just dug it out and became better. I kept at it and they didn't. They were farm kids that came over to make their $4 or $5 and go home. I would make $80 or $90 some weeks, a lot of it from shagging balls for the professional while he gave his lessons. I would get only thirty-five cents an hour, but the members, rich people, would often give me a dollar tip.

When I began giving lessons as an apprentice I was putting from $500 to $700 a week into the till, in cash. I didn't get what I made in golf lessons. I got paid a salary, and the lesson money went into the pro's till. In those days the club repairs and cleaning went the same way. Many weeks I would do as much as $500 in club repairs, but that was all the pro's money, while I was getting a salary of $75 or $80 a week. But that was the rule in those days, that's the way it worked, and I didn't feel I was getting a bad deal. I felt I was fortunate. I was learning a profession and getting paid for it. How much better can you do than that?

Between 1920 and 1930 I won the Arkansas State Open four times and had good jobs. I was at the Concordia Country Club in Little Rock, where they only had about forty members. It was a Jewish club and the members were pretty much wrapped up in business and only played on Wednesday afternoons and Sundays. The rest of the time I practiced. On average I would hit 600 balls a day, although a lot of them were short pitches and chips, because I recognized early that I had to be very good at the short game or I wasn't going to go anywhere. All my playing career I was made fun of for my small size and being a short hitter. And I lived with being an unorthodox player. See, I swayed way back behind the ball intentionally and lunged past it to get more leverage. I never learned to hit it far, because I was afraid to go into a strength-building program for fear it would make me muscle-bound and ruin my career.

Sometimes you have to recognize things for what they are. I had a great break at Concordia. I got to play a lot, as well as practice. I met a man there named Harry Tennenbaum—his father owned a junkyard in Little Rock—and he loved to play golf. Many times we'd play thirty-six holes a day, sometimes seventy-two, on the hottest summer days in Arkansas. It was a nine-hole course and we'd spin around it in fifty minutes.

Then I left Concordia to become Craig Wood's assistant at the Forest Hill club, in New Jersey. Forest Hill was a kind of hell-bent-for-leather place where nobody had much money but spent what they did have. Even then, in the depths of the Depression, you could get a $5,000 nassau going. The people at Forest Hill weren't professional gamblers or that kind, they were businessmen who enjoyed their golf and the excitement of playing for a lot of money in the Depression times.

Anyway, it wasn't the kind of place where I could get the kind of opportunity I got at the Metropolis Country Club in White Plains, New York. I was offered the head job there by Mr. Gerald Rosenberger. One night he had me and my wife come to his house in New York, at 865 Park Avenue, for an interview with the club board. Everyone was there in black tie—they had had a dinner—and I was very impressed. They agreed to take me on at $7,500 a year guaranteed, and anything I made over that was mine. It was a great break, because Metropolis was the highest-grade establishment I have ever worked at. It was the way they ran it. Mr. Edwin Waterman ran the place like a czar. He was president of the club the fourteen years I was there, and he guided me into becoming a good golf professional. He said he wasn't going to tell me how to teach, but he did tell me how to run the business correctly, and how to comport myself. He said I wasn't to call any of the members by their first name until they insisted on it. Mr. Rosenberger was the first to insist on it. Anything I accomplished in golf was influenced by him. After finishing my very first season at Metropolis, Gerald Rosenberger had seventy of the members put up $50 each—a pot of $3,500—to send me and my wife on the winter tour. They drew up an agreement that I was to send any checks I won back to them and if there were any profits we would split them fifty-fifty. This was the tour of 1931–32, which began in November. It was my first full tour. I had made two partial tours when I was at Concordia; members there sent me. I went from California through Texas and back to Arkansas. So I didn't go to Florida until December 1931, for the Miami Open.

Anyway, the members of Metropolis put up the $3,500, which was a little more than enough to pay for our whole expense, because you got a train ticket from New York to Florida to southern California to northern California, back down to southern California, then through Arizona, Texas, and Louisiana back to Florida and up to New York for $202. There was berthage, of course, that was extra. You paid about $8 a night for a berth, but it was overall a very reasonable rate.

Well, that first full winter tour I won about $4,700. I figured, pretty nice, made my winter expenses and lived quite well, didn't have to spend any of the pennies I saved during the summer, and got fifty percent of the purse money I won— another $2,200 or so. When I got back home, nothing was said by the members, and they had a dinner party for me; the whole membership was there and me and wife were wined and dined, and they didn't take their share of the profits. They gave me my share, plus a nice big check which I've still got, canceled, for $1,500. They did the same thing the next winter. They didn't give me any more bonus, but all the profits. But I was pretty well established by now, and beginning to make some money, maybe $14,000 a year, which was darn good in the depths of the Depression.

The touring days were fascinating. There was so little money that we didn't take ourselves too seriously. We fought like cats and dogs for the titles, but the money didn't seem to make that much difference. So there were a lot of antics, fun, camaraderie. People like Frank Walsh, Al Watrous, Tommy Armour. Watrous had such a great joy for the good things of life. You'd see him frequently having dinner on the balcony of his hotel room all by himself. He'd ask you over, but was as happy to be by himself. Oh, and he was a tireless practicer.

Hogan at his best didn't hit as many practice balls as Al Watrous.

We all usually stayed at the same hotel in town. One year for the L.A. Open we stayed at the Hollywood Plaza Hotel and had to take a taxi out to the course—Riviera Country Club. That was a big trip, $7.50, so three or four of us would share it. I remember going out one morning with Frank Walsh, Tommy Armour, and Cyril Walker. Armour and Walker were good friends. They played in the Mid-South, in Pinehurst, every year as a team.

I'll digress a minute here. One time in the Mid-South, Armour shanked his ball into a bunker on the tenth hole and Cyril put his second shot on the green. The most you could be was twenty-eight or thirty feet from the hole, because they were little sand greens only about fifty-five–sixty feet in diameter. Tommy didn't make a good shot out of the bunker; he still wasn't on the green, so he picks it up. When Cyril was ready to putt, a fly lights on his ball. He's trying to brush it off and his club hits the ball backward off the green. It might have been all right, but Armour laughs at him. Cyril got so mad he took a seven on the hole, and they were out of the tournament.

Anyway, in this taxi going out to Riviera, Walker kept us enthralled all the way telling funny stories and singing. He sang quite beautifully. Well, this was the day he was carried off the course by two policemen, literally. He played so slowly they asked him to hurry up, and he became abusive. He said, "Who the hell are you? I'm an ex-U.S. Open champion." This was about 1931, he won the Open in 1924. He said he came out 3,000 miles to play in their diddy-bump tournament and they couldn't kick him out, he'd play as slow as he damn well pleased. Well, when he came to the ninth hole, they told him he was disqualified and he said, "The hell I am! I came here to play and I'm going to play." So these two officers picked him up by the elbows and I can still see him being carried up the hill, kicking his legs like a banty—he was a small man. They threw him off and told him not to come back or he'd go to the pokey.

There were a lot of fascinating guys out there. Leonard Dodson was another. He was involved in five playoffs and never lost one. That's remarkable, because Dodson was so unpredictable. We're playing a tournament in Glen Falls, New York, and the day before it starts, Dodson gets into a discussion with a fellow named Johnny O'Connor, who was a big bettor. Dodson agrees to play O'Connor a $500 nassau playing on one leg, if O'Connor gives him one up each side. If Leonard touches the ground with the other foot before the club hits the ball, he gets a two-stroke penalty. Well, he lost the first three holes, then beat O'Connor all four ways. He shot 69, starting par, bogey, bogey. Next day in the tournament he's standing there on two feet and takes 77.

Ky Laffoon was another character, although he was more serious about his golf than Leonard. Ky was the first person to go a full season with an average under 70 strokes. November to November, 69.1. But he had a pretty good temper. He was playing poorly at one time and, after he finished a round, said he'd never take more than 72 strokes in a tournament again. *Never.* The next week he goes out and shoots 67, 69, then 65, and by this time he's close to the lead or in it—a tournament in Sacramento. Well, in the last round he comes up to the eighteenth green with about a six-footer for a two, misses it, picks up his ball and puts it in his pocket. He never finished the hole and was either disqualified or he withdrew. I asked him, "Ky, why did you do that?" He said that the first putt he hit was his seventy-second stroke and he'd vowed he'd never shoot more than a 72 in a tournament again. So he picked it up.

I never weighed much over 125 pounds, but the only player who ever intimidated me was Gene Sarazen, and he wasn't an especially big man himself. He did it with his demeanor, and his playing, too. I happened to meet him in the fourth round of the first PGA championship I ever played in, in 1931. In Providence. I played superbly in a twenty-five–thirty-mile-an-hour wind and he beat me four up with three holes to play. With me *three under par.* I didn't believe anybody could play that kind of golf, because I would have beaten anybody else in the field that day. About his demeanor, Sarazen was so arrogant. I always hoped he didn't get mad, because he played better. If there was nothing happening that got him excited or mad, he would just pick it up and put it in his pocket out of boredom. He wouldn't pick it up in the U.S.

Open or the PGA, but in regular tour events he had it in his pocket at least twenty-five percent of the time. He shouldn't have done it, because he was a big drawing card, one of the three best in his era.

I've taken some pleasure out of being the little guy who has beaten the big fellows. At match play, don't think that isn't an advantage, because a big guy would rather lose to a big guy. And I had a cocky attitude that boded well for me, especially if they had a tendency to get ruffled. Some were easier to ruffle than others. Henry Picard gave the air that nothing could ruffle him, but that was the exterior. Inside he could get ruffled easily. Frank Walsh was another one. For dollar nassaus in practice rounds Harry Cooper would beat me nine out of ten times, but when the tournament started I beat him three times out of four. Harry threw away more tournaments than anybody because he was too excitable. And he believed everybody was lucky and he wasn't. Golf is so much an emotional game. It's made up of one part physical excellence, which is God-given. There's one and a half parts that is acquired physical excellence. That's how you take care of what you have; you understand cause and effect and how to use those characteristics. Then there are three or four parts for emotional excellence. That's the summation of all the things that let you go on and envision success, not failure. The minute you begin envisioning doing something poorly, just as sure as you're sitting there you will fail.

I believe this had a lot to do with my victory over Sam Snead in the 1938 PGA championship at Shawnee-on-the-Delaware. That's the one event in my competitive career people seem to remember best, because Sam was outhitting me. But there's one thing I still can't understand about that championship. There was the famous bookmaker, Doyle I think his name was, and even though I'd been the PGA champion four years before, when I played a fellow named Levi Lynch in the first round in '38 Doyle made it even money. I'm a previous champion, and this fellow hasn't done anything. Now, the next round I play Tony Manero, and I'm 3-to-1 underdog. Of course, Manero had won the U.S. Open. Then I play Ray Mangrum, Lloyd's brother, who was as good as Lloyd, and I'm 2½-to-1 underdog. I play Henry Picard and I'm 3-to-1 underdog, and when I play Sam Snead in the final he's the favorite, 10-to-1.

Well, when Tony Manero won the U.S. Open in 1936, Doyle had him at 200 to 1 to win, 100 to 1 for second, 50 to 1 for third. Tony said that was an insult and he was going to bet $20 across the board on himself, and he did. That only changed his odds to 100 to 1, 50 to 1, and 25 to 1, and he said that was still an insult, so he bet another $20 across the board and goes out and wins the tournament. The Open at that time paid $1,000 to the winner, so Tony won a big chunk of money besides.

Anyway, in that PGA in '38 I was smarter than they were, all of them. There wasn't a one of them who knew how to take care of himself in 100-degree sweltering heat. It was 100, 102 with a humidity of ninety, and it just wilted them. In match play I knew how to take care of myself. They had very cold water in that valley [Delaware], and before I'd go out to play in the morning I'd soak in a tub of cold water. Usually there was a five-hour difference between your morning starting time and the afternoon round, and even if you were playing with a slow player you'd go around in two hours and forty minutes. So I'd have my wife draw the water and before I had my lunch I'd take another cool bath. I'd stay in it until I actually was chilled, then I'd go back and have my lunch and a warm-up. Oh, I was getting stronger as the week went on, and they were all wilting.

Everyone says Sam was outhitting me 100 yards, but it was only forty-five yards. Sam's average in those days was 280, and mine was 230, but he didn't outdrive me by that much at Shawnee. The interesting part of it was, he lost all four of the par-five holes, where he figured to have the best chance because of his length. But he lost them to birdies. I birdied every one of them in the morning, and two of three in the afternoon. He never birdied one of them. He never hit the greens in two. He kept hitting his second ball long to the left in the long grass, and I was out in the fairway a little short of the green and would pitch up and get my four.

I think he was the best sport under the circumstances. It must have been one of the most galling experiences of his life. Got to have been. Because he drove it bullet straight. But a 71 in the morning on a course where he can reach all but one of the par-fives in two is not such a good score. He drove it magnificently, but didn't do much after that.

I felt quite confident after nine holes that I could beat him, because I went out in 31 and was four up and he wasn't playing that well. I was 66 in the morning. His length didn't bother me, because I was the shortest hitter in the annals of golf to be as successful as I was.

Paul Runyan lives in Pasadena, California, and remains very active as a golf teacher, traveling to many parts of the world and throughout the United States as a member of Golf Digest *magazine's instructional schools staff. He also plays in senior tournaments, and says he's hitting the ball a little longer now than he did when he was thirty.*

HAROLD SANDERSON

Photograph by Al Barkow

"This game, you never lick it."

My golf career was virtually 99.9 percent in America, and I never was to feel like an employee or something less than a first-class citizen. Why? We're an immigrant nation. Everybody comes over and, Lord, if you made a lot of money and joined a country club but you know your old dad was a coal miner in Czechoslovakia, why should you put on airs? Oh, there were some who got snobby. The *nouveaux riches*. Boy, nobody can be snobbier than they are. But you take the real old family lines and it's a pretty democratic country. I never considered golf a rich man's game in America, although I did in England.

My two elder brothers were golf professionals. One of them, Archie, was the first to come over from England. One of his cronies, Charley Mayo, was coming over to play in the U.S. Open, and Archie was going to join him. He was turned down by the Army because of varicose veins; in those days they turned you down for that. They were supposed to leave on the *Lusitania*. But it was sunk, of course, on the inward voyage, so Charley Mayo backed out. He didn't want to go with all those subs around. But my brother said, "Aw, heck, I'll go anyway." So he came over, played in the Open at Baltusrol, and decided to stay. That was in 1915.

Harold Sanderson

In the meantime I became an indentured apprentice to Charley Mayo. This was at Burhill, in England. You see, I had worked for him as a kid of fourteen and fifteen, but he had some crackpot system I got fed up with, so I quit. This time, he said, I couldn't quit him. My father and I had to sign an indenture form, a regular legal document. I signed for a three-year indenture. Actually, they had indenture in the United States, too; for toolmakers, for instance. The English form was kind of funny, because you were not supposed to frequent public houses—hit the booze, in other words—and you had to keep good company and all. Which was a lot of . . . Well, in any case, I couldn't quit Charley. In other words, he was going to teach me clubmaking and he was going to be doggone sure he got something out of me. That was the idea, and it really wasn't as bad as it sounded. He was protecting his interests, which was fair enough. When I think of all the assistants I've broken in, trained, even taught how to swing a club, who then left me just when they were becoming useful . . .

I was born in Surrey, England, at Walton-on-Thames. My father was a harnessmaker. There was a golf course nearby and we caddied, the classic entry into the game, although not so much now. I began caddying when I was around eleven, just about that time when kids could be trusted. I was good at sport, a better-than-average athlete, and when I started to play golf I thought, with all the cocksureness of youth, oh, this will be easy. And, of course, I fell flat on my duff. But I went at it, and eventually worked up a pretty good game.

I was seventeen when I came to the United States to work for Charley Mayo at the Edgewater Golf Club in Chicago, where Chick Evans was the topnotch amateur. This was in 1920. Charley got a lead on the job from a friend, and went over to take it. That put me in the scheme, although by then I was only with him one year. I had two more years of indenture, which was valid in England but not in the United States, but I followed him to Chicago and stayed with him. He liked me, he wanted me, and I learned just about everything from him. I've been in the United States ever since.

Charley Mayo was a well-recognized pro when he came over, but there is some truth to the old story that many a Scot would get a job here in those early days simply because they were Scots and people wanted a Scot in the shop. I knew several fellows who had pretty good games of golf in Scotland, but were more professional soccer players than golfers. Or they were toolmakers. That's where the term "shoemaker" for golfers came from. I can still hear old Fred Brand in Pittsburgh saying, "Ah, he's nothing but a bloody shoemaker." But, you see, they were craftsmen who could make and repair clubs, and that was what people wanted then more than anything else.

It's too bad we can't hear from old Jack Jolly, who's dead now. Jack was the one who used to meet these Scots coming off the boat here, and help them make a new life. He'd get them pro jobs, establish a line of credit for them. Help them. It was commercial on his part. He sold the old Colonel golf ball, which MacGregor made, to the pro trade. So, of course, those fellows he helped set up did their business with Jack. But he was a wonderful old guy and, because of his personality, had a great appeal to everybody. Jack played a good game, too.

Anyway, I stayed with Charley Mayo for two years in Chicago, then went with him to Druid Hills in Atlanta. When Charley went home to England for a visit, I ran the shop there, but when he came back he got some bee in his bonnet and just didn't like the job anymore. So he asked to be released from his contract, and was. Before that, Charley had sent another experienced assistant over from England to be with him, a guy who had been a major in the British Army. He wasn't much of a golfer, but was a very fine clubmaker, and in those days a clubmaker was a jewel. If a pro had a good clubmaker, brother, that was an asset, more so than if he was a good teacher or player. But the club had come to like me, and I was starting to play good golf then, so the club suggested I take Charley's job in partnership with this major. He's a mature man about thirty-six, and here I am a half-baked kid. So I had enough common sense in me to say no, I didn't think that would be right. I was a much better golfer, and the arrangement they wanted would have made for bad blood. So I thanked them and went to work for my brother Archie at the Sleepy Hollow Club in Westchester County, New York. Archie was there for twenty-six years.

Then a job opened up at a resort course nearby, Briarcliff Lodge. I had an interview for it, and got the job. It was a nine-hole course with a unique feature. This is one for the books. The first tee was on top of the pro shop! Apparently, the pro shop had once been a toolshed underneath this jutting ledge. So I'd be in the shop working on a shaft or something and would hear the thump, thump of the golfers above trying to hit the ball. Well, the place was bought by a syndicate and they were going to promote it, so from my angle the question was who knew Harold Sanderson, although I finished in the first six in the Westchester Open that year. They hired Gene Sarazen, and I'm out of a job. But, you know, none of those guys—Armour, Cruickshank, Sarazen, Hagen—ever gave lessons then. They were free-lancers. They played with the members, or others, and if they had a club affiliation they always had some good assistant to run the shop. They would just float around. But they had all the business in the golf shop, and just paid the assistant a salary. I played with Sarazen a lot. I never did play with Hagen, but he was my favorite. He was the best of the bunch, a great guy. Sarazen was not very communicative, by comparison at least.

So I wind up in Pittsburgh. I was there for a couple of years at Thornburg, which later became Chartier Heights. The pro who was there quit because the place flooded in the spring, and only around July 4 would the course be fit to play. He said dead pigs and wild hogs were floating around in the water. While in Pittsburgh I won the Tri-State Open and a few one-day events, then I moved to the Hollywood Golf Club in New Jersey.

That winter, of '29, I went out and played some of the national tour. In fact, I played the very first one that went to California. It was gotten together by Hal Sharkey, a Newark [New Jersey] sportwriter. He managed it. We played Sacramento, Fresno, Los Angeles, Long Beach—about five tournaments out there. I finished third in Sacramento. Eddie Luce won the tournament, Jim Turnesa was second. I got $350 for third and was in clover. Three hundred and fifty bucks! For playing golf! Of course, in those days the pros were really like pure amateurs. By that I mean the prize money was always welcome, but it was not of compelling importance. There wasn't enough of it. It was just frosting on the pie. We played because we loved to play, and got just as much fun out of our practice games for a couple of bucks. It was a winter vacation, or almost so. You practiced and played golf and made contacts for jobs.

When I saw California for the first time I thought, Boy, this is where I want to be. But the pro jobs there in those days were terrible. The club ran the shop and just paid the pro a flat rate. It was not too good a deal. It's hard to say why they did it that way out there, and not in the East. Some bigwig, maybe, in the state golf association there didn't like pros.

After I'd been out on the tour I decided it was not for me. I was a conservative young lad and never did any running around, no drinking. So the tour was pretty monotonous. I mean, the golf was fine, but you had the rest of the day and the night. It was a precarious life, financially, but mainly it was for me monotonous, or it would have been.

I had great hopes of becoming a great player when I was young. Everybody has that. I think I could have, had I elected to stick with it and not become a club pro. Had I been born thirty years later, then there would be the money and I would have stuck with it. Because I had the game, the equipment, with the exception of the putting stroke. I would have worked that out, though, with the constant playing. When you play golf every day, something gets fastened in a young body, particularly if you're under thirty, so you can do it in your sleep. You can visualize everything. I used to get up and take a practice swing and I could visualize my tee shot being down the center, and it would go down the center.

But then again, I remember in the last U.S. Open I played, in Rochester in 1955, poor Ben Hogan, after what he went through from his accident and the nerve strain of golf. He had that putt to tie for a playoff which would have given him his fifth Open title, or a chance for it. It was a putt of only a few feet, and he stood over it, stood over it, stood over it, and I said, "Brother, when is he going to take it back?" Finally he did, and it came nowhere near the hole. I was on the plane with him that evening, going back. Now, here was a man who had done everything in golf, and you would have thought that by that time, at his age, he would have thought, "So what! I missed." But on that plane he had the look of the most abject misery on his face. That man was suffering. So I thought to myself, Boy, oh, boy, what price glory. What is it, huh? This game, you never lick it. You can tell how much Nicklaus suffers now that he misses short putts. He's suffering, and if he won two more national championships it wouldn't enhance his stature any more. But the guy who makes his first million wants two.

Once you say you're going to teach the game, you can say goodbye to your career as a player. I gave a tremendous amount of lessons, always. At Hollywood it was a short season, so I'd be teaching from morning to night. I liked to teach, but it was wearying. You get a lot of people that can't hit a haystack with a . . . The only thing is, you have the realization that some of those very poor starters develop into very good golfers. So that keeps you on your toes. You say, This might be the one.

In the winters I used to teach in Newark, at Bamberger's, in the sporting-goods department. A net was set up. I would get some of the minor-league baseball players in there, and they were the quickest golfers you could make. It was a cinch. If you're a good baseball hitter, you can make a good golfer.

I was interested in the Ernest Jones method when that was popular, but I thought it was mainly good salesmanship. It must have been more than that, though, because he was pretty effective. But the best book I've ever read on golf was Ben Hogan's, the one he did with Herbert Warren Wind. Hogan had a fine golf swing. It was compact. It reminds me of this fellow Madlock, who led the league in hitting for the Pirates. That little, short job he does. In fact, I think a short swing is an asset for the average golfer. When I get young kids I always tell them that the short swing develops the long ball, not the long swing. When I say short, I mean short of the horizontal on the backswing. I think it makes you learn to apply your power better.

When I was a kid I was kind of skinny and I made a long swing. I had a very supple body, which made it a little tougher under pressure. With a short swing, under pressure, there is less time to think and go wrong. Swing within yourself is the way we always put it. And if you notice, on the tour there are very few golfers who reach the horizontal or dip a little below it. In my day it was common. Like Harry Vardon, he was way over. They may have done that because they played in those big, heavy sports jackets. But you'd think that would have been more restrictive. I think it was a relic of the old gutta-percha days, when they had to take a different swing to hit that guttie ball.

There's nothing new in golf instruction. It's a regular merry-go-round. You keep coming back to things. The basics will never change. After all, the clubs are virtually the same, except for the development of newer metals that allowed them to reduce the weight of the hosel; that's where the neck of the blade fits into the shaft. That was a tremendous improvement, because it allowed the weight to be distributed better. With that old thick neck they couldn't do that. It also added more speed to the clubhead; because the shafts became slimmer and there was less air resistance.

But whether these more modern shafts—powdered manganese, graphite, and whatnot—accomplish anything is a moot thing. Even the hickory shaft was a great-feeling club to hit. You know, the pros would buy hickory shafts by the gross and have first pick out of them, and there were probably a dozen that were really topnotch. You tested them for the spring in them. After a while you got so you were like a piano player. You were handling the shafts so much that you gave one a nudge and could tell if it had the proper yield. The pro would get that one. It would be laid aside, very carefully.

You see, they couldn't make hickory shafts with different flexibilities the way it can be done with steel. To get a really stiff hickory you'd have to leave it as thick as a post. If you took it down as slim as you dare, then you would have to have a very high-class piece of wood in order for it to hold up under the smack of impact. Some of those shafts would last for years in the hands of a good golfer. It was amazing. Of course, it was the hacker who allowed the pro to make a living repairing those shafts, or replacing them.

Being a club professional now is much different. Something younger golfers will never know is the smell of the old pro shop: glue, shellac, varnish. There were shavings all over the floor. Now you go into a pro shop and it's like a boutique.

Was the older way better? Well, yes, in that the very smell of it represented craftsmanship. There were clubmakers as well known as old violin makers. Some golfers would insist on having a club made by an individual clubmaker.

The clubs came to us in the rough cast, a rough wooden block and bored, although you could change that a little. Then you shaved and sanded them and finished them. Then you had to fasten the shaft to the head, put the face in, and sole the woods. In those days the driver was the only one that didn't have a sole plate, because it didn't make much contact with the ground. The brassie had a sole plate—of brass—and the spoon did, too, because it was used to hit the ball off the ground. And always you had to pour the lead in the back to get the weighting right.

Along with that work, my brother Archie, when he was in England, used to cut the greens in the morning, and he also had to have time to teach and play. And sometimes on weekends he used to have to tend bar in the clubhouse. That was part of his duties. He made I would say £2 a week. And these guys these days moan and bellyache about their lot!

You develop a lot of insights about the game over a period of years. Some you hang on to, others you reject. Often the ones you reject are the ones you should have hung on to. For instance, I used to think putting was mainly luck because some days I knock in those ten- and twelve-footers, and other days I couldn't get a one. It was a bad mistake on my part. I had a pretty good golf swing—some people thought it was an excellent swing—yet at putting I was always mediocre. Because I did not follow a specific formula.

You know, they say they are better putters today because the greens are better now than in my day. But that's a fallacy. A lot of courses—I'm speaking of the top-quality courses now, like Oakmont—had putting greens that were flawless. The fairways are better now, what with the watering system we have. But the greens were actually better fifty years ago, because they didn't use insecticides as they do now. The insecticides eliminate worms, so they have to keep watering, watering, watering to keep the greens soft. You see, worms aerated the greens naturally; kept the subsoil alive, you might say. In the early days the greenskeeper, earning $5 a day, would take care of the worm castings with a long bamboo pole, swishing them off. Many people have thought that was to clear the dew in the morning. Well, it did that, but the main purpose was to clear away the worm castings that came up overnight. Then the greens would be cut.

But, you see, without the worms the soil beneath gets hard and the water only softens them for a moment, whereas the worms keep them regularly soft. The worm is the most marvelous trigger there is. It makes topsoil out of nothing, out of subsoil. It ingests the soil, and it goes through and comes out as topsoil. I learned that from my own gardening. That's why you look at many of these modern greens and they're rock-hard because they put on water, but what you get is a film on top and the greens bake. I remember when they used to cut the greens in the spring, before power mowers came in. The fellows would run to get up speed with the push-mower, because the grass was so lush and heavy at that time of year. Brother, they really had to get a burst of speed up, like a pelican taking off from the water.

No, I don't think the greens are anywhere near as good as they were.

The ball has improved—oh yes. I still play, of course, and I get distance that amazes me. I'm 81 at the moment, but I'll play 75, 76. Last year I broke 80 about seven times.

I have two daughters, and they play a bit, but I never rammed it down their throats. Now, if I had sons I would have figured yes, because they could get a free education, a scholarship to college. In my day I could have gotten one if the present rules were in vogue. But in my time there was no such thing, because it made a golfer a professional. As it was, I went to school only until I was sixteen. The rest of my education I had to acquire on my own. I've always read a great deal, and taken courses. I took a course in English at Columbia University years ago. And I did some writing, but only for the club publication, and a piece for a program for a women's tournament in New Jersey.

Golf, of course, always keeps you fresh. It's always got you licked, you're never ahead of it. You have your days of glory, but . . . I'm amazed at the way those elbows stand up among the players of today who practice so much. I remember the first year I got tendonitis, I would flinch when I hit a shot. It only takes one bad swing, or divot, or hitting a hard piece of ground. Well, I went to an orthopedist and he told me to quit for five weeks, which I did, and then it was okay. But a couple of years later it hit me again. I stopped for six weeks. Fine. I go play. Then after I retired, I was in my seventies, it hit me again. So for three and half years I didn't touch a club. The pro at Canoe Brook who replaced me, Jack Kiefer, was always nagging me to play, but I said nah.

Well, one day my grandson comes over and he wants a lesson. We go to the driving range and he says, "Grandad, let's see you hit one." So I say okay. I tee it up, take a couple of practice swings, and whoosh! Right down the slot. I hit three balls, every one of them as good as I ever hit it. The next day I'm back at the driving range, and I hit a small bucket. I was about seventy-five then. So finally I said to Jack Kiefer that I'd go play. I went out and shot 75. Now, I went from that, and don't ask me why—the psychology of it—to somewhere around 84 the next time. And the next time 85 or 86. It's so odd. Often the first round of the season, or the first round in three years, will be a very good one. You hit the ball well, even putt well. Oh, it's a cockeyed game.

Harold Sanderson

Harold Sanderson is held in very high regard as both a player and teaching professional by all who have been around golf for the past fifty years. He won the New Jersey PGA championship at the age of fifty-seven, the New Jersey Seniors five times. Harold won the last National PGA Seniors title— the Bourne Trophy—before the age requirement was lowered. At age sixty he won with rounds of 70–67. He played in three U.S. Opens, his best showing coming in the 1932 championship, when he was but one stroke behind the eventual winner, Gene Sarazen, after thirty-six holes.

Harold's last head-professional post was at the Canoe Brook Country Club. He retired from there after thirty-eight years. He now lives in retirement in Florham Park, New Jersey.

FRANK WALSH

Photograph by Al Barkow

"If there's one secret . . . it's to do as many things as possible with the left hand."

I can't tell you how many stories I've heard and read about how many poeple actually saw Gene Sarazen knock that ball in the hole for a double eagle in the Masters. In one of them Bob Jones was sitting in a cart. First of all, there were no carts then. And Jones wasn't there anyway, he was back at the clubhouse. I had left him there with Craig Wood—we had been drinking some of Bob's corn and waiting for the rest of the field to finish so my friend Craig could be crowned the winner—when I decided to walk out and see just what was happening. There were only six or seven people there on the fifteenth hole. Gene's playing partner, Walter Hagen, was away over on the other side of the fairway playing short of the creek, and, of course, there was Sarazen with his caddie, and I recall three or four people talking about Henry Picard being their man. Henry wasn't in the group, but he was close in the tournament and some of his fans were out there. Henry was a big name in the South, a favorite son.

Anyway, Sarazen just put his right foot back and hit a low hooking shot. Just the wrong kind of shot for the circumstance. If Picard was there, he would have thrown it sky-high and dropped it onto the green softly. Sarazen's wasn't the right type of shot at all, but it hit on the right front corner of the green—there's a bunker there now—and it curled around on the slope and went in the back of the hole.

After it went in, Gene just moved quickly forward the way he always did and kept his eye on two fellows up at the green, spectators who were going onto the green as though to take the ball out of the hole. I remember Gene shouting at them, "Get the hell away from there!" or something to that effect. I turned and headed back to the clubhouse after I saw the dreadful thing happen—taking my roommate out of the championship. I started back in a rush to tell everyone at the clubhouse, but then I slowed down, saying to myself that no one would believe me anyway, and, besides, it would be a half-hour or so before Sarazen and Hagen came to eighteen. So I had plenty of time.

Gene played the right type of shot on eighteen, where he had to kite it—get it high—and get it to the back part of the green, because the pin was at the top level. Which he did. The thing is, at fifteen Gene didn't think about winning the championship. He was just going through the motions. But at eighteen he knew he needed par to tie Craig. So this was, in a sense, the greater shot of the two. He had a three-wood to eighteen from down below the hill, so we couldn't even see him from the back of the green. Bob Jones, myself, and Craig had come out to see the shot, and when Gene's ball came up to the back of the green about ten or fifteen feet from the hole, maybe a little more, we knew there would be a playoff. When Gene hit it on the green the way he did, Craig spilled his drink. But to show you what kind of fellow he was, I remember he cleared away the ice that had fallen so the reporters behind the green wouldn't slip on it. He didn't want anyone to tumble just because he got upset and spilled his drink. Grantland Rice, O. B. Keeler, and others were back there on their haunches, watching.

We never saw Gene hit his first putt. We began walking back to the clubhouse with our heads down, no conversation whatsoever. We knew that if he made it for birdie, we would hear the applause. Well, he two-putted and, of course, beat Craig in the playoff, and that was that.

I was invited to play in the Masters because I knew Bob Jones very well. We had played some golf together around the country, and at Augusta. I hadn't won anything in the '30s, but Sarazen did beat me out of the Florida Open sometime in there. I never won any tournaments on the tour. I don't think I even came close; maybe a second or third occasionally. I wanted to play tournaments all the time, but a good club job would always come along. And, frankly, I didn't latch on to the knowledge of the golf swing that I have now.

Me and my brothers grew up living right next to the Auburn Golf Club on the south side of Chicago—the Englewood section. So, of course, we caddied there, and also at the Beverly Country Club. Then my older brother, Tom, became the superintendent of golf at Olympia Fields. He was in charge of the caddies and the starting times and all. It was a big job, because there are four courses there. Through Tom I went to work in the pro shop at Olympia Fields, and from there got my first head-pro job, at Butte Des Morts—it means Hill of the Dead—in Appleton, Wisconsin. That was a summer job, and in the winter I would play the tour a little wherever there were tournaments. But I also took some winter club jobs. I had stints at the Miami Biltmore and Normandy Isle—I opened up Normandy Isle.

Then Craig Wood wanted me to replace him at Rumson, New Jersey, so he could take the offer he had from Winged Foot, and I couldn't refuse my friend. So once again I didn't get out on the tour. Then Rumson closed up during World War II and I was walking the streets of Red Bank, New Jersey, after I was told I didn't have the proper education for the jobs I wanted in the Army. I was hurt, feeling badly. Well, as I was moping along the street, one of the Rumson members saw me and said Al Watrous was trying to reach me on the phone at the club, he said Watrous had a job for me. I called Al and asked him what the job was, and he said, "Golf professional. What the hell else can you do?" It was at Red Run, in Detroit, and he said to get there as soon as I could, and I told him I'd be there in fifteen minutes. So I was at Red Run for ten years.

It was on the tour where I got to be friendly with Craig Wood. We were thrown together somewhere along the line, and it wasn't even to do with his car; he wasn't looking for someone to ride with him. We had fun in those touring days, but we practiced a lot, we worked at it. We'd get to the next town and as soon as we could we'd all be out on the practice tee. And there were some unusual things, compared to today. I remember a time we were playing in El Paso in the winter, and they had cottonseed-hull greens. When the sun came out, steam would rise up over them, so when you finished a hole you walked off the front of the green so the people behind could see you were leaving and it was open for them to play up. The other thing was, on these greens the metal part of the cup would sometimes rise above the edge of the hole. They left tampers by the greens to tamp them down, and to smooth down the line of your putts. Well, one time I'm playing with Bill Mehlhorn and he has a putt for a birdie, but he didn't examine the cup well and his ball hit the metal rim and went around it. Oh, the fire in his eyes as he tamped the cup down with his putter so the ball could drop in! Bill came over to me as we walked off the green and said, "Give me the card, Frank." He said he didn't want me to put down the five, that it would punish hell out of him for his carelessness if he put it down himself. I loved him for that.

Another time we played a tournament on Catalina Island. I don't remember how much we played for, but there were about thirty-five of us invited over, and after the third round I was about thirty-third in the field. I wanted to go back to Los Angeles, but Al Watrous said to wait and see what kind of pairing I got for the last round. This was in 1929. The pairings came out and I was put in last, to make a foursome with Hagen and two others who were leaders. Watrous said he wanted me to play with Haig because he hadn't seen me play and I might get a lot of help from him. He said he'd talk to Hagen, and he did.

So we went out and played. It was a course where on one hole, a par-three, Hagen played it with a putter because the green was way down below a hill. Anyway, I went wild. I went around that course in 57—par was 69. I'm not going to talk any more about it, but the part I love is, for the next thirty years, including the ten at Red Run, where Hagen spent a lot of time, Haig would never fail, when Watrous came over, to say to Al, "Is this the fellow you wanted me to help with his game, who can't play a lick?" And he'd point to me. It was a funny happening at Catalina. Everything I did was right, and I picked up a big chunk of money for passing some thirty players and finishing third.

But I never got to play enough tournaments . . . never did. I don't think I would have done well out there then, anyway. I couldn't do with the ball what I saw the other fellows doing. It's a funny kind of statement for me to make, but they didn't like what they were doing and I didn't like what I was doing, but I'd rather have had theirs than mine! Damn, how they hated to hit the ball right to left, and how I would have loved to do that! They all hooked the ball, and I sliced it, and— can you imagine?—all the stars came over and studied me because I'm a slicer, a fader. They wanted to see how I popped the ball up into the air. Theirs was going low along the ground. They wanted to fade the ball because they couldn't control the hook, and they couldn't get the ball high enough. They hated the hook. I could fade it because I couldn't turn my left hand counterclockwise the way they could.

I learned how to play golf, mainly, by watching. George O'Neill was the pro at Beverly when I caddied there. He was an elegant man, dressed beautifully, spoke so well, and he had a smooth, lackadaisical way of playing that I tried to emulate. In those days, the '20s, you made a forward press with the club after your waggle, then started the club back. Everybody had it, we were all doing it, but it was all wrong. Because it got the body in first, instead of hitting with the hands—swinging the arms down and hitting the ball with the hands. You see, we practiced to get a fine-looking follow-through, with the body turned away. It looked good, but it was wrong. It had nothing to do with hitting the ball with force. We were posing all the time. We didn't know it. I had to change it all and get more arms and wrists and hands into it. Turn that left hand over, instead of sweeping the ball. I was watching Lanny Wadkins the other day on television. That's the way. *Hit* it! He slaughters the thing. We didn't see any of that when I was young. Armour started teaching it in the '30s—hit the hell out of it with the right hand, he said.

It's a question of manipulating, turning, rotating the left hand counterclockwise in the downswing. It's much easier for a right-handed person to rotate his left hand clockwise, because that's natural. And most people are right-handed. But the club has to be turned counterclockwise when hitting the ball to make a good shot. That's why the game is so hard for most people. Many of the stars on the tour are left-handed people playing with right-handed clubs, so they turn counterclockwise naturally. They're geared that way. Hear me out! They can't fade the ball. Some of the best players in the world can't fade the ball, even though they always talk about trying to.

I tried to teach people to hook or draw the ball. If there is one secret to the game, one thing I would tell a beginner to do to become a good player, it's to do as many things as possible with the left hand. Learn to eat with the left hand, take the club out of the bag with the left hand, and between shots carry the club in your left hand and rotate it counterclockwise, from right to left. I watch people playing right out of my window here, and they carry the club in their right hand and upside down as though they never hit a ball in their entire life. They could do a lot for their game if they carried the club in the left hand to give it some exercise. They never use it in the swing, and they won't ever use it right until they learn how to use it between shots.

It's not that the left hand is weak, physically. It has nothing to do with strength or flexibility, but with agility and going against what the left hand wants to do naturally, which is to turn clockwise in the fingers. People can't grasp the immensity of how important it is to spin the club counterclockwise! It's not a matter of just holding on to the club with the left hand, but *using* the left hand to hit the ball.

An engineer once told me I'd lose my audience, because you have to be an engineer to understand what I'm talking about. And he was right. The counterclockwise idea throws them for a loop. And, let's face it, what are our chances of announcing now that children have got to be taught to take the fork and put it to their mouth with their left hand, to not shift it to the right hand to shove the food into their mouth? Or to take the soup up with the left hand. What the hell for, someone will say, so they can play better golf? But I'm afraid that's what I mean. I think it's awful that for myself in my later years I can't take a cigarette lighter and flick it with my left hand.

Frank Walsh

Oh, I've got one more story about the tour. When I think of 1929 I think of being on the boat headed for Honolulu. There were twelve of us, with our expenses paid, going to play for some money. I have with me a Victrola, because I've got to learn to dance. I didn't realize at the time it was going to be a perfect place to learn how to dance because I had a perfect alibi for my goofs—the boat swaying back and forth. If I stepped on a girl I had a perfect alibi. So I danced all the way over. The point of the story is the beautiful retort of Tommy Armour. I danced all the way over to Honolulu. I didn't jog around the boat with the rest of the fellows. I was just lifting the girls up—Mrs. Espinosa, Estelle Armour, and so on. Dancing all the way. So after the tournament's over, we're back on the boat and someone asked Tommy Armour, "Tom, whatever happened to Frank Walsh? He'd been playing well until he got to this tournament and then he finished last. He got the smallest amount of money." And Tom said, "You know, I was interested in Frank from a teacher's point of view, and when I played with him the last day I was curious and watched him on the short holes. I think he danced too much coming over. Because it seemed to me his navel was trying to knock the flagstick out of the hole before the clubhead got to the ball."

Of course, that was right in line with the way I learned to play, and wanting to look so elegant on the follow-through. Tall and pretty. Which was the wrong thing to do. You have to have your head looking back at the ball while the hands and arms are ahead. You have to be a striker.

What made me want to look so pretty in the swing? That's the way all the pictures were. You only saw the players in the follow-through.

Frank Walsh's brother Tom was a successful golf-course builder and operator, and his brother Packy was a longtime professional in the Chicago area. Frank lives in retirement along one of the fairways of the PGA National Golf Club in Palm Beach Gardens, Florida.

SAM SNEAD

A portion of Sam Snead's ever-classic swing, as it appeared in the mid-1930s.

" 'No, you grunted. When you grunt you made an effort, and it counts.' "

I have a picture of me when I first started caddying—seven years old. I had a little Sunday bag with about four clubs in it. The driver was as tall as me. It looked like I was going to beat brush or something. Not long after, I started playing golf.

My uncle used to come up on Sunday and get me by the ear or the hair and say, "C'mon, damn you, let's go pitch horseshoes." We'd go out back of the barn, and he couldn't beat me. So one day I was out back fooling around chipping—see, I put some tomato cans in the ground to make some holes and I'd chip with a jigger, which was like a five-iron—and my uncle said, "Gimme that," meaning the jigger. So now we stopped pitching horseshoes and started chipping. I beat him at that, too. Then one Sunday he came up with this bag of clubs, half left-handed, half right-handed, and he said, "C'mon, damn you, we're going up to the Goat." That was the name of the little nine-hole course at the hotel [the Homestead, in Hot Springs, Virginia] where we could play. You'd play six holes up the mountain, and three of them off of it. Well, he'd whiff a ball, see, and I'd say, "What'd you have, Uncle Ed?" and he couldn't count above five. He'd say he had five or four and I'd say, "Yeah, but you whiffed it down there a couple of times," and he said, "Son, those were practice swings," and I said, "No,

77

you grunted. When you grunt you made an effort, and it counts." So that was my first golf, up and down the Goat. Oh, they wouldn't allow us on the regular golf courses—Cascades, Upper Cascades—but we'd slip back in a wooded area where a green was and chip and putt. If we saw somebody, we'd head for the brush.

I was the youngest of five boys, and we all played except the oldest, Lyle. He never played any sports, because he had trouble breathing. Poor devil choked to death. I wasn't the best from the start, but I was after I got up. My brother Jesse and I would play Homer and Wilfred, who always called himself Pete, and I could beat their best-ball. That's when we could play on the big courses, because I started working there at the Homestead.

I started out as clubmaker. I put wooden shafts on the heads. The shafts were spliced then, there was no hosel. You fit the spliced end over the head, glued it, then wound it up. I had to trim those shafts down with a piece of steel or glass, and be very careful because if you trimmed too much they got too whippy. I learned from Freddie Gleims, who was the pro. He was the most apt man I ever knew in running a pro shop. He would figure out a way to give lessons when it was pouring rain. He'd take 'em up in the summerhouse—it was like a shed—and have them hit the balls out of it. Just to get his lessons in.

Well, one time Gleims and Nelson Long, the other pro, were out playing and this woman came down—a big-busted woman—and asked if she could get a golf lesson. I said both pros were out and she said, "Couldn't you give me a lesson?" and I sort of hummed and hawed and the guy there named Keeser, who was taking greens fees, said, "Go ahead, I'll look out for you." I didn't know whether she should swing over or under her bosom, but I knew a few tricks, like laying out the clubs for alignment, and I worked her. Boy, she was sweating after I got through with her.

After the lesson was over, she said, "Young man, you should have a club of your own." I said I was working on it, I hoped to someday. Well, she was the right type of person. She spoke to the manager of the hotel and said he had a kid down there that knows his business. Two days later the athletic director, Toby Hanson, said to me, "Come upstairs, I want to talk to you." I thought maybe I'd done something wrong or somebody was laying something on me, but he said, "How'd you like to go over to the Cascades course as pro?" There hadn't been anybody there since the Crash in '29. He said I'd get whatever I could and a sandwich and a glass of milk for lunch. So I went over there and, of course, I had a chance to practice, and I beat sod. Oh, I beat sod. They said, "Hey, you're beatin' all the grass off." And I broke the course record twice the first two weeks on the job. But that was a rough year, because then people weren't traveling much. If a pigeon lit there, he didn't leave with one feather. Boy, you got it all. I would rent my clubs out for a buck and a half—half of them, so I'd have the other half if somebody came along who wanted to play.

I was about twenty when I gave that lesson and got my first pro job. I actually got into that part of the game kind of late. I ran a restaurant for my uncle for a year or so, and I worked in the drugstore while going to high school. I'd go down there at five o'clock and be there until eleven at night. Soda jerker and everything else. Then I'd walk home, which was two and a quarter miles and in some places through these woods on both sides of the road. You could imagine hearing panthers and wildcats and bears and everything else. I tell you, you didn't tarry.

I played golf in high school, and baseball and football, and basketball when you had to go back to center after each point and have a tip-off. I was fast, I could run the hundred in ten seconds when I was in my last year in high school. Then I played bush-league baseball. We played those coal miners over in Marlington, Slade Fork, and those places, and they'd be drinking and we got so if we won we just went over and got us a bat to go to the car. We said, "Okay, buster, we don't want to truck with you, but if you want it, come and get it." They backed off when we had those bats in our hands.

Yeah, I was a pretty good athlete. They've always said I'm double-jointed, but there aren't no two joints. I'm just loose-jointed. That's the proper way to put it. And if my vertebrae were in line, I'd be two inches taller. I could have gone to college on an athletic scholarship—baseball and football. And, of course, I could have made the golf team, but they didn't have very many then. But I went to my high-school coach, Harold Bell, and we talked about it and he thought that by the time I spent four years in golf I'd be farther ahead than if I went to college. I wanted to be an athlete, and Harold thought that was best.

Nobody really taught me how to play. I'd ask Freddie Gleims to watch me hit a few and he'd say, "You're a pro now, you ought to know." See, when I got that pro job at the Cascades and started shooting those low scores, he didn't like that at all. He thought he was a good player, better than he actually was. He'd say, "Oh, you think you're hot stuff now, huh?" It was just jealousy.

Like the first time I went down to play in the Miami Open I had this two-wood that belonged to Gleims. He was down there, too. Well, I won about $150 or $200 and he said, "I've got to have that two-wood back." I said I was going over to Nassau to play, but he said he had to have the two-wood. So I don't have a club to play with, and have to go back home. Gleims leaves for Nassau and I go look in the locker he was using. I just wanted to see if that club wasn't there. Well, it was. Gleims didn't take it to Nassau. He just didn't want me to go there.

Now later that year, 1935, I'm playing the last round of the Cascades Open with Cruickshank and Gleims. I was the only one to break 70 in the first round—shot 68—and was leading by three. So Gleims says to me on the first hole, "How do you ever expect to be a pro with that left elbow coming out like that?" I had it sort of like Palmer did. I'd drive with a three-wood and kind of close the face up and set that dude with a kind of low-running hook. Well, after he said that, on the second hole I tried to keep the elbow down and the ball went halfway up the mountain. I took an eight, shot an 80, and finished third. Hell, I could shoot 80 around there with two clubs. I mean, he really upset me, Gleims, but that served me the rest of my life. It cost me that tournament, but afterwards when anybody started to say something to me I'd say, "Hey, beat me with your clubs." So I learned it the hard way. I could imitate anybody and I'd say, "Gee, that must be the way to do it," but that didn't last very long. I'd always go back to my way.

When I went to Miami in '35, that was the first time I went out on the tour. I drove down in a Model-A Ford and it took about two and a half days from Hot Springs. Going down through Georgia, there were one-way wooden bridges that might be 300, 400 yards long and you had to look ahead to see if there was anyone at the other end coming on. If he was on it first, then you'd have to wait your turn to get over. Cows would be sleeping in the middle of the road, and you'd have to be careful at night, because they were black and black-and-tan and blended with the road. Before you knew it, you were right up on 'em. There were many wrecks from ramming into cows. You'd hit hogs, too. I ran over a lot of shoats, pigs about twenty pounds. I thought it was going to upset the car, but there was just a rocking.

I went back to Miami in 1936, and this time went over to Nassau. Johnny Bulla, Bobby Dunkleberger, a boy from Greensboro, and I went over on a small freighter, about a forty-five-footer, and that thing went chug-a-lug, chug-a-lug. It didn't move but about ten miles an hour. It took us all afternoon and night to get there, about 200 miles, and Bulla and me got deathly sick. Dunkleberger was running all over the place, and we wanted to kill him because he wasn't sick and was eating everything we couldn't eat.

Well, a few weeks earlier I'd won over $300 for finishing third in the Cascades Open, and I won some more money in Miami, so in Nassau I asked Henry Picard and Craig Wood what my chances were if I went on the tour on the west coast. Picard said I'd have to finish one, two, or three in order to make expenses, and Wood said, "You want to know whether you're going to stay home and teach or be a player?" and I said yes, and he said, "Well, why don't you go?" I had just signed up with Dunlop Tire and Rubber Company and was getting $500 a year from them, a set of clubs, and a dozen balls a month. But I still hadn't gotten the money from them, and I had only three hundred-and-some of my own. Then Wood said if I couldn't make it he'd let me have money enough to get back home on. I said, "My goodness."

A friend of mine, Leo Walper, said I could go out with him if I paid half the gas, but he was pulling a trailer and it would take us a week to get there and, Lord, I'd use $300 up just for gas. So Bulla said, "Hey, Jackson, I'll go." We drove out in his '36 Ford, and the deal was we'd split the costs. But then in Greensboro John picked up this fella he knew who was

81

going out, a football player, and he paid half the gas and oil. So it only cost me and John a quarter of it. When we got there we wouldn't let him out of the car until his sister came down with the money.

Then, I had an uncle living out in L.A. and we stayed with him, which saved us a pretty penny. Bulla and I slept in the same bed. That sonofabuck could go to sleep like you cut off a light. He'd run his hand over his nose twice, pull the covers over him, and, bam, gone. Now, six o'clock in the morning, ping, he walks on his heels to the bathroom and shakes the building. John weighed about 235 then. Then he'd come run jump on the bed and we'd begin to wrestle. We tore up more rooms like that. . . .

Hell, I think as much of John as I do my brothers. The first time I saw him was in 1935 at the Louisville Open. Nelson Long and I see this guy with hair hanging down over his eyes hitting two-woods at a sand trap out there, and every time he missed the trap he'd beat the ground with the club. I said, "Look at that bastard beating the ground with his club." We stood there and watched him hit, and any time anybody watched John he'd hit 'em till the cows came home. I never saw a man so happy as John when he won the L.A. Open. He said, "Now, Jackson, I'm king for a day." Well, you know, his father gave him hell for playing golf.

Anyway, in the '36 L.A. Open, John is low qualifier and I just get in. Afterwards I'm down in the practice area, and Henry Picard is there and I'm looking at his clubs—he's also on the Dunlop staff and has a lot of them. In fact, Picard was instrumental in getting me that contract with Dunlop, which was pretty good for someone who hadn't done much yet. So I pull a driver out of Picard's bag and say, "God, this is good." He says to go ahead and take it, because it's too big for him. See, one trouble I was having was with my driving, because I had a whippy-shafted driver I couldn't control. This driver from Picard had a stiff shaft, and my driving improved forty percent right then and there.

Now I go up toward the clubhouse, all elated, and Leo Walper's on the putting green and he says, "C'mon, Sam, I'll putt you a quarter a hole." I didn't have a putter, so he said to get one out of his bag, and, oh boy, I got a beauty—a model of Bobby Jones' Calamity Jane. It sat upright just the way I liked. I made three aces in a row and Leo says that's enough putting for quarters. Then he asked me if I wanted to buy that putter for $3.50, and I could hardly contain myself getting the money out of my pocket. Now I've got the two most important clubs in the bag, the driver and putter, and I say to Bulla, "You want to split what we win in the tournament?" He says, "Hell, no, you can't play a lick." I said, "I'll play you five dollars every tournament." Because now I've got these two clubs. He says, "You want to make it more?" but I say five's enough.

The first round in L.A., John played ahead of me and came back to watch me. I'm on seventeen looking over my second shot and John says, "Jackson, you've got six-iron to the green." I said it didn't look like a six and he said, "Well, I just played the hole and I ought to know." I asked him what he shot and he said to never mind. Well, I hit a seven-iron and put it about ten feet under the hole, perfect. I said, "Uh-hunh, if I'd a used a six-iron I would have been over the green," and Bulla said, "Yeah, but you forced that seven." See, he shot a high score and he was protecting his $5 bet.

Well, Bulla didn't win anything in the tournament, and I won $600, plus my $5 from John. Then we drive up to Oakland. I'm hanging in there in third place the last day. Revolta's leading, but I pass him after nine—made a birdie three to his six—and I come to the sixteenth hole and here come the people over the ditches and under the fences to see me play. People were lined up from the tee clear to the green. I never saw so many people at once. So I birdie the last hole to get the lead and a guy wanted to take my picture, but I wouldn't let him because the tournament wasn't over and there were still some good players out there. I was superstitious. Then Fred Corcoran, who had just come on to manage the tour, told me to come up to the press tent because I had won the tournament, there was nobody out there that could catch me. I didn't know the word could get around that quickly. So they did take a picture of me, sitting on a bench, and it was sent to New York as a wirephoto and a few days later they showed it to me in a New York paper and I said to Freddie, "How could they get my picture in New York? I ain't never been there?" I wasn't quite that naïve, I knew what was going on, but Freddie made quite a thing out of that crack. He became my business manager.

Now I'm back in L.A. and see Harry Cooper surrounded

by some reporters and I hear him say, "What goes with this Snead? He's getting all the publicity and I'm winning." Well, he wasn't winning then. Anyway, the reporters say, "What can we write, Lighthorse Harry Cooper wins again? Here we've got a hillbilly, some new blood, something to write about. It makes pretty good reading." I overhear this and get the notion that playing the hillbilly thing wasn't a bad idea.

Then I go down to Del Mar to play in the Crosby tournament. I win it, and the pro-am. They paid $1,000. I won $600 in L.A., $1,200 in Oakland, $1,000 at Del Mar. I've got $2,800, and I say, "Hey, looka here, I'm a rich man!" Then I won the Miami Open and the Nassau Open. So after my first whole winter tour—'37–'38—I was way up there and on my way. Those two clubs I got in L.A. made a big difference.

The traveling was tough when I started out. You had to drive everywhere. At first I drove with Bulla, but after a while I drove by myself. I didn't care about having anybody, because then I could just get up and go when I wanted to. Although George Low used to drive with me now and again. You know George. When I stopped in a filling station he'd go into the men's room and stick his head out to see if I paid the station manager before he came back to the car. When we went in a restaurant I'd say, "Now, George, you eat like you were going to pay for it." We didn't have a deal to split, and George never paid for anything. I don't know whether he had it or not—money—but, well, he was pretty good company. You know how I'd beat him out of a little bit? When I drove by myself, to keep from going to sleep I would guess how far it was from one hill to another and check it on the speedometer. You get pretty good at that, doing all that driving, so I'd bet George I could guess within three tenths of a mile how far it was to a hill and I'd beat him just about every time. Finally he said, "That's it." He wouldn't bet anymore.

One time I took my father on tour with me. When my mother died in 1940 I brought him down to Florida and out to California. His brother had moved out there—his son was a dancer and working in show business—and they saw each other and hugged, and both cried because they knew they'd never see each other again. I brought Pop back through Phoenix, and when we got to Texas I could see he was nervous and

I said, "You're getting homesick, aren't you?" He says, "Yeah, well, kinda." I asked him if he wanted to go home and he said any time and I told him, "You're leaving in the morning, seven o'clock, you'll be home tomorrow night." "Ohhh," he said. I called him the next morning and said, "Pop, come on down and have some breakfast." "Don't believe I want any." "Well, come on and have some coffee." "No, don't think I want any coffee, either." I said, "You know how you're going home?" He said, "I've been surmising that."

You see, he'd never been on a plane and was scared as hell. I gave him his ticket, put him in a taxi, and told him what to do. The plane only went to Greensboro, and he had to take a bus from there to Hot Springs. But he said, "I couldn't get those dad-blasted bumblebees out of my head." He didn't know to hold his nose and blow to pop his eardrums when they got blocked from cabin pressure. He said those bumblebees stayed in his head for a long time.

My father was a strong man. He was an engineer over at the hotel. I'll tell you, we had a firemen's team and we'd pull this heavy reel of hose off wheels that were six feet high. Ten guys. We'd run 125 yards pulling that hose and hook it up to a hydrant, put a nozzle on it, and have water coming out in twenty or twenty-five seconds. My dad would run down there with the team when he was seventy years old. But another thing, my daddy was a haughty man. He would speak to you in passing with only "Howdy." And if you touched his head you had a fight on your hands. He'd go to the barbershop and say, "Hurry up and get this over with, and do as little as you can. I don't want you to fool with my head." Boy, I never saw a man so touchy. I suppose I got a lot of that from him, but I'd like to have all my characteristics and character from my mother. She was easy-going, and one of the few people I ever saw who had front sight as well as hindsight. We never went to my dad for anything, we always went to my mother.

The biggest thrill over all the years? Usually your first tournament win is your biggest thrill, but it wasn't necessarily with me. I think the one I enjoyed the most was in '42, the PGA championship. I was in Washington, D.C., in line ready to take that one step forward to be sworn in the Navy. There was all these fellows with the scrambled eggs on their bills, and I said to one of them, "Hey, what's the chances of me skipping this one and doing it next week? They're having the PGA championship over in New Jersey, just below Atlantic City," which was not very far away. One of the scrambled eggs said why don't you go ahead and get inducted and they'll probably let you go. I said no, I understood they were really tight about the pros, they wouldn't let us move, and he asked me what it meant to me. I said $2,000 if I win plus $2,000 from Wilson Sporting Goods, who I represent, and maybe a few testimonials and whatnot. I said I might get $10,000 out of it, and at that time that was a helluva lot of money. Well, it just so happened I talked to the right guy. He said to go call the draft board and tell them I'd had my physical and want to go play and I'll be inducted the following Monday. I said, "Thank you very much." So I got on the phone and they said okay, and I went over and played Jim Turnesa in the final.

Jim was the giant killer. He had beaten Nelson, Hogan, and Harrison before we met in the final. I loved match play. I would study a guy I was playing just like Ted Williams studied pitchers. You look for a weak spot, or a weakening of his character. I would notice if he changed his mannerisms, which was a way to read him. Now, in the finals I'm playing Jim, and at the tenth hole I noticed he changed his mannerisms and I said to myself, "I got you now, Jimmy." Well, I had won the ninth hole to get even, and at the tenth I threw a fade around the dogleg and he changed his mannerism and hooked into the trap. That just shot me right up. I said, "Uh-huh, that's it." You see, he got to taking two more waggles than he usually did. I knew he was getting tight, and now I have more confidence in myself, and I beat him two and one.

So the '42 PGA was my first big championship. Of course, all of them are big as far as I'm concerned. I mean, they talk about the majors and how important they are. But you're playing the same guys you play every week, just on another golf course. If I could have shot 69 in the last round every time, I would have won nine U.S. Opens. *Nine.*

I'll say this, though, they have better communications in the tournaments these days, so you can know what the rest of the field is doing—from the scoreboards that are all around. That would have made a difference in that U.S. Open in Philadelphia. I wouldn't have hit so dumb a second shot, with a wood out of that bunker. I didn't know I didn't need a birdie so badly. And now they pair the leaders together the last round, which is much better. At Oakmont in '53, Hogan and I were one-two playing the last round and Hogan is going up the ninth when I'm going down the first. We should have been either playing together or only one group apart.

I loved playing Hogan head-to-head, and I beat him every time we did—three times—because I knew he wouldn't say anything to me. That was good, because it helped me concentrate better. Also, because I knew he'd play well. Of course, when I played with Hogan I never watched him, because it was jit-jit—fast back and fast through. I'd watch him address his ball, and when he did his forward press I'd look down the fairway. I'd never watch his swing, because I'd want to get fast, too. I enjoyed playing with Jim Turnesa and Johnny Palmer. They had nice, slow, easy swings that kept me slow and easy.

But, no, I don't feel my career has not been fulfilled because I didn't win the U.S. Open. It's like the guy said: you going to crucify a man because he missed a putt to win a tournament? Does a three-foot putt mean his whole life? Another guy said, well, he couldn't win the big one. Well, Jesus, what do you call those others? What's big and what's small?

Samuel Jackson Snead has won over 135 tournaments during one of the most remarkable careers in golf history, not only for its achievements but for its longevity. He has continued to play on the senior tournament circuit into his mid-seventies, and, despite some ailments including impaired vision in one eye, and some loss to time of his storied flexibility, will still shoot rounds in the 60s. He is the oldest man to win a PGA tour event, the 1965 Greensboro Open, when he was fifty-two years and ten months old. And at age sixty-seven he shot rounds of 67–66 in the Quad Cities Open. Sam won the Masters three times, the PGA championship twice, and the British Open once. He played on eight U.S. Ryder Cup teams, and was once a non-playing captain. He won the Vardon Trophy four times.

Sam winters in Boynton Beach, Florida, and in the summer is back in his native Hot Springs, Virginia, where he has a big home at the top of a hill from which he can almost see the small house in which he grew up.

BYRON NELSON

Byron Nelson shakes hands with Clayton Heafner after they finished tied for first in the 1942 Tam O'Shanter tournament, outside Chicago.

Photograph by Al Barkow

" . . . winners are different. They're a different breed of cat."

I was twelve when I went to caddie for the first time, in the fall of '24. There were more caddies than players in those days, so you kind of had to work your way in. You ran the gauntlet, they had a kangaroo court and everything, because they tried to keep you out. A new kid would come in and they'd all line up—all the regular caddies—and you had to run between them. They'd have belts and sticks. They didn't really harm you, but they warmed you up good. And there was a big hill and they had some barrels and they'd put you in one and roll you down the hill. That's what you had to do. If you toughed it out, then you became one of the gang, and when someone new came through, you got to give it to him.

I started to swing a club shortly after, because I liked anything you could play where you were hitting something. I seemed to have coordination for it. But my first round of golf? Each year at Glen Garden Country Club they had a party for the caddies at Christmas. The members caddied for you, and would let the caddies use their clubs if a kid didn't have any. I didn't have any that first time and used the clubs of Judge J. B. Wade. I shot 118, and I don't think I counted when I whiffed it. I actually hit it 118 times. But I went from 118 that year to 79 the next. I just fell into it, and started hitting the ball. The thing about it, in that day and time the pros weren't interested in teaching juniors and you didn't just go up to them and get them to help you. They weren't approachable, most of them. So what I did when I got interested, I got every book that was around, watched good players, and started piecing together my own game.

But there were two or three people that helped me in the beginning. When Ted Longworth came to interview for the head-pro job at Glen Garden I had probably my first big thrill in golf. At the time he was the Missouri State PGA champion, and I got to caddie for him. The pros back in those days didn't pay the caddies, but you were so glad to caddie for them you did it as an honor. Well, I became good friends with Ted Longworth. Then Jack Grout came down as his assistant and we were about the same age, so we became bosom buddies. Then Dick Grout, Jack's older brother, replaced Ted Longworth at Glen Garden, and when I asked him a few questions about how to play he answered them.

Then in the early '30s, when they switched from hickory to steel shafts, I had to start restructuring my game. I was still pronating the way you had to do with hickory because of the torque in the shaft, which would open the clubface. But steel didn't have that same torque, and I would hook the ball around a house. I had to stop the hook, so, just by trial and error—I'm going over a period of time now—I found that the more I moved laterally through the ball and kept the club and hands going in front of the ball, the straighter it would go. I could stop the pronation and carry my hands high if I stayed down and through the ball a long time and did not raise up.

See, in that day and time you pronated the hands and hit against a stiff left side. The way I taught myself to not do that, I would only practice against the wind so I could know I was moving on a lower plane through the ball. Going downwind or crosswind, the ball blew around too much. So I kept working on that, but I got too much lateral motion down below, and I was moving some up above, and I got to be the worst shanker that I guess ever lived. Because, moving the lower body laterally, and the head, too, I'd get the heel of the club into the ball first. I got so bad I would shank for weeks. And I'm not a kid now, I'm a young man. Eventually I determined, by trial and error, that if I would hit out from underneath myself, if

Byron Nelson

I'd keep my head back, I wouldn't shank. The more I did that, the better I got.

So in 1932 I turned pro. Ted Longworth started a tournament in Texarkana, where he was now head pro. The total prize money was $500 and there's people playing in it like Dick Metz and Ky Laffoon, but I rode a bus over there from Fort Worth, carried my little Sunday bag and a suitcase, paid my $5 entry fee, and played in my first tournament as a pro. That was November 22, 1932. In that day and time all you had to do was go pay your entry and say you were playing as a pro, and you were a pro. Well, I finished third and won $75. Boy, did that encourage me. That next spring, of 1933, I got a telephone call from Ted Longworth. He said, "Byron, I know you don't have much experience, and it's not much of a job over here, but I think I can get it for you." Head pro at Texarkana Country Club. Ted was leaving to go to Portland, Oregon. Texarkana was a small town, and the job wasn't worth anything, but it was a job and I didn't have one, so I went over there. I made about $60 a month at the start. That's not salary, it's what I made from my lessons and so on. Things were rough at the time, and I lived with some people named Battle; room and board right close to the club, $7 a week. It's hard to believe, isn't it? And Mrs. Battle was a good cook.

Very seldom did anybody come to the club before noon on any day, so I had an excellent practice field and I'd hit balls. I hit 'em down there and go down and hit 'em back. I didn't need anybody to shag for me, although there wasn't anybody to shag anyway. So I got better and better. Then, in June, I met Louise. I'd already met her father and mother and one of her sisters at the Church of Christ, where I was a member. They had sent Louise to beauty school in Houston, and she came back and got a job in a beauty parlor in Texarkana. I met her at Sunday school. The second time I saw her we became engaged, and I never after had a date with another woman. We didn't get married until June of 1934. We'd like to have gotten married sooner, but we couldn't afford it, even though her father had a grocery store. You can't save any money on $60 a month.

I played a lot of golf with a man at the club named Arthur Temple. Par at the Texarkana Country Club was 73, and when

I played with Mr. Temple he would bet me a dollar I couldn't break par. If I broke par I got a dollar; if I didn't, why, *he* got a dollar. So any time I won I could have a date with Louise. We could go to a show and have a Stuttgart, which is ice cream and a very thick chocolate. There's a place up in Arkansas called Stuttgart where they made a very thick chocolate—like a fudge. We could go to the show and get a Stuttgart after for a dollar—if I broke par. If I didn't, we stayed home and swung on the front porch swing. Anyway, I got to where I did it pretty regularly—break par. It was almost as though he was just giving me a dollar.

Now then, come that fall I decided I wanted to go to California and play part of the winter tour. So what happened was, a very wealthy man at the club named J. K. Wadley liked me, because he was a Baptist and didn't like anybody who smoked or drank, and I never did either, and he told me he'd give me the money to go to California and whatever the profits were, we'd split them. That's the way a lot of the boys got started. So I told Louise about it, and one day she said, "Daddy wants to see you." Well, I knew I hadn't mistreated her, but back in that day and time when the father wanted to see you, well . . . So I went into his store and he said, "Byron, Louise was talking to me about you going to California for four or five tournaments. I don't like the idea that if you make anything you have to give half of it back. If Louise has enough confidence in you to marry you, I'll loan you the money to go out there."

I had bought a car. A member of the club named Dyer was a Ford dealer and he had some cars he carried over from the previous year and he sold me, on time, a roadster, a Model-A Ford convertible. So I went out. I won $50 here and there in California, and made some decent showings, but when I got back to Texas I had just enough money in my pocket to play at San Antonio and Galveston before going back to Texarkana. I wouldn't have any money left and I'd owe Mr. Shofner, Louise's father, $650.

I'll never forget, I get on the first tee at the Texas Open at San Antonio, and the starter, a man named Wilson who knew me, gives me this big introduction . . . a coming tour player and all that stuff about making a few good showings up to then. So I almost whiff the ball. I dribbled it down the fairway maybe 100 yards. Well, I hit my brassie, then put an eight-iron about eight feet from the hole and made the putt for my par. I made a par after topping the drive badly, and the thought popped in my head, you dunce, if you can miss it that bad and make a par, if you ever hit it right you're going to make a birdie. So I wound up shooting 65 or something low like that. I finally finished second in the tournament. Wiffy Cox won. Bill Mehlhorn was there, and Harry Cooper, Craig Wood, Bobby Cruickshank, all the great players, and I finished second. I think I won $375. Now I go to Galveston and finish second there. Craig Wood won. Then I go home to Texarkana. I don't even stop. I'm flying. I want to see Louise and pay back her father. I had enough money to pay him. I asked him how much interest I owed and he said, "You don't owe me anything, I'm proud of you." So I had $100 left and I went down to the jewelry store and bought Louise a little diamond engagement ring, and I was broke. That was the spring of '34. In June we went ahead and got married, broke or no broke.

Now in the fall of that year, 1934, we go to California, Louise and I in the roadster. It had a little rumble seat in the back, that's all the room there was. It was just a one-seater, the one seat across the front, and it had isinglass windows. You know, curtains, and they flopped in the wind. There were no glass roll-up windows then, not in a roadster. There was no heater in the car, either, and when we left Texarkana it was cold. I heated some bricks and put them in a big pasteboard box, to keep Louise's feet warm. And her mother gave us a lap robe, which we still have, to throw over her legs. But before we got to California Louise got what is called the croup. It's almost like asthma. She'd just choke up, and she coughed a lot, and it scared me to death. I had never seen her with it before, had never seen anybody with it before. So I had a doctor in California come to our apartment—we had an apartment because we played in the same place for four weeks—and he gave her some medicine. It cost $5. I'll never forget that, because you counted every penny in those days.

Jack Grout rode with us some on that trip, but with his

golf clubs and everything Louise finally said it was either Jack or her, so I told Jack he'd have to get a ride with someone else. See, there were three of us up front. We stood the golf clubs up in the rumble seat and stacked the suitcases behind us up front.

Anyway, we made our way, and then something happened during the San Francisco Match-Play championship. All the pros had to qualify except the defending champion and Lawson Little, who was the National and British Amateur champion at the time. Lawson's father was an army colonel and ran the club where we were playing, the Presidio, so when the qualifying was over they gave Little to the least-known player in the field, which was me. The PGA didn't do the pairings in that day and time, the local committee did. Well, I was worried. Here I am, a beginner playing the best amateur in the world on his home course. I can tell you, I didn't sleep very well that night. But I got keyed up, because the next morning every pro patted me on the back. They were upset not that Little was playing in the tournament, but because he didn't have to qualify. Then Leo Diegel said to me, "Kid, I'll tell you how you can break this guy. I've played with you and you can knock the ball a long way. When you get on the first tee he won't be expecting anything out of you. He's a big-headed little brat"—that's what Leo called him, and worse than that— "so what I want you to do is tee it up and just jump on it. If you miss it, okay, but if you hit it and knock it past him he can't stand to be outdriven." So Lawson has the honor on the tee and flicks one down the fairway. I get up and my knees are shaking, but I jump at that thing and fortunately hit it dead solid. I carried it right over the top of where he was.

This was a par-five hole, and in this day and time they had a line around the edge of the green in white lime to keep the gallery off. The gallery could walk in the fairway with the players, but they didn't want them on the green, of course. So Lawson hit his second and is short of the green, and I put my second inside that white line. I saw him kind of give me the fisheye . . . you know? Well, he didn't birdie the first hole and I did, and, to make a long story short, I just ate him alive. I shot 33 or something on the front nine and beat him five and four. I didn't win the tournament, though, Jug McSpaden did.

94

Byron Nelson

Okay, now I have become friendly with Ed Dudley, who was the pro at Augusta, and because of what happened to me that winter, beating Little and all, I got invited to the Masters, the second one, in 1935. George Jacobus was down there and told Ed he was looking for a good young playing assistant for his club in New Jersey, the Ridgewood Country Club. Ed recommended me, George interviewed me, and I was hired.

So Louise and I went up to New Jersey in the spring of 1935. We roomed and boarded with some people named Hope in the town of Ridgewood. They took us in and treated us great, especially Louise, because she was so homesick and lonesome it was pitiful. She was there in the house all day long, she didn't have any money to spend, and I had the car and was away all day long. But Mrs. Hope was awfully good to her.

So, anyway, when I got up there I had some conferences with George Jacobus about what my duties were, and then we talked about the game and teaching. I told him I'd developed this new style of playing, and I went through the whole thing—the lateral shift and more use of feet and legs, no pronation, hands high on the backswing, staying down through the ball, low trajectory. George was from the old school, but he was a smart man and knew golf real well; he was a real long hitter and had been a pretty fair player. I asked him what he thought about all that and he said it was exactly right, that we were going to have to develop a different style of play because of the steel shaft. He was already moving in that direction, he wasn't teaching pronation anymore. So I said to him, "What I'd like you to do, to help me, is whenever you're on the practice tee and I'm practicing, you interject what you think about what I'm doing. Because I can't feel it a hundred percent." He said he would, and he did and it helped me. He gave me confidence, because he confirmed in my mind that I was on the right track. I started becoming more consistent. I won the New Jersey Open, then the New Jersey PGA—I beat Clarence Clark, Vic Ghezzi, Craig Wood, Paul Runyan, they were all up there. Then I beat a great field for the Metropolitan Open, at Quaker Ridge. I would have to say the Metropolitan Open was my first important victory, because in that day and time it was a major title. Harry Cooper, Denny Shute, Henry Picard, they were all there.

There wasn't any one of my contemporaries on the tour who influenced my game, because no one was doing what I was. I've been given credit for starting this type or style of playing, but they do it better now than I did. They still use their feet and legs, but I probably overused mine some. And everybody always said I dipped into the ball. I remember Gene Sarazen said, when I first came out, that I wouldn't become a great player because I dipped. Of course, Gene hit against a straight left side, and everyone was used to seeing golfers straighten up at impact, so by comparison it looked like I dipped. Actually, I was just staying down with my body. There was a sequence of pictures of my swing in *Sports Illustrated*—the old one, not the one that is published now—and it proves I didn't dip. You can see how the head is still held back, and how the club extends. I really just stayed down and through. Even today I don't think you can improve on the position. How's a ball going to go anything but straight from there? I had very little deviation in the flight of my ball. I might push or pull it a little bit, but I had very little curvature of the ball in flight.

In 1930, when I was eighteen, I had made up my mind that I wanted to play golf, but I didn't know I was going to become a professional. I knew I was going to play golf as much as I could, because I had been a halfway decent sort of kid player around Fort Worth and the members at Glen Garden had given Ben Hogan and myself playing privileges. Ben was a caddie there, too, but we weren't real close friends. He lived on one side of town, I lived on the other, and we didn't fraternize except at the golf course. I lived right close to the club, so I could play and practice a lot. Clubs don't seem to do that much anymore—give promising youngsters playing privileges. I think that's one reason why Texas produced a lot of fine players back in those days. We all had no problem finding a place to play, and most times we didn't pay any green fees. They were just glad to have the junior golfers around. As long as you conducted yourself all right, why, you were welcome, and if you could play well, there was no problem playing the tournaments.

As a matter of fact, the Fort Worth *Star-Telegram* published at the beginning of the summer season all the tournaments over the whole state, and there was one you could play in absolutely every week—amateur tournaments, that is. That's one reason why Texans kind of dominated the game for a time. And another thing about Texas was the wind blew a lot, so you had to learn how to cope with it. The wind still blows a lot, but in those days you also had hard greens, and had to play off hard fairways. You really had to learn how to manipulate the ball. When we got off Bermuda grass and went to bent, boy, that was heaven.

We don't produce golfers down here like we used to, because everyone in the country plays under the same conditins—watered fairways. So you can say that great golfers are created under bad conditions. Personally, I don't think there's any question about it. It was tough, playing back then. You had to learn to play diddy-bump shots, chips and runs, and on hard greens.

Well, it all came to a head, I guess, in 1945, with that streak. I won eleven straight tournaments, eighteen for the year. But I think it started in 1944. Of course, I'd had some good years before. In 1937 I won my first Masters and the International Match-Play championship. And '39 was a great year. I won the Western Open, the North and South, and the National Open. Anyway, I won six tournaments in 1944, and averaged 69.67. I played very well, and the thing I did, I kept track of every round, made little notations, just like when you take inventory at the end of the year, and I found two things. I chipped poorly too many times, and played too many careless shots. By that I mean I didn't concentrate hard enough. For instance, there'd be an out of bounds on the right and no trouble on the left and I'd just walk up and hit it and get into trouble. Because the truth is when you're playing well you quit concentrating. You can get a little complacent if you just hit it good, good, good. It can get kind of boring when you're playing as well as I was, and then all of a sudden you quit paying attention. I had people say to me it was no fun watching me play, because it was just on the fairway and on the green, two putts, and once in a while I'd make a birdie putt. The average person may not understand that it can get boring for the player, it sounds like a silly thing to say, but it's true. Anyway, I made up my mind to do some practice on my chipping for the 1945 tour, and I said, "I'm not going to play one careless shot." Those were the only things I had to change.

In the third tournament of that streak, in Charlotte, Snead and I tied, then tied again, and I beat him in the second playoff. See, you had to play eighteen-hole playoffs then, and we had two of them. In the first playoff he had a good chance to beat me on the last hole, but he three-putted. But that was the only close call. I won most of them by three or four strokes, and sometimes more. The last tournament I won that year was at Glen Garden. Yes, a beautiful irony, right where it all began.

Of course, the pressure built up something terrible. I know one time I said to Louise—this was along about the seventh or eighth tournament—that I wished I'd blow up today, I don't care what I shoot, I just want to get rid of this. And I came home and she said, "Well, did you blow it?" and I said, "Yeah, I shot sixty-six." I think I had twenty-five 66s that year. Bill Inglish, the newspaperman from Oklahoma who does all the statistics for the Masters now, came up with the fact that during that year I averaged 67.45 for the last round of each of the tournaments.

The pressure was created not just by the press, excepting there would be a lot of questions about whether I expected to make it six or seven or whatever in a row. But the other pressure was worse than that. You see, golf in that day and time was so small and needed help so badly that when we'd get into town for a tournament we had to go to the Kiwanis Club, the Lions Club, all these types of clubs to promote the tournament, and because of the streak all they wanted was me. I dodged some of them, but not many. The tournament committee would say I had to appear. Then, too, in that day and time they didn't have radio remote capability for interviews, so I'd have to go from the course into town to the radio station, which took time and broke up my rhythm.

Byron Nelson

I know people have said that the streak wasn't as great as it seemed because the competition wasn't as strong as it could be, what with so many fellows being away in the military. I can understand the feeling. It happened just after the war and there weren't that many good players around. I'll admit that. But Charlie Price called me up one day and said, "Byron, I've done you an injustice. I was one of the writers that said during that run you had in 1945 that the competition wasn't all that good. But I went back and found that Snead and Hogan played in almost every tournament you won."

See, the thing of it is, during that year Hogan shot twenty-five under par at Portland, Oregon, in a tournament, so he wasn't exactly hacking it around. And I played with Snead more that year than I've ever played with him before or since. I played exhibitions with him, one at the Navy base where he was stationed, and he shot 62s and 63s. But most of the time when people make that comment I say I'm just glad I played when I did and I never backed off from anybody and never had any problem beating people I wanted to beat.

The thing I'm more proud of than anything else about my playing career is the degree of consistency with which I played. I won money in 113 consecutive tournaments, and you have to realize we had a lot of tournaments where they only had fifteen or twenty prizes, not forty or fifty the way they do now. It showed that my ability to concentrate and keep on playing if I bogeyed a hole was good, and I could still come in with a respectable round of golf. Because it's easy, especially after you've been playing well, to have a bad day and say, Oh well, there's always next week. But, of course, I didn't feel that way.

Is there a psychology for winning? I don't understand the psychological function of the human mind sufficiently to answer that very well, except to say that winners are different. They're a different breed of cat. I think the reason is, they have an inner drive and are willing to give of themselves whatever it takes to win. It's a discipline that a lot of people are not willing to impose on themselves. It takes a lot of energy, a different way of thinking. It makes a different demand on you to win tournaments than to just go out and win money. I know when I first started playing out there, I thought, Well, if I can just finish in the first ten, I can make a living. Because the purses were $5,000 in those days and tenth place was worth $180, and that would get you by for a week if you lived conservatively. But I soon realized that if I was going to try to win only $180, I was never going to win $500 or $5,000.

It's hard to explain about winners, or champions. There's a certain aggressiveness. That's the thing I saw in Tom Watson the first time I watched him play. There is something about the mannerisms. I know the first time I won the Masters, in 1937, I just felt like I had springs in me. I didn't hardly feel like I was walking.

Byron Nelson

Byron Nelson won the 1939 U.S. Open and lost a playoff for the championship in 1946. He won the PGA championship in 1940 and 1945, the Masters in 1937 and 1942. In all, he won fifty-four events on the pro tour. He played on three U.S. Ryder Cup teams. His record of eleven straight victories on the tour may very well stand for all time.

Byron lives on his ranch, Fairway, in Roanoke, Texas, which is on the outskirts of Fort Worth. He remains active in the game of golf as a member of Golf Digest *magazine's professional advisory staff, and especially as honorary chairman of the Byron Nelson Classic, one of the most prestigious annual events on the PGA tour.*

CHANDLER HARPER

Photograph by Al Barkow

"What you did was gamble. In those early days . . . I guess we all gambled."

I hit my first golf ball in 1923, when I was nine years old. My father had played once before, on a vacation in Maryland, and had bought a set of clubs. So he joined the club here when it opened, in 1922. It was the first golf course in Portsmouth. A nine-holer.

My father was born on a little farm in North Carolina, near Whitakers. He came down here as a telegraph operator making $40 a month. He sent $20 of it home, because his family needed it. From being a telegraph operator in the railroad station he got a job on the railroad as a conductor, the Atlantic Coast Line. Well, somewhere in North Carolina they had a wreck and he was fired on the spot. He asked for a ride back to Penner's Point, which is a part of Portsmouth, and they gave it to him. You see, Penner's Point had practically no homes on it, it was wide open, so he decided to go into the real-estate business. He knew a man high up in the railroad company who loaned him $500 to start out with. This was way back in the 1890s. My father was forty-three when I was born. He eventually became very successful. He wasn't a millionaire, but he was considered very successful for that time.

Anyway, I went out and caddied for my father and my brother a couple of times, then started to play. In the beginning, like everybody else, I couldn't play at all, but I took to it

103

pretty quick. When I was fourteen I won the city championship, then won it two more times in a row and retired. By that I mean I quit playing in the local tournaments because, you know, there weren't many good players here at the time.

In high school I was also playing baseball, and loved it. I wanted to be a big-league ballplayer. Of course, I was interested in golf, too, and trying to do both. Well, I went up to Winged Foot in 1929 to see the National Open. My father took me and my brother. Bob Jones won it, and when I got back my baseball coach told me I had to do one thing or the other, baseball or golf, because my baseball was suffering. I picked golf.

Why? I was getting very interested in Walter Hagen and Bob Jones. They seemed to be so great. They were winning, they were the best golfers we had, and I thought they were making big money. Of course, Jones wasn't making anything because he was an amateur. But Hagen was getting $700 for winning a tournament, so he was a helluva player. Anyway, I thought that's what I wanted to do. I played amateur golf for two more years, won the Middle Atlantic, and state amateur twice, the state open, then turned pro in 1934. I was twenty.

My very first tour event was in Indianapolis in the spring of '35. It was supposed to be a big tournament. Five thousand dollars total money, a $1,000 first prize, and they had the British Ryder Cup team over here, so both Ryder Cup teams were playing. I finished eighth. But let me tell you what happened.

The next tournament was in Louisville, Kentucky. This fellow who was also in the tournament offered to give me a ride, and on the way through town I stopped by my hotel so I could pay my bill. I used my check from the tournament, a hundred-and-some dollars. We went on to Louisville and when we got there I heard that none of the checks from Indianapolis were any good. But I had cashed mine, paid my bill with it, and I got away with it. I think it was a year before they straightened it out.

I suppose it was kind of a wild thing to do during the Depression time, go out and play the tour. But, you see, when you come up in the Depression, you don't realize it. When you look back, you know how tough it was, but when you're in it, it doesn't seem that bad. You know things are tight, but they don't seem that bad because everybody else is in the same condition. Almost everybody.

What we were all trying to do was make a reputation so we could make money some other way. Nobody had any idea of making any on the tour. The year I turned pro, Paul Runyan was the leading money winner. He won $6,800 for forty weeks, and he played them all. Then I remember a little later, '38 I think, that Snead won $19,000 and we sat around in a hotel lobby somewhere and wondered if anybody would ever win that much again. Because Sam won so many tournaments. He must have won seven that year, and he had seconds and thirds, and he got $19,000. We said nobody will ever get that much again, because nobody is going to play that good. We didn't think. We were all trying to do something that would put us in a position to get a good club job and make a good living.

I wasn't overawed playing with all those great players I saw there in Indianapolis. I was young and brash and I thought I was going to be good. I kind of thought I should have won that tournament. Of course, I played with Sam Snead a lot when we were amateurs, I played with him in high school. He turned pro a little later than I did, because he didn't have any money. He was the caddie master in Hot Springs. They say Sam played barefoot, but I didn't see it. Anyway, it took me a long time to win. It wasn't until 1942. I kept trying, and could finish in the money, but that didn't mean anything, you could finish third and win $100. What you did was gamble. In those early days on the tour I guess we all gambled. Guys like Lloyd Mangrum. He was a tough gambler, let me tell you.

In the winter of 1938 I went out to the coast. I borrowed $3,000, took $1,500 to buy a LaSalle, which was made by Cadillac. I borrowed it from a loan company in Norfolk. My bank wouldn't loan it to me. The banker asked me if my father knew about my plans to go on the tour, and I got mad and said, "No, why don't you go tell him?" My dad knew I was going, but he didn't ask me how I was going to do it. I could have asked him for the money, but didn't want to. Well, the banker wanted to know what it was all about, and I just walked out and went to the loan company and paid more interest. It was like eight percent, but they take that out first. I borrowed $3,000, but you don't get that much, you get eight percent less. Then you pay monthly installments, so you're actually paying a lot more. In six months you get half of it paid off, so you get the use of but half the money, on average. So you're paying a helluva lot more. Like about sixteen percent. Which was terrific in those days.

I was gone for four months. I played the whole winter tour in '38, and when I got back I was playing golf with my father and he told me I had gone off and fouled him up. You see, in those days the banks were charging three cents for checks you wrote, and my dad said I left owing three cents. What happened was I drew all my money out of the bank but didn't allow for the three cents, and I'll be damned if that banker doesn't go to my father about it. He paid it, and said I owed it to him. Nowadays banks are delighted to do business with you.

So in 1938 I went out to the coast, and I was green as hell. I didn't take anything but summer clothes, and it started raining in the L.A. Open and it rained right on through the whole tour. Six weeks of it. Up around San Francisco, if you lost your ball in the fairway you didn't have to find it, because they were burying. If they knew you were in the fairway, you just put another ball down. Now I'm going to tell you one here.

The last round at Sacramento I'm paired with Lloyd Mangrum and a guy named Joe Ezar. Now, Joe Ezar had played in Portsmouth in '33. He came for an open tournament, at the Cavalier [Yacht and Country Club]. Paul Runyan won it. I don't know how Ezar did, but the next day he's over at a place called Truxton Manor that I hung around and played a lot of golf at. The airport is there now. Ezar wanted to play everybody. He was a gambler. And a character. So everybody's making a game with him. It was on a Monday, and we had a gang of guys around, pros and amateurs. I was still an amateur. One of the guys was Mr. Jones, who I went to work for when I first turned pro, and he wouldn't play Ezar. Ezar asked him why not and Mr. Jones says, "Mr. Ezar, for either one of two reasons. You're either too good for me, or you're not going to pay me if I beat you." Ezar said, "Why don't you get out of my hair?"

106

Well, everybody beat Ezar, and he didn't pay off. He said he'd see us tomorrow. So he came back the next day, but [President] Roosevelt had declared a bank holiday and Ezar said he couldn't pay because his bank was closed. He never did pay me: $125.

That was in 1933. Now in 1938 I'm on the tour in Sacramento, and me, Mangrum, and Ezar are paired together. We're all out of the money, pretty much, and it's raining and sleeting—the worst damn weather—and they're playing through it; thirty-six holes the last day. So Ezar says, "Let's play two-dollar cuts." Skins. He called them cuts. I said, "How about that money you owe me, a hundred and a quarter?" and he said what's that, and I said, "Don't you remember back in Norfolk in '33?" and he said he paid everybody off and I said he didn't pay anybody and that I didn't care for his deal, but that I would play him cuts except everybody had to put up after each hole. So I shoot 68 in the morning, 68 in the afternoon. Making him pay after each hole, I end up with a pocket full of $1 bills that are wet as hell. When I got back to the hotel and pulled them out of my pocket, there was absolutely no way to separate them. So I just laid them out on the radiator all night long to dry out.

By the way, with those two 68s I ended up in a three-way tie for last place in the tournament and got $16.66—three-way split of $50.

Our next stop was New Orleans, believe it or not. From Sacramento to New Orleans. It was just me and wife driving the LaSalle. That's about 2,000 miles. We left on Sunday night and I played in the pro-am Wednesday afternoon. The reason I remember this is, in the pro-am I play with an optometrist named Ketchum who had a partner named Cheatham. I asked him if he had that up on the store and he said, yeah, right up there: Ketchum and Cheatham.

The next stop is St. Petersburg. They got to doing the scheduling better, but that's the way it was then. So we drove all the way to St. Petersburg and I finish 68, 68, and tie Johnny Revolta for first place. They were putting up a $3,000 purse and the club said they were having a hard time—this was during the Depression—and how about us splitting the gate receipts for the playoff three ways? Normally then the players got the playoff gate money. I said fine and so did Revolta, then he said to me, "Boy, you want to split the prize?" Of course, he was older than me, and was the leading money winner right then on the winter tour. I thought, Hell, I'd like to play this guy. But we did split.

He beat me, by a shot. When we got our checks, first and second split, and the gate, we got $608 apiece. Then I went home, because I'd lost seventeen pounds during that trip and I didn't have it to lose. I wasn't used to playing so much golf.

The next year I was back in St. Pete and . . . Some things you never forget. They had a fifty-four-hole tournament that year, and on the last hole I hit a drive down the middle of the fairway and somebody came up and said I needed a four to tie. It was a par-five, but I could reach it in two. We get to the middle of the fairway and can't find my ball. Right in the middle! Finally we find it. See, a woman had walked across the fairway in high heels and stepped on it—sunk it right down; it was a very sandy course there. I had to play it! I knocked it out fifteen feet, put the next ball on the green, made a five, and lost the tournament by one stroke to Henry Picard and Snead. I told this to Grantland Rice and he wrote a helluva story about it. First thing he said, I was the unluckiest sonofabitch he ever saw. I've got the article someplace.

But I finally won. The first one was what they called the International Four-Ball in Miami in '42. Herman Keiser and I were partners. Gene Sarazen and Ben Hogan were defending champions and we beat 'em six and five in the third round. I'll never forget. Herman was a helluva putter, and going down the first fairway after lunch—they were thirty-six-hole matches—Gene said to me, "This guy can't putt like that, can he? Meaning Herman. I said he was even better, he's just been making six- and eight-footers. So on the third hole Herman rolls in about a forty-footer and I say to Sarazen, "I told you." Walking in after the match, Gene was saying something about our being lucky and Ben said, "No, Gene, we just got the hell kicked out of us."

Funny thing, talking about Mangrum. He was a better player than I was. He won more tournaments. But it seemed like I beat him every time we played. We played in the quarter-final of the PGA the year I won it—1950. It was at

Scioto, where Nicklaus was brought up. It was long and narrow, the course, but I could hit it straight and had Lloyd four down at lunch. But in the afternoon he caught me, and we were even going to the thirty-fifth hole, a par-three. We both hit the green about fifteen feet to the right of the hole. He was a little outside of me, and I knew what he was going to do. See, we were still playing stymies in those days. So he putts first. I knew it broke left and that if he didn't make it he would leave it short of the hole. And that's exactly what he did. Right in front of me. Well, I hit probably the best shot I ever made. I took a nine-iron and chipped it. It hit just short of his ball, jumped over, and went in the hole. All Lloyd said was, "Let's go to the next hole."

I had been thinking I had to win that hole, because the eighteenth is a long par-five, 540 yards, that he could possibly reach in two and I couldn't. I could only hit it 500 yards with two shots, and I was afraid he would get close enough to make four. Well, he outdrives me by about fifteen yards. I hit a pretty good second about forty yards short of the green, and he hits his a ton—a driver off the fairway, I'll never forget it. He put it on the extreme left corner of the green. Well, I pitched and thought it was perfect. It hit short of the pin, but took a big bounce and went about fifteen feet past. Now I've got a downhiller, Lloyd putts from over seventy-five feet and almost makes it for an eagle. *Man!* I'm one up, so I have to make mine to win. And I make it. I'll never forget it. There must have been 5,000 people there. Lloyd took off his cap, bowed, and said, "Take the goddamn game."

That was the greatest match of my life. In the semi-final I beat Jimmy Demaret three and one, and in the final I played Henry Williams and didn't play well. But it turned out I didn't need to.

When I think back on all those days on the tour, I guess Tam O'Shanter would be in my thoughts a lot. That shot Worsham hit to beat me in 1953. It was $25,000 for first, $50,000 total, because then you got to play twenty-five exhibitions, all expenses paid at $1,000 per, representing the George S. May Company. George was sponsor of the tournament. That was by far the biggest money you could make out there at the time.

The circumstances were, there was four of us tied going

to the last round, and Lew Worsham was one of them. I come down to the last hole in the next-to-last threesome. Worsham is behind me in the last group. The hole is 400 yards, with a creek in front of the green. I had a perfect lie and hit a nine-iron. The ball hit on the front part of the green and went right at the cup. I knew it was awfully close, but I couldn't tell how close. Frank Stranahan was standing up there and he told me the ball lit maybe a couple of inches from the hole and spun back about fourteen inches.

Anyway, I knew that through sixteen I was even with Worsham, and I'd birdied seventeen. Now I know he's got to play pretty good, since I've put this ball dead to the hole on eighteen. So I walked up and tapped it in, and George May comes over and tells me to get ready, he wanted to give me the first-prize check. It was running late, it was about seven at night. I said, "Let's wait for Worsham to finish." See, I heard this roar before I hit my second at eighteen, so I assumed Worsham birdied it, which he had. So he needed a birdie on the last hole to tie me. Meanwhile I got on the radio with Jimmy Demaret and he was congratulating me on winning, but I said we'd better wait till Worsham came in. You see, several times that year I had been robbed. I had four or five seconds. At Palm Springs, Freddie Haas eagled the last hole to beat me. At Tucson, Bolt and I were paired together and he's got me one shot going to the last nine holes and I shoot 31 and he shoots 31 and beats me. I shot ten under par at Baton Rouge and thought I won and when I got in they told me Toski birdied six of the last seven holes, so he beat me by a shot. So it was happening. And it did at Tam O'Shanter.

I saw Worsham's shot. I don't think he hit it right. A lot of people think he bladed it a little, but it wasn't so low in the air. He used a pitching wedge—of course, he made it a little strong: you know, decreased the loft—and when the ball hit I wouldn't have been surprised if it had spun back off the green, because it hit in front and there was a rise there. But somehow it had overspin on it and when it hit it just went like a football, end over end. It just kept coming and coming right up and into the cup. He makes an eagle two and wins the tournament.

Oh God, my stomach sunk. You see, I was thirty-nine years old then and I knew that in any big tournament the chances of me being up there again weren't very good. In fact, two years later I built my golf course here and got busy with that, and I didn't play well again until I was a senior.

Well, of course, I think golf's a great game. It's the challenge. It's so damn hard to play. You can't hang on to anything. When I think back I don't know how I beat those guys ever. I never practiced, I didn't have the patience. And I never gave golf all my time. I had club jobs, and I was in the small-loan business for about thirty years. I helped organize that with my father-in-law in 1947. That took some time, in the beginning. But I still think I should have won more. Maybe I got mine some other way, other than golf.

I mean, I've done real well, won a major title, which most people don't do, and made a good living. But they'll have a hard time making me believe I got mine in golf. You know, you're always calling your opponent lucky, and, in sixty-one years of playing, someone should have called me that. But no one ever has.

Yeah, maybe if the Worsham shot hadn't come so close to the end of my tour career I might feel differently. Oh, that shot took the wind out of me. After the tournament I said to Mr. May, "Look, you're going to send Worsham on this exhibition tour. Well, I haven't got anything to do right now, why don't you send me along with him? Give me five hundred. Let 'em see who he did it to, you know." He said no, no, I should come back next year and win it.

You know, I named a dog we had at the time Wedgie, after that shot. And our fourth hole here at Bide-a-Wee I called Wedgie, because it's 140 yards long, which is close to the distance Worsham holed out from.

Chandler Harper won eight PGA tour events, and the 1968 PGA Seniors and World Senior championships. He played on the 1955 U.S. Ryder Cup team, and set the tour's fifty-four-hole scoring record of 189 when in the 1954 Texas Open he played the last three rounds in 63–63–63. Chandler lives in his hometown, Portsmouth, Virginia, and plays golf as often as possible, usually at the Bide-a-Wee Golf Course he built in the 1950s.

JOHNNY BULLA

Photograph by Al Barkow

"I hit more balls than Ben Hogan ever thought of."

The only thing on the tour I had a bad reputation for, if I had one, was I got so frustrated with my golf. See, I'm left-handed, but I never hit a golf ball left-handed until I was forty years old, and I shot 76 the first time I played left-handed. It got so I could play par golf and was a club longer in distance, playing left-handed. But when I was a boy they told me I wasn't going to be any good unless I played right-handed. Well, that just absolutely ate my lunch, because it was so hard for me. But I didn't know anything about it then.

You know, if you're left-handed and play right-handed you will probably not be able to turn the right side away as well on the backswing, because your natural coordination is not that way. You can handle it when you're younger, you can adapt and force against nature, but as you get into middle age it becomes harder to do. Because the body loses flexibility. Which is why Johnny Miller went into his slump.

Or take Bobby Jones. He had to work so hard at his golf. It wasn't a natural game for him. They say he didn't practice a lot, but the heck he didn't. He retired at twenty-eight because he knew if he went further he wouldn't have been as good. You see, Bob Jones was left-handed. Jones loved to shoot trap, and he couldn't shoot. He'd hit maybe ten or twelve targets. I said to him one day, "Bob, let me show you some-

113

thing. You're shooting right-handed and there's no way, because you're left-eyed." That's the reason he turned his head to the right before he started his golf swing. Well, Bob started hitting twenty, twenty-two targets shooting left-handed soon as I showed him how. He was one of the few left-handers who switched and was really successful at golf, but I think he would have started to lose it in his thirties.

Now, Ben Hogan was not really left-handed, as everyone thinks. He's what we call a skip generation. According to Mendelian Law, four percent of the species takes after their grandparents. What happens—and it's so easy to see if you take a look at it—the right side of the body is the masculine side, the paternal side. The muscles are bigger, and the turn of the elbows and knees; they turn out for masculine, in for feminine. But if you skip a generation, the left side is the masculine, not the right. So Hogan's strong side is his left side, because of the skip-generation law. He's a natural right-hander, but with great strength in his left side.

Considering how good I played left-handed at forty—I shot 62 once on a good course right here in Tucson—I believe I would have won more on the tour. But I continue to play right-handed because I don't have the time to work on it left-handed so I could get to the level of play I reached right-handed. You know, they broke me from writing left-handed my first year in school. The teacher used to hit me with a ruler when I went to write left-handed. That's why I stuttered for two years, and also stayed in the first grade for two years. But I don't resent having been turned right-handed when I was a kid. What I've done is try to help others. I have more statistics on handedness than anybody. I give a lot of lectures on it.

No one ever played golf in my family. Oh Lord, no! My father was a minister—we were Quakers—and he tried to keep me from it. He wouldn't let me caddie on Sunday. He never accepted the fact that I played golf, but my mother finally did. They just thought it was wrong, frivolous. It was like musicians, or actors, or anything that wasn't manual labor was wrong. That's just the consciousness they grew up with.

I'm from North Carolina—Burlington—and it all happened at once how I got into golf. I started out caddying and thought twenty-five cents for nine holes was a great deal. But I also thought it was the silliest thing I ever saw, grown men chasing little old golf balls. Then we had a caddie tournament, and I shot 87 for nine holes and was last. I said right then that I was going to learn how to play this game. That's the day it started. I was eleven years old. Well, all through high school I played on the golf team. Then the clubhouse of the Burlington Country Club—which is where I started caddying— burned down and the pro left, and as soon as I got out of school that summer I was the professional. By that I mean I took care of the clubs, shafted them when they needed it, and all that stuff. I knew how to do all that because I'd worked for the pro there in the years before. There was no actual pro shop, though.

I saw a lot of big-time golf at Pinehurst every year when they played the North and South tournament. I think my first one was in 1931, when Paul Runyan won. I was born in 1914, so I was seventeen. One of the players who impressed me so much with his rhythm was Joe Turnesa. I loved to watch him hit a golf ball. And MacDonald Smith. I played with him later. But they didn't influence how I would swing the club. There was a fellow at Greensboro by the name of Andy Gray that I tried to copy. He was tall, like me.

Anyway, in 1933 I hitchhiked up to Chicago to see the U.S. Open at North Shore Country Club, then stayed on and caddied there for about three or four weeks. The caddie master was real nice to me. One day I went to a driving range in Chicago, on Touhy and Western avenues. They had a great big high fence at the far end, and I asked this fellow who owned the place how far it was over that fence. He said, "Don't worry, sonny, you can't hit it over." I told him I thought I could and he said to go ahead and try. So I started carrying that fence, and he asked me if I'd like a job teaching there. So I taught there for the rest of the season. The next year I went over to Big Run, on the southwest side of Chicago. The following year I went to the Woodridge Country Club, then I went with the Walgreen Drug Company. I went over there and promoted their golf balls. The PoDo golf ball and the Golden Crown. The PoDo was the Walgreen ball for years. The Walgreens had a little bulldog named PoDo and they named the ball after him. We sold the PoDo to the retailer for fifteen cents and he sold it for a quarter, and he paid twenty-five cents for the Golden Crown and sold it for forty-five.

I won the L.A. Open with the Golden Crown. I wasn't a teaching pro anymore, because I worked only for Mr. Walgreen. I promoted the golf ball, gave trick-shot exhibitions at driving ranges, and played the tour winter and summer. I had a good arrangement, but the pros hated me. Oh, they hated me, because so many golf balls were sold in drugstores. I was the first one to really promote retail golf. L. B. Icely, who ran the Wilson company, he didn't want Sam Snead to travel with me—Sam was on Wilson's advisory staff—but Sam told him, "Look, you can tell me what to do on my golf, but don't tell me who my friends are." Icely kept me out of the PGA, wouldn't let me join because I was selling in a retail outlet. He kept me out until after the war. I could have been on the Ryder Cup team, because I played well enough then. But I wasn't because I didn't belong to the PGA. I was an outcast.

I minded to some extent, naturally, because it's never nice to be shut out. But I remember one time in Cleveland when Ed Dudley was the president of the PGA and he said, "John, I can't accept your application." This was for the $10,000 Cleveland Open. I asked him why not, and he said I was bad for golf because I was selling retail golf balls. So I called Justin Dart, who was the son-in-law of Mr. Walgreen and my boss, and he said, "John, you better hope they keep you out. We'll both be rich. I'll sue them for every dime they've got." I went back to Dudley with that and they had a meeting and decided they weren't going to bother me anymore.

I never did get to play Ryder Cup golf, but in 1941, when the matches were canceled because of the war, Bobby Jones got up a team to play our Ryder Cup team. Up in Detroit. And we beat the hell out of them. Hogan was on our team, and Clayton Heafner, a lot of good players. See, the Ryder Cup in those years was all political. Can you imagine that the year before Hogan won four tournaments and wasn't selected for the team?

Mr. Walgreen gave me my first trip to the British Open, in 1939, but not because they were selling a golf ball over there. This is quite a story. When Walgreen first hired me he said, "John, I've got a friend named Mudd, my insurance man, and we're always pulling jokes on each other. He doesn't know who you are, and I want you to come over to Beverly"—he was a member of Beverly Country Club, on the south side of Chicago—"and play just as bad as you can until I get all the bets down. Then I want you to really clobber him." So I played terrible for five holes, just awful, and he got all the bets down and I *still played terrible* and he lost every bet. Hah! I thought I was going to get fired, but he thought it was a big joke. I was so embarrassed. Well, they went to Orlando in the winter and played together all the time, so I'm playing in St. Petersburg one day and get a call from Mr. Walgreen. "John, I've got a game for you. We're going to get even. Mudd thinks this amateur over here in Orlando can beat all the pros." I said, "Not Carl Dann," and Walgreen asks if I know him and I said he owns the course and nobody beats him over there. Ky Laffoon and those guys got killed over there. But Walgreen said I had to come over, he'd made a lot of bets already. Now I know I'm really going to get killed, but, wouldn't you know, I shot 29 on the first nine and something like 61 or 62 for the round. I just killed him. So in the locker room Mr. Walgreen ways, "Well, we had a field day, what would you like?" I said I'd like to go to the British Open. He said, "You've got it." And that's how I got to go to my first one. Later I went on my own, or for Sears, Roebuck.

I had left Walgreen's by 1946. The old man died, and Justin Dart quit the company. Walgreen's son took over and everything changed. I went with Sears in '46 and ran their golf department. They had a line of clubs with my name on them. See, the fellow who was head of the sporting-goods department at Sears knew what I did over at Walgreen's, so he wanted me to come over with him. But that didn't keep me out of the PGA. After the war they made a rule that anyone who had been playing on the tour for so long got in. Things had begun to change, and they couldn't keep it the old way. Sam Snead was having his clubs sold in department stores—he was making $35,000 a year in royalties—so they couldn't say anything about the retail business keeping me out anymore.

Johnny Bulla

I owned my own plane before the war, and flew the tour some. I guess I was the first one to do that. I had a four-place Fairchild. I took a lot of people who had never been in an airplane before. Back then flying was not so common. After the war I bought a DC-3 and would take twenty at a time, pros and their wives. I charged them. Oh heck, yes. I had always been interested in flying. I remember I caddied all of one Fourth of July, carried doubles in the morning and afternoon, to make enough money to go for my first airplane ride. When the war came I went with Eastern Airlines. You see, all the commercial pilots were Army and Navy pilots and they were called back into duty. So they were short of pilots. I had enough air time, and they hired me as a co-pilot.

I was interested in a lot of things. In 1932 I hitchhiked down to Augusta, Georgia, and stayed for about six weeks to watch them build the Augusta National Golf Club. I saw them cut down all the trees around Amen Corner. I was interested in golf architecture. Donald Ross was my hero. He was over at Pinehurst, and because I asked him so many questions about golf architecture he took an interest in me. He took the time to give me answers. He explained his concepts. I remember a lot of it. Like he said, never build a trap to try to catch somebody. Always put it out to show him where not to go. Always have it where the poor player can play the hole. And always be fair. If you missed a green, he would have it so you weren't in water so the poor player could still play without taking a penalty. I was always a great believer in that. And Ross said to always make the course look like nature left it there. He was the greatest, I don't care what anybody says. I'm such a traditionalist from being around Donald that I can't stand these penalty golf courses they build now. They're always looking for how they can catch you and penalize you. But they'll change again.

Another time I was trying to find out the modulus of elasticity of a golf ball. I'd heard of the fellow who designed the dimples on the golf ball, an English engineer who was working for a glass company in Butler, Pennsylvania. I went up to see him. I asked him how he worked out the dimples. He told me he developed a homemade driving machine with a spring so he could throw the club at the same speed every time. So he knew what he would get every time, and he began to realize that the dimpling on the ball made it stay in the air longer. People already knew that when the old gutta-percha balls were nicked up they would go higher, but they didn't know why. But the engineer knew something about aerodynamics, and understood the dimpling. Then he worked out the right depth and size, and they kept that dimpling pattern for years and years. He got a patent on it, the engineer. His name was Taylor. My mother's maiden name was Taylor, English, so that's why I always remember the engineer's name. My father was English, too. Bulla was originally Bull, but my ancestors added the A to it. I guess they didn't like to be kidded about the bull. They came over before the Revolutionary War.

How did I get to be so close with Sam Snead? I'm still probably the closest friend he's got. But if you could know the reason for it you would know the whole reason for life. There are certain people where the chemistry is right. There are certain people you don't like, certain people you do, and you form these things pretty quick. I first met Sam in Louisville, Kentucky, in 1934. We played a little tournament there. We met on the golf course and hit it off right away. Then we decided to travel together. We took my car the first year, his car the second. I was the only one who ever traveled with Sam.

Sam had the reputation over the years for being rude and tight with money, but I always say that what you have when you're young you always have more of when you're older. Sam was always afraid people would take advantage of him. See, he grew up in an environment in Virginia where everyone had to look out for themselves. Everybody outside of Hot Springs was a foreigner, as far as he was concerned. So most people couldn't get close to Sam. He wasn't as bad as he sometimes seemed, he just wanted always to protect himself. He was a kid that never had anything, and then all at once he falls into the public eye and it spoiled him, no question about it. It's like he said once when we were driving through Kentucky: "Boo Boo"—he always called me Boo Boo—"we're finally going to have dinner where nobody is going to bother us." So we sit down in the corner of this little old restaurant in a little old town, and of course they bothered him to death. Everybody gets to the point where they'd like to be alone.

I remember in 1939 Sam was playing so good he was just winning everything, so, at the Miami Biltmore, Nelson and Hogan try to copy Sam's swing. I think it was the funniest thing I've ever seen. They were down there practicing and, of course, trying to make that long, full swing of Sam's, and there was just no way. They never got back to the ball. It was so funny. For my swing I loved to play with Byron. He had the kind of swing I could use, both of us being tall. Sam didn't. I couldn't use Sam's swing.

Sam talked with me often about his never winning the U.S. Open. He thinks it was just destiny. I do, too. If you're supposed to win, you'll win. I don't think he got nervous after those first two he sort of blew. Sam didn't miss a shot at Spring Mill in '39 when he took that eight. He just used the wrong club in the bunker, that two-wood, and didn't quite carry it. It only lacked about an inch of getting out. You know, I was leading that tournament going into the last round. I had the lowest fifty-four-hole total that had ever been shot. But I had some putting trouble, shot 76, and lost by three shots. Then I went to the British Open and finished second by two shots. I finished second again in the British Open in 1946, with Bobby Locke. I talked Sam into going over for that one, and he beat me and Locke by four shots.

I only won one big tournament on the tour, the L.A. Open. Oh, and I won the Peoria Open in 1934. Beat Gus Moreland. But I was not a winner. I just didn't have it. So I didn't enjoy the tournaments. No. I enjoyed the excitement of travel and all, but it was so frustrating to me, the playing. I worked so hard. I hit more balls than Ben Hogan ever thought of. But it never came.

So you ask if I'm satisfied with my career? Well, how I did has nothing to do with that. The bottom line is, if you've helped someone else along the way, you've accomplished life's purpose. I'm a great believer that life is made up like a three-legged stool. There's the physical, the mental, and the spiritual. I've seen ministers just fall over because they have too much of the spiritual side and don't get the other two. I think you've got to have a balance. I'm not talking about going to church. Your temple is inside, not outside. You show me a man who treats his fellow man right and I'll show you a religious person. I have not been a Quaker for a long time, and don't go to church anymore. I did when I was a kid, but I remember my mother raised Cain when I wouldn't go to church with her. I said, "Mother, when you invite those colored people across the hollow to come to our church, then I'll come." "Oh, they've got their own church," she said. I said, "Don't give me that. If we're all made in God's image, then we're all the same. That's what's wrong with the world."

Golf just happened to be my medium. Millions of times I wished I had done something else, but on the other hand I feel that was what I was supposed to do. I'm a great believer in fate being written for you. Golf gave me the opportunity to meet a lot of people, and it gave me the opportunity to control my emotional feelings. See, golf upset me. I wanted to play better, and it bothered me that I couldn't.

Johnny Bulla lives in Phoenix, Arizona, and presently has in the works a project to manufacture (in Japan) and distribute in the United States and elsewhere a set of golf clubs he has designed. They are a complete set of irons in the shape of traditional wooden-headed clubs. He also lectures on sidedness, and plays golf occasionally . . . right-handed.

WILLIE TURNESA

Photograph by H.W. Kartluke

The Turnesa boys, with their Dad, probably the most accomplished golfing family in the game's history. From left to right: Mike, Joe, Frank, Phil, Mike, Sr., Doug, Jim, and Willie.

Photograph by Al Barkow

" . . . through golf you get to know the inside of people."

The story of how the Turnesas got into golf is, I think, a very good one. It started when our father came to the United States from Italy when he was fourteen years old. When he got here he went to live in Greenwich Village with some *compadres*, which in Italian means uncles or friends. You see, he was an orphan but there were some people here from his village in Italy, including the lady who became our mother. His first job was shining shoes on the Delaware-Lackawanna ferryboats that ran between Manhattan and Staten Island. But he was unhappy living in the big city, with the pushcarts, the concrete, the noise, and whatever. As a boy he worked in the hills around Naples with sheep herders. So one day—he was maybe twenty now—he decided to take a walk. He walked all the way up to Elmsford, New York, which is in Westchester County. That's about twenty-one miles. When he got there he saw workers digging in the ground and he went over to see if he could get a job like that—pick 'n' shovel work, it was called. He loved working in the ground. Sure enough, the foreman gave him a job. He didn't know what they were building, but he wouldn't have known what it was if they told him. It was a golf course—Fairview Country Club.

After the course was built he stayed on and a few years later became the greenskeeper at Fairview. He kept that job

123

for the rest of his life. The club retired him when he was eighty. He learned about being a greenskeeper through nature, not from books or anything like that. But they didn't have chemicals in those days, anyway. They didn't have watering systems either. My father would taste the soil to find out how much acid there was in it. And he would water the greens by hand, with a hose. He put his finger over the end of the hose to get a spray, because they didn't have nozzles then. I want to tell you, you need some strength to do that, because the water came out with a lot of power.

My father built our house with the help of some *paisanos* who came up from Greenwich Village. It was only a half-mile from the course, and it was nothing for him to walk over at night to water the greens and stay sometimes till two o'clock, then be back there at six in the morning. He loved the course, every blade of grass on it, and never once lost a green. It's now an industrial park and not well kept. If my father could see it now, he would turn over in his grave.

Our last name in Italy was something like Turnazah. That's the way it sounded, nobody knows how it was spelled. My brother Phil, the oldest, changed it for euphonic reasons to be Turnesa, pronounced "Turnessa," which isn't that bad. Either way, in Italian it means money. Which is a funny thing, because back then we never had any money. After he had some security in his job my father got married and started raising a family. Nine of us, seven boys, two girls. All the boys became golf pros except me. At one time we all lived in that small house my father built, and in the winter my brother Jim and I would haul wood in from the woods to feed a big potbelly stove. There was a well outside, and whoever got up first in the morning had to bring in the water for all of us to wash up. When my brother Joe did well on the tour we built a new house with three and a half bedrooms. It cost $5,000, a lot of money before World War II. But money was always short. Sure, my father had a regular job, but we're talking about fifty bucks a week, and with nine children his pay didn't go too far.

All the boys worked on the course for my father, picking weeds by hand and doing every other kind of job. We also caddied. Joe, the third born, was so fascinated by the game he was always trying to find extra time to practice. My father had him cutting the grass with a team of horses pulling the mowers. The horses wore big rubber boots on their hoofs so they wouldn't chop up the place. Now, the tenth fairway at Fairview was very flat, a 440-yard hole with no bunkers or anything, and Joe trained those horses to cut the grass by themselves so that while they were doing that he could hit golf balls. He always had one eye out for my father, because if he got caught he would've gotten killed. That's one way to learn to play golf, teach horses to cut grass so you can hit shots.

Joe, of course, went on to do very well as a player. He was the first in the family to play the tour. My father raised some pretty good players. I'm not bragging when I say that, it's just that we did have a good record. Joe was runner-up to Walter Hagen in a PGA championship, runner-up to Bob Jones in the 1926 U.S. Open, and played on three Ryder Cup teams. He won the Texas Open and some other tour events. Jim won the PGA championship in 1952, and was runner-up in it to Sam Snead in 1942. And I won a couple of U.S. Amateurs and a British Amateur.

I was swinging a golf club when I was five, six years old. We all started young, because we were always around the course. Jim and I were only three years apart, so we were close, and we would hit balls back and forth to each other on a big hill that was right beside our house. I preferred hitting them downhill, because I was small—I'm the youngest—and it was easier to get distance. It was about a 125-yard shot. We would also play matches at the club, many times for the use of our brother Mike's car, which was the only one in the family. My father never owned a car, and didn't even like to ride in one. When we knew Mike's car was going to be available, Jim and I would play a match to see who would get it for a date with a girl. Well, I won that car a lot of times, which may be why Jim never had many dates and never got married—he's the only one of us that didn't. I'm only kidding about that, but if you want to know about playing golf under pressure, try having a big date and needing that car to make an impression on your girl.

Joe was a contemporary of Sarazen, Hagen, Leo Diegel, Johnny Farrell, Willie MacFarlane, and all these great players came around fairly often and I played with them. MacFarlane was one of my favorites, which is why I never minded being called Willie. He gave me a very important piece of advice about playing golf that I never forgot. This was when I was around thirteen and playing in the Westchester Caddie tournament. I used to dream about playing in that tournament. I could hardly wait for it. I used to have my shoes shined and my whole wardrobe laid out way ahead of time. Anyway, this one time when I'm thirteen I shoot 73 in the morning round, then a 77 in the afternoon. I must have won by ten shots. I could hit it pretty good. I turned over on the ball and that baby would go. But that's what MacFarlane's advice was about. I used to hit a seven-iron when it was a five-iron shot, and he told me to hit everything three-quarters, to never swing all out except maybe when you just had to have something extra. From that time on I played the way MacFarlane suggested, and I'd have to say he was right.

But one of the best pieces of advice about golf I ever got was from my brother Phil, who was pro at a club here in Westchester for about fifty years and was also a greenskeeper. He took a six-month course in agronomy at Columbia University. A lady he caddied for, Mrs. Herzog, paid the tuition. And Mike has been pro at the Knollwood club for over fifty years. We Turnesas are a steady family. You learn to be that way when you're poor, because you understand the importance of security. Anyway, when I was a kid on the way up, around sixteen or seventeen, I would sometimes get beaten by fellows I knew I could give two up a side, and I couldn't understand it. When my opponent hit a ball onto the green, or holed a long putt, I would get upset because I thought I was the only one supposed to hit greens and make long putts. So Phil said to me one day, "The only way you're going to learn anything is by losing. You lose enough now, and you'll win something big later. But if you keep winning these little caddie tournaments and the like, when you get to playing people who can really play you won't be able to do anything."

What Phil was saying to me was that you try to win all the time, but you should expect to lose now and then and shouldn't worry about it because it will make you tougher. Well, it all came to a head when I traveled all the way out to Portland, Oregon, to play in the 1937 U.S. Amateur. Everybody in the family chipped in to pay my way; they all used to finance my golf. Now, there were thirty-two places for the championship and, don't you know, I get into a playoff for the thirty-second spot after going that far from home. Fourteen of us in a playoff, and it eventually got down to myself and a fellow by the name of Jamieson from Alabama. This was after seven holes. On the eighth hole, if Jamieson misses a ten-footer, I'm in, and by now we're playing with car lights turned on around the green so we can see the hole. But he makes the putt, and I have to sleep on that because it is too dark to go on. The next morning we continue. Now, the dew in Oregon is like glue, and I hook my drive into the rough on the first hole, make a double bogey, and lose to his bogey.

I get on the train for a very long ride home, and I think a lot about what my brother told me about taking your losses and getting tough, and I say to myself over and over again that nobody is ever going to beat me again. I said, "I play with all the pros and can play up with them, so what am I doing losing to amateurs?"

The next year the U.S. Amateur was at Oakmont, in Pittsburgh, and I decided no amateur could beat me on that course because it was too tough. And I won it, the 1938 U.S. Amateur championship. But there's another aspect to that victory that has to do with Gene Sarazen's sand wedge. It's a yarn not too many people know about, including Gene.

I was known as "Willie the Wedge" after I won the Amateur at Oakmont, because I played out of a lot of bunkers that week, and in most cases very well. But it all started at the Quaker Ridge Golf Club in Westchester County. I was playing a round there with a very good pro friend of mine by the name of Danny Galgano, and on one hole I hit a bunker shot and nothing happens. It doesn't come out. At the time I was using a nine-iron for that shot. So Danny says, "You can't play with that club at Oakmont, because the bunkers there are furrowed and the ball sinks halfway down." He said I should get a wedge. I didn't own one. The sand wedge was invented only a few years earlier, by Gene Sarazen. He used it to win the U.S. Open in 1932, out on Long Island—at Fresh Meadow. He was getting it up and down like magic.

Well, my friend Lester Rice, a great sportswriter and a

close friend of Sarazen, had the wedge Gene used to win the '32 Open—the very one, not a model. And Lester gave it to me. Now I've got it, but I'm not sure how to use it. It wasn't that simple. But I got the hang of it, and down at Oakmont the ball came popping óut every time and close to the hole. The other players weren't moving the ball at all out of those furrows. So the same wedge Gene Sarazen used to win the U.S. Open, I used to win the U.S. Amateur. From one Italian to another, right?

I used that club to win the British Amateur in 1947, and over a period of time used it so much I must have worn half an inch of steel off of it. There were little dots on the clubface, and those were worn smooth. Finally, it got too light and I had to give it up. It's in the USGA Museum now.

I've been asked many times why I didn't turn professional. For one thing, I didn't like to teach. But, mainly, my brothers didn't want me to be a pro, because none of them ever went to college and they wanted me to have that advantage. My brother Frank, for instance, wanted to be a doctor, but where was there money for that at the time? He worked in a pharmacy once, and everyone called him Doc, but that's as far as his medical career went. Also, the pro life was not a good life, as I saw it. I'm talking about playing golf for a living, which is all I was interested in. Today, playing the tour is a career, but in my early days you did it because you couldn't do anything else. If you were going to be a pro golfer, there was no sense in going to school, and hardly any golf pros went beyond high school. Sam Parks did, and Craig Wood, but they were rare. Before them I don't think anyone did. I'm talking Mehlhorn, MacFarlane, Sarazen, Hagen, that generation.

The thing about being a professional in my day was this. You went up to a certain point age-wise and ability-wise, then you were cut off because of physical reasons. You can't play at your peak anymore. You've had your ups, but all of a sudden those leaves start falling off the trees and you go down and down and down. Now where're you going? You pump gas. How're you going to raise children and educate them? Even today, with all the money they're playing for out there, out of all the fellows only about twenty are making good. They all have to maintain a permanent home, raise children, and on the road pay for motels, cars, airplanes, food, caddies, and so on. If they win $100,000 they aren't making that good a living.

So the question for me was what am I going to do when I'm forty or fifty years old? Am I going to make a living on the tour? No way! I don't think I was strong enough to make the tour, anyway. I only weighed around 135 pounds. Hogan was small, too, but he was strong. Boy, let me tell you he was strong! Besides, I had to listen to my brothers. They wanted a better life for me, and it turned out pretty well. I went to Holy Cross on a golf scholarship, and studied business. When I came home for the summers I played in all the local tournaments, and tried for the national Amateur, but usually only when it was east of the Mississippi. If I could drive to it, I would go. I never played the amateur circuit, such as it was, in tournaments such as the North-South in Pinehurst, because it was a question of money and I didn't have that much. I had to work, too, during my summer vacations. I was the golf writer for the Worcester newspaper when I was at Holy Cross, and during the summer I wrote golf for the White Plains *Reporter*. They paid me ten cents a word and I would write a lot, turn in 1,000 words, but they would always cut it down to 300 or so. Which is what I got paid for.

I won my first U.S. Amateur championship right after finishing at Holy Cross, and this was a big help to me. Everywhere I went I was treated and greeted well. My first job after college was with Fruehauf, the trucking concern. My boss was Mr. Fruehauf, the owner of the company. He loved golf, and I went all over the United States calling on clients and potential clients and playing golf with them if they were interested. I was a sort of public-relations representative. I covered all seventy-two branches, and spent three months during the winter in California. I covered all this territory by car, by the way, just the way the tour pros did on their circuit. I'd go to a branch manager and he often had a customer who wanted to play golf. So that's how it worked. At the same time, if the manager had some gripes he would tell me and I would send the message back to the home office in Detroit. I was doing well. Back in 1939 I was making $200 a week, which was a tremendous amount of money at the time. Then again, I was never home and was not married.

Willie Turnesa

When World War II started I went into the Navy, and after that into my own business—fire extinguishers, a dry chemical which is now the top fire extinguisher in the country. But I didn't have the resources to finance research and development, so I made a few bucks and sold out. After that I went to work for Binghampton Container, a box company, and worked for them for thirty-seven years. My business life has been okay. I never made a tremendous amount of money, but enough to educate four children, maintain my wife and home. And I kept up my golf game. You see, sales enables you to play golf. There was never a week went by that I didn't play golf with a customer. I would play at six on a Sunday morning if that's when they wanted to play. It could be well worth it. I remember a time playing at Westchester Country Club with a potential customer. At one of the par-threes, a long, tough hole with the green on top of a hill, the customer said he'd give me the account if I could reach the green with a three-iron. So I hit the three-iron on the green and won a $300,000 account.

There were only two things that were important to me in my golf: playing in the U.S. Amateur and winning it, and playing on our Walker Cup team. I also played in five British Amateurs. So I played all my career at match play, which I liked best. I played very few stroke-play events. I wasn't geared up for stroke play. In match play you can free-wheel it. If you're on a tight hole, the worst you can do is lose the hole, so you take a chance. Give you an example. I played once in George S. May's tournament at Tam O'Shanter in Chicago. I did it because the branch manager in Chicago wanted me to meet some customers out there. Well, one day I hit my approach over the back of the eighteenth green, way back near the parking lot. The pin is up front beneath a huge tree overhanging the green at that point. I figure, what the heck, I've got nothing to lose, so I try something wild. I figure the tree is thick enough to keep the ball from going through and into the creek beyond. It did just that. The ball rattled around in there and came down not far from the hole. I made the putt and scrambled out a par. It was the only shot I had. That was a stroke-play tournament, but the idea for the shot came from match-play competition, where you can take chances. I played a lot that way, although not usually in such a bizarre style. I

130

could never stand having to chip a ball into the fairway when I was in trouble. Still can't.

Golf for me was always a means of introduction to many things in life—people, mostly. Rather than have a roundabout association, through golf you get to know the inside of people. Let's say you meet someone new who's a golfer. You don't even know his name, but right away you're friendly because he's a golfer. All criminals stick together, you know.

Now, there's been a lot said about Italian fellows having a difficult time in my day getting head professional jobs at clubs around Westchester County, and elsewhere—at the good clubs. But this was not the case with the Turnesas. If anything, I felt that sort of thing more at college. Never in golf. I touched base with some of the finest people in the country, and always felt I could handle myself. I didn't try to be a good guy, I *had* to be. I could have been the other way, but I realized I couldn't make any mistakes on my way up because in amateur golf you weren't only accepted as a golfer—you had to be accepted as a gentlemen, too. You had to get invitations to this tournament or that, and being a gentleman had to do with that. You build up a series of good friendships or acquaintanceships. A pro is not concerned this way. He's playing for cash, but I'm playing for glory, as an amateur, and for business connections, I have to admit. For instance, I always played my practice rounds with Jess Sweetser, who was an establishment guy, and he got me my first job, with Fruehauf. Jess liked my golf, but he also liked my personality.

Golf has been good to me and the whole Turnesa family. And it all began because my father didn't like the concrete down in Manhattan and decided to take a walk upstate. Not bad, huh?

William P. "Willie" Turnesa is retired from business and lives in White Plains, New York, very close to the town where he grew up. He plays much of his golf in the old neighborhood, at the Knollwood Country Club in Elmsford, New York, where his brother Mike still holds sway as the head professional.

SAM PARKS, JR.

Photograph by Al Barkow

"Yes, I was the dark-horse champion."

I started taking golf lessons in 1922, when I was twelve. I was an only child, and got all the goodies. My father was a member of the Highland Country Club in Pittsburgh. He got as low as a four handicap, and was a great student of the game. He read all kinds of books on it, and was also a rules expert. He was on the Western Pennyslvania Golf Association board of directors, and I remember often he would get calls at home late at night from golfers still at the course having their after-round celebration, asking about a rules call. Gene Sarazen was my first golf teacher. He was the professional at our club, and in June of 1922 he won the U.S. Open. The club gave him a leave of absence for a year to take full advantage of his title—play exhibitions—so he was back only a few times. But in March, April, and May of that year I took lessons from him. Gene and I were at a function recently, and he was telling someone that I was his favorite pupil. I bet Gene he wouldn't take credit for any part of my swing, though. He laughed. Because it was a little unorthodox, by the usual standards—a very slow backswing, and I was a little more wristy than many.

Gene's lessons were influential in my golf game, yes, but you can imagine the impact of how important golf could be when my teacher went away and won the National Open. All that publicity. After he won they had a big banquet at the William Penn Hotel in Pittsburgh, honoring Gene. Dad took me to the dinner—I was about the only young kid there—and I can remember they brought a great big papier-mâché golf ball into the ballroom, and at the proper time it opened like a book and out stepped Sarazen. He came over to our table and said hello to my dad and me. I was so impressed.

This all had a big influence on me wanting to become a real good golfer, but I had no intention of ever being a professional. My dad had a lot of friends in business—he was a real-estate insurance broker—and I figured that when I graduated from college I would probably go into some business. I went to Penn State for a year, then my father's business was in trouble and I transferred to the University of Pittsburgh so I could live at home and commute to school. Which I did for three years. When I graduated the Depression had hit bottom—1931—and all these people who I thought might hire me, many of them presidents of big companies, were losing their jobs. So, due to the exigencies of the times, I turned to golf. I had an opportunity through some friends to take a pro job at a little resort near Uniontown, Pennsylvania. I was up there for about a year and a half, then got a real good job in Pittsburgh, again through the influence of my father, at the South Hills Country Club. I was professional there for nigh onto ten years. You see, once I won the National Open, in 1935, being in golf was too good to let go of. It took a world war to get me out of golf. I didn't break out of the golf profession until 1942, as we were gearing up for the war. I was not classified as being a desirable draftee—wife and child, that sort of thing—so it took a world war to get me out of golf. The steel industry needed people, because many were lost through the war effort, and I went to work for U.S. Steel. I was with them for about thirty years, as a steel salesman. I'm sure my winning the U.S. Open helped my career with U.S. Steel.

There may have been a certain amount of aloofness or resentment toward me from the other pros because I came from money and had a private-club and college background. But I don't really know if that was true. There were very few college graduates playing the tour when I was out there. Myself and Lester Bolstead, who I palled around with. I believe Craig Wood went to college. Perhaps the other fellows were a little self-conscious at having to struggle so hard up through the caddie ranks, then cleaning clubs and being assistants before becoming head pros. But when I won the Open they were nice. I daresay they were a little surprised, but they arranged exhibition matches at their clubs, and I went on an exhibition tour with Jimmy Thomson, who finished second.

Yes, I was the dark-horse champion. But it was only because so many people told me so, and what's my opinion against that of thousands of others? Well, I'm the best repository of the memory to defeat that suggestion. Namely, the number of times I finished in the first twenty when I was playing the tour. It was fairly often. The summer before I won the Open I finished eighth in the California Open and was fourth in the St. Paul Open. In the spring of '35 I tied for eleventh in the Masters with Walter Hagen, who won his last tournament two years later. That wasn't hay. And the year after I won the Open I tied for tenth in the Masters. In 1937 I tied for sixteenth in the U.S. Open; finished ahead of Ky Laffoon, Byron Nelson, the Turnesas, and Craig Wood, and a few other top players.

So, about me being a 100-to-1 shot to win that Open, as it came to be said. In 1935 there were people in Pittsburgh who thought I might have a chance to win the Open, because it was being played at Oakmont and they knew my local knowledge of the course and that I had finished second there in the 1934 Pennsylvania State Open, with 298. You see, the U.S. Open had been played at Oakmont only once before, in 1927, and Tommy Armour won with 301. I had broken 300 by two, playing from the same tees, and in a field that included Al Espinosa and Willie MacFarlane. Now, there was a guy by the name of Doyle who was the biggest bookmaker of those times, and people around Pittsburgh thought they might get good odds from him on me winning, because I hadn't won anything yet. The only thing I had ever won was the Western Pennsylvania Junior Championship. Never even won the Western Pennsylvania or Pennsylvania State Amateur. So they got in touch with Doyle, and the best he would give them on me was 20-to-1. He was very knowledgeable about golfers, he followed the tour and knew who was finishing in the top twenty, things like that.

He said this guy Parks was a seasoned tour player and he couldn't see him going off at more than 20-to-1.

I think over the years, subsequent to my winning, people began to exaggerate the odds. They wanted to say how much of an outsider or upset winner I was, especially since I didn't win another major championship after that, which is true. But I did win a few things afterwards. The Youngstown Open, the Erie Open, the Pennsylvania Open. And I won the Tri-State PGA three times. They don't sound impressive, but they gave me the taste of winning.

See, after 1937 I gave it up, tournament golf. I was a married man with a young son, and I became a club pro. Then in 1941 the war came on and the tournaments were pretty much kaput, and I went to work for U.S. Steel. Now, had I continued to play and got the additional experience of playing around the tour, it's altogether possible I would have revived my game and maybe won some big tournaments. But I wasn't particularly eager to do that. I wanted to get into something more substantial. Because mind you, in 1928 Horton Smith was the leading money winner with $20,000, and in 1934 Paul Runyan was leading money winner with $7,500. This wasn't a very good goal to dedicate your life to. I could see that the best steel salesman in the country could make, say, $25,000 or $30,000. Why should I fool with the low-paying other job? I had a college education in business administration to make the switch-over. So, at the first opportunity, I promptly did switch. I don't regret it at all. It was the best thing that ever happened to me.

Well, at the time I won the Open the local papers were kind. It was: "Hometown Boy Wins." And they mentioned that it was on one of the world's hardest golf courses. I think part of the reason I didn't get the most favorable reaction from the national news media when I won the Open was because a lot of those newsmen had preconceived ideas about what their stories were going to be like for the final day. They may have been partially written already. Then, all of a sudden, this upstart comes in and they have to throw out all their notes and start from scratch. There were some who made a good story out of it, like a Horatio Alger thing, a guy comes out of the woodwork and confounds the experts. But I was crossed up by some of the guys. This Henry McLemore was a dirty writer. He called me Lonesome Sam, I guess because I'd never won anything before. The term I always heard among newsmen was "What's the angle?" John Kieran, Bill Richardson, even Grantland Rice would say, "What's the angle? What are we going to play up? How are we going to make it different?" Well, I made it different for them.

But it's no fun talking about how much of an upset winner you were. It's just a crock of marbles. I'll just say this: there were other fellows for whom the U.S. Open was their first major championship—or only one. It takes considerable discretionary power to determine what major tournament you're going to win as your first, and I had great judgment.

It's much more fun talking about the winning of it. I figured I could maybe finish in the first ten, because of my performances on the winter tour of 1934–35, and also because I knew the course well. I'd played Oakmont many times as an amateur and, being the pro across town, was able to get over there regularly in the spring and early summer before the Open. Mr. Fownes, who sort of owned the course, and the pro, Emil Loeffler, always made me welcome. What I did was I went over to Oakmont maybe twenty, twenty-five times—it was about twenty-five miles from my club. I'd get there early in the morning and play nine holes. I'd hit a couple of balls on each hole, and practice putting from the various corners of the greens until I knew the rolls. And I made notes. I would take a blank scorecard and mark on each hole what club I hit from certain locations—two-iron from the big tree on the right, and so on. I didn't pace it off, I just noted what club it took to reach the green. The actual yardage wasn't important. In the blank box where the score goes, I marked with arrows which way the grain ran on the greens. I don't recall that others made notes like that in my time. Most of them could remember that stuff in their heads. But that was hazardous for me. I wanted to be a little more accurate. I suppose my college education had something to do with that kind of methodical playing. I hate to think those four years were totally wasted.

So I got more practice there than anybody else. Furthermore, all the courses around Pittsburgh specialized in having very fast greens—they copied Oakmont, which was the local

ideal to try for—so I was accustomed to very fast greens.
Many of the players weren't. Well, it turned out that after the
third round I was tied for the lead with Jimmy Thomson, and
it was then I began to have ideas that maybe lightning had
struck and I would be pretty close and there was a chance
these other guys might fall dead. But I didn't visualize winning. I expected somebody to beat me. In other tournaments,
no matter how well I played, somebody would always come in
better, you know. But it turned out they all had their pitfalls.
I can remember after I finished I was sitting up in the locker
room with my father, who was a very devoted follower. People
would come in and say, "Sam, Hagen just went through nine,
he needs par on the back nine, thirty-five, to beat you." Then
somebody came tearing back: "They played down the tenth,
Hagen had a bogey." "They played eleven, Hagen had a bogey.
Now he has to shoot even par or one under on the last seven
holes to beat you." I figured he wouldn't do it, and it turned
out he didn't.

Then I had reports on Jimmy Thomson. He was the long-
ball hitter of the time, and he was sailing along pretty good
until he had a six on the fourteenth hole. Some well-wisher
came tearing in—the fourteenth green is very close to the
clubhouse—and said, "Sam, Thomson just had a six." Well,
then I knew he was going to have a hard time getting any birdies on those next four holes. So it turned out I had a great, and
beautiful, surprise.

My father was very proud of me winning the Open. As I
say, he followed me in tournaments for years. I can see him
now. When I was playing the little tournaments around Pennsylvania he would come out and I'd see him hiding behind
trees. He thought he'd bother me, whereas the contrary was
true. I enjoyed his being with me. I felt comforted and sup-
ported. Of course, he walked all the way with me during the
Open. I can remember going down the fairway in the last
round and fellows who knew me were crowding around, putting their arm around my shoulders and saying, "Now, old
boy, keep on, you're doing well," and that kind of stuff. Some
of them were real bores, and I finally said to my dad, "Listen,
whatever you do, keep Carl so-and-so or Joe somebody off my

back." So he would start talking to them so they wouldn't talk to me.

What was it like coming down the stretch? Well, I knew I was crowding the top place and I was nervous. Awfully nervous. But I was schooled in playing before galleries around the tour. I remember getting a lesson from Paul Runyan on how the crowds could help you. He said that when there's a big gallery behind the green, it's farther away than you think. It had to do with depth perception. I didn't play a lot of memorable shots near the end, but there was one very good one, and in any case I certainly recall a few of them. Take the last three holes, a par-three, which is 235 yards. I hit the green with a brassie. But the hole was in a tough place, and I three-putted. So I figure I'm pouring out my life there. Then on the seventeenth hole I hit a magnificent pitch shot to within four or five feet of the hole. But that's the fastest green on the course and the hole was up on a promontory, and I miss the birdie. On the eighteenth I hooked my drive into a bunker and played out with a six-iron in front of a cross-bunker, leaving a long seven-iron to the green. I got that on the green and took two putts. The national news services have a picture of me putting out on the last hole. I've seen it many, many times. I left myself about a two-footer—the final putt. I choked down on the putter it seems clear to the hosel. I'm bent over right down close to my work, and it went in. I won by two shots.

I can remember that I made around $17,000 out of that Open, mostly for exhibitions. I mentioned that to Gene Sarazen years later, and he was very much surprised, because in 1932 he won both the U.S. and British Opens and got only $20,000 for exhibitions and all. We played for the gate in many places, and in those cases we'd get maybe $150 apiece. That is, myself and whoever I played with. I remember a couple of outstanding exhibitions that paid $350. There weren't many of those. One was at Bedford Springs, where Joyce Wethered was playing an exhibition. She was the great British player, and was on tour here in 1935. They called me up and asked if I would like to play with her, and I asked how much they were paying her. They said $350 and I said, "Well, don't you think the U.S. Open champion is worth $350, too?" Reluctantly they said, "We guess so." So I ended up playing with Joyce Wethered for $350. She was just as good as everyone said she was. Magnificent. An interesting thing, a sidelight. She dragged her right foot in the follow-through, the way Billy Casper did.

There were some guarantees. I remember IBM had me and Paul Runyan up to play an exhibition match, and they gave us $500 apiece. I've often thought what a magnificent thing it would have been had they given me IBM stock at the time instead of the $500. It would be worth a fortune by this time . . . if I'd hung on to it. So there wasn't that much money in it, my Open victory. Like the other day Calvin Peete won $81,000. It's unbelievable that they pay that much. I once had an interesting conversation with Joe Dey while he was still the executive director of the USGA. They had just raised the prize money for the Open to $25,000. I said, "Joe, this thing's got to stop. Before you raise it any more, you're going to have to pay retroactively all us old winners and bring our winnings up to that." He thought it was a great joke. But, in truth, I don't resent how much money the fellows make now. I think it's a wonderful thing. People say it's spoiling the game. Not at all. It's great public relations and publicity. In this day of baseball and football players making one and two million dollars a year, who's going to begrudge the leading money winner on the golf tour making $450,000? It can further dignify golf as also being a great sport.

Sam Parks, Jr.

Sam Parks lives in Largo, Florida, and sells condominiums for a subsidiary of the U.S. Steel Company that owns and operates the famous Bellevue-Biltmore Hotel and its two golf courses.

LEO FRASER

Photograph by Al Barkow

"They were the show, the dancing girls, and they could call the shots."

My dad, who was known as Jolly Jim Fraser, came to the United States from Aberdeen, Scotland. He wasn't a golf pro in Aberdeen, he was an amateur, and, like most of the Scots that came over around the turn of the century, he became a pro here. He was the pro at Van Cortlandt Park in New York City, then out on Long Island, and in 1916 he became pro at the Seaview Golf Club in Absecon, New Jersey. The next year my younger brother, Sonny, was born. Sonny developed into one of the finest amateur golfers in the East, became Speaker of the House of the New Jersey Assembly, and was on his way to becoming governor of the state, but he had Hodgkin's disease and died at thirty-four. I mention that because he was such a tremendous influence on my life, even though he was six years younger than me.

My father loved being a club pro and he was a fine player. In 1920 he and Walter Hagen beat Harry Vardon and Ted Ray in a match over in Pottstown, Pennsylvania. I caddied for my father—I was ten years old—and I remember he holed a putt on seventeen, a real holy-ghoster, that won the match. Then, at Whitemarsh in Philadelphia one year, my dad and Willie MacFarlane, who had also come over from Aberdeen, lost to Vardon and Ray. The one thing I remember about that time was the four of them sitting in the locker room before the

143

match and polishing off a whole fifth of scotch whisky. Then, as true as I sit here, Vardon and Ray both made threes on the first hole, and one of them made another three on the second hole. From that point on, no one could convince me of the evils of drink.

Seaview was an ultra-private club owned by one person, Mr. Clarence Geist, who was the biggest utilities man in the United States. He owned the Philadelphia Suburban Water Company and had the franchise on maybe 400 other utilities in the United States. Geist used to play here at the Atlantic City Country Club, but when it started to get too crowded he built Seaview, which is up the road a few miles. This was around 1912. There was nothing else like Seaview in the rest of the country, except when Mr. Geist later bought Boca Raton in Florida, which he made even grander. How many other clubs at the time had an indoor swimming pool, a French chef, liveried chauffeurs who drove Rolls Royces and Pierce-Arrows? Every affluent club used Seaview as their standard. There was no dining room in Philadelphia or New York that could excel Seaview's. We had a swimming pool, horses, squash courts and tennis courts, a trap-shooting range, and a beautifully manicured and great golf course. Sam Snead won a PGA championship there.

It only cost $100 to join Seaview way back when, but it took more than money to get in, and if Mr. Geist heard anyone complain about the price of anything he'd just go up to the person and say, "Your resignation has been accepted." That's the kind of guy Mr. Geist was. He despised dogs, thought airplanes were the product of the devil, couldn't stand cigarettes, and his feet always hurt. He had a one-lane road built practically parallel to every hole at Seaview, and as he played a limousine would accompany him carrying several changes of shoes, extra hats and sweaters, a change of underwear, whiskey, special drinking water, and a small machine gun. Geist frequently shot in the 70s, but he was the slowest golfer I've ever played with. If he wasn't changing his shoes or having a drink or putting on a sweater, he'd delay the game telling some long-winded story. If a group on the first tee saw him as far out as the third hole, they would say the first nine was too crowded and go start on the back nine. And, of course, Geist would take golf instruction from anybody. I lived with my mother just off the first fairway at Seaview and one morning around five a.m. the phone rings. My mother answers, then comes in and says to me, "Quick, Mr. Geist wants to see you immediately." I get over to the club and he's wearing a night-cap, a long, flowing nightshirt, high-top slippers, and he's got a golf club in his hand. First thing he says, in his gruff voice, is "I've got the secret. You pros don't know a damn thing." I asked him what it was and he said, "All you have to do is turn your right foot out a little."

I talk so much about Geist because he was of the greatest characters I've met during my whole life in golf. And he had a lot to do with my career in the early years. But, you know, he was also a part of the game's history in this country with the golf resorts he built.

As I say, we lived beside the first fairway at Seaview and I got my start in golf as a caddie boy. I was very small, and the only way I could get out was on rainy days, when the older caddies went home. Then I'd run across the first fairway and grab a couple of bags—they were those little, light, round ones. I was nine or ten when I started. It was at this time when I caddied for Robert Todd Lincoln, the son of Abraham Lincoln. That sounds incredible, I know, and people think I'm fabricating when I tell them that, but figure it out. It was around 1920, and he didn't die until 1926. I've been a Lincoln-ophile ever since I was a boy. I read everything I could about Lincoln, Sandburg's books and all the rest. I'm not a Lincoln scholar, understand, but I love all the folklore about him. Well, Robert Todd was a small edition of his father. He looked just like him, and I'm sure he was the most frugal Lincoln who ever lived. He'd give ten-cent tips. I'm saying he was very astute with a dollar.

My father was killed in an automobile accident when I was thirteen, and after that I caddied for a while, played some with members, and next thing I know I'm in the pro shop after school sandpapering shafts and putting on grips and learning how to make clubs. Every once in a while one of my clubs shows up—all clubmakers of that time put little marks on their clubs, their initials or something, which was kind of an egotist-ical thing. When I was sixteen I went out to Detroit to visit a favorite aunt of mine. I had gotten into a scrape with Mr. Geist. He wanted me to go to work in the local gas company and I didn't want to.

Anyway, I remember they had the damnedest golf school you ever saw in the General Motors building. It was indoors, but it had bunkers in it, and maybe fourteen nets. But one day I'm in the Spalding store in downtown Detroit—Spalding had stores in all the big cities then, and the pros would gather at them to buy equipment and make contacts—and a golf representative named Frank Farrell asks me if I'd be interested in an assistant's job at the Plum Hollow Club. I wasn't sure what I wanted to do, because the pros I had worked for didn't inspire me much. They did things that bothered me, like saw a guy's shaft in such a way, or leave a rivet out of the club so it would break and they'd get the repair business. I was brought up differently. My father wasn't real strict, but he was an ethical man, and this didn't sit right with me. Well, I meet the man who's looking for an assistant—Mr. Arthur Ham. I took one look at him and he doesn't impress me very much. He's got hair down to here, is wearing an old Scottish cap—he's from New Zealand—and I'm accustomed to flashy, tailored people. So right away—big, mouthy me—I tell him I can make a lot of money back in New Jersey. I was getting $40 a month at Seaview, but I told him I was making $100, and he said to me, "This job pays better than that, it pays $140." Well, I never heard of that kind of money, and besides I would get one third of my lessons. I didn't know how to teach, but I taught.

I got to liking Mr. Ham, and I told him I had about 300 Stewart and Nicoll iron heads that my father had left to me, and that I'd make them up for him. He didn't know I made clubs, and actually I had mostly done only repair work up to then, but we made a satisfactory arrangement and I started making up complete sets. I could make a set a night. We were using bamboo and hickory shafts—half and half—so you didn't have to do as much work on them. Ham sold every one of those clubs as fast as I could make them. Fifty dollars for a set of six. I worked for Mr. Ham for a year, then he got dismissed. He was referee of a match between two women in the finals of the club championship and apparently ruled against the wrong woman, for reasons best left unsaid.

Ham was offered a job up in Saginaw, Michigan, but it wasn't big enough for him and he recommended me for it. He really took good care of me. I baby-sat his kids, took care of his dog. I enjoyed the man, and he was like a father to me. I received a couple of references, although not one from Mr. Geist, and I got the job in Saginaw. So I'm a seventeen-year-old head professional. It's a semi-private, semi-public course, but right next door is the Saginaw Country Club, and now I get the break of my life. Saginaw Country Club had a husband-and-wife team of golf professionals. It was very unusual to see a woman professional in those days—this was around 1928— and a lot of ladies didn't want to take lessons from her. So a feisty little gentleman named Hess comes over to me one day and says he wants me to teach his daughter. Well, if I ever saw a natural in my life, this was it. All you really had to do was tee it up for her. So the first year she wins the club championship, then she wins it again, and I get the reputation for being a great teacher. Then some other guy sends a fellow named Bob Montague over to me, and he wins the city championship, and thanks to all that I become head professional at Saginaw Country Club. Understand, at the time I didn't know too much when it came to the golf swing. I didn't learn anything about it until I ran into Ernest Jones some years later, which was a great experience.

Sometime in the 1930s I went down to Pinehurst to play in the North and South Open, and on the train coming back is Ernest Jones. I introduced myself to him, because I'd been reading some of his articles. He was a very well-known teacher. We both had sleepers, but we never opened them that night. We talked golf swing all night long, and I mean all night long. Jones was famous for his theory "Swing the Clubhead," but he didn't say there were no other mechanics to the swing, which a lot of people thought. He allowed there were other mechanics, and certain variables in the golf swing, but it had to be a swing first. You could make all the adjustments you wanted, but you must always make the clubhead swing. He said the hands are the only part of the body attached to the club, so they must swing the club, and I remember distinctly asking how you could use your hands that way and not be kind of flippy, and he saying that was using your wrists, not your hands. I remember we got a porter to get us a golf club out of the baggage compartment, and right there in the aisle Jones showed me what he meant, and about how the palms of the hands should face each other, where the pressure points were, and so forth.

I remember Jones saying, "There's tension in the swing, but no tenseness." He stretched a rubber band to its utmost and said that was tension, and beyond that was tenseness, which is when you lost it all. He said you play golf by feel and that there are three fundamentals of the swing—"and don't let anybody tell you any differently," he said. The three fundamentals have nothing to do with keeping the elbow in, with shifting weight, turning hips, stuff like that. They are control, balance, and timing. Control is with the hands, balance is with your feet, and you get timing by making the club swing. One of the tricks he showed me was to walk down the fairway in between shots swinging the club in time with each step—that's how you get feel and timing.

You see, Jones lost his right leg in the service and that's when he developed his theories. The thing was, he could no longer make a big body shift and found he didn't have to; he played well with one artificial leg. One of his favorite expressions was "The body should give to the swing." In other words, you shouldn't worry about pivoting, you just make the clubhead swing with the hands and arms, and everything else follows. You know, Jones once gave a talk at a PGA meeting and was booed off the stage by the other pros, I guess because they didn't like his concepts of the swing. Jones was a very scientific man. I used to go up to his studio on Fifth Avenue in New York and watch him teach. I'd catch him about three o'clock, then we'd go out and have a drink at Schrafft's. That's how I learned to teach golf.

I was the pro at Saginaw Country Club for nine years, and came back to New Jersey when Mr. Geist called and offered me the job at Seaview. I was open to the idea because I wanted to spend some time with my mother and my brother,

Sonny. So I went through the usual trauma of breaking my contract, because I had a wonderful relationship with the people in Saginaw—I grew up there, you know—and took a plane back. When Geist heard I flew back, I was fired before I was hired. But he hired and fired me many, many times. Anyway, I told him I was not going to work for the money he was offering. I said I wanted $15,000, guaranteed, and here was a man who paid people $100 a month. But, you see, I knew I wasn't going to teach because Mr. Geist would want me to play golf with him all the time. He would only play with good players. So I'd have to hire a topnotch assistant to do the teaching, and I'd have to pay for that out of my salary. In the meantime Geist shows me a picture of Edith Quier swinging—she was a fine player at that time—and he asks me if his swing looks anything like hers. See, Geist was the greatest golf nut you ever saw. He had this beautiful green carpet in his office all chewed up from practice swings with his irons. Well, I told him he had a better swing than Edith Quier, and I got $15,000. I'm sure I was the highest-paid professional in the area at the time, but I had to pay my assistant $5,000, so I wasn't that far ahead.

But Geist wouldn't let me play tournaments. Don't ask me why. My brother, Sonny, could play in anything, and was winning many of the amateur events, but I couldn't play. I did slip away once in a while, and one time in a tournament that had a bunch of good players—Vic Ghezzi, Craig Wood, Jimmy Thomson, Clarence Clark—I got around the first day in 70 and there was a big headline, "Fraser Leads." Everyone thought it was Sonny, because I hadn't been around much, and Mr. Geist didn't say anything for about two weeks. Then someone said to him how great it was that Leo played so well, and he fired me. Again. I did everything he didn't like—fly in airplanes, I had a dog. My father and Geist got along fine, and Sonny patronized him and kidded him so he didn't realize it. I was the only one who didn't get along with him, because I talked back to him, which I shouldn't have done.

I played some of the winter tour for a few years. The first time I went out was in 1929, when I was nineteen years old. Emerick Kocsis and I went out west from Detroit in the first gearshift Ford. Before that you just had a clutch pedal and an emergency brake. You'd put the clutch down, turn on the ignition, let the clutch out, and go. One drive. Ours was a Touring Ford, with a gearshift. It went for $695.

The first place we went was Sacramento, California. We rented a room for $5 a week and played at the Del Paso Country Club. We won about $25 that week. The next tournament was on the Monterey Peninsula, but it was before the Bing Crosby event. It was a small tournament—some members put up $3,000. Then we went to Pasadena, and I'll never forget playing with this little teeny guy who has a gold watch fob on with a black ribbon that says, "Arkansas Open Champion." Of course, it was Paul Runyan, who had this little driver—God, it was little—and he would hit it full smack on the face and it would go only 210 yards. I remember distinctly that I didn't qualify. I shot an 80. The next one was the L.A. Open, and I qualified but didn't do anything. Then I made a couple of hundred bucks in Agua Caliente.

You know, in those days there was no such thing as a thirty-six-hole cut. You had to stay on in the tournament even if you had no chance, because they needed a field for the gallery. It wouldn't look good to have only twenty players the last day, so you couldn't leave town and save caddie fees. Caddies were the biggest expense. Five dollars a round in California. We could stay two fellows in a room for $15 a week, which wasn't bad, and eat for a $1.50. You could get breakfast at a Pig 'n' Whistle for thirty-five cents. But caddies were expensive.

I would like to have played more tournaments if I'd putted better, but I'd jerk the stroke, you know. I could play a little, though. I won a few Michigan championships, and I qualified for the U.S. Open and PGA championships.

You never know who's going to be good, at least by looking at them. When I qualified for the '32 U.S. Open, I played with Ky Laffoon and Jug McSpaden and I wondered how these guys got in the championship. I didn't think they could play at all, then. Like at the eleventh hole at Fresh Meadow, a par-three about 220 yards. Jug will remember this. I say to myself, "I want to see this dude play this hole," because Jug was a terrible slicer. Well, he took a slash at it and it was knocking down all the tree limbs on the left side; he was playing his slice. But, later, if it wasn't for Byron Nelson, Jug would have been the premier player during the World War II years.

And Laffoon I could never figure out. He stood with his feet spread very wide apart, and he was such an intense man—not mean, just intense, and a perfectionist. I remember at Glen Falls neither of us played too well. On the last hole I roll in a putt from all the way across the green to beat him, and he said, "You aren't going to take the money, are you?" It was for maybe $6, but neither of us were holding very much at the time.

Now, also in '32, I qualify for the national PGA championship in my local section in Michigan, and Jose Jurado comes into the picture. This is a pretty interesting story about how the championship was run then. Jurado is a great Argentine player who almost won a British Open, and they want him in the championship for some glamour, a big-name player, because the PGA wasn't drawing too well. The U.S. Open and Amateur were the only ones that drew crowds in those days. I shoot 71 in the morning qualifying round to lead the field. In the afternoon I get back on my game with a 76, but it's good enough to tie with Jurado for the last qualifying place. The playoff is the next day, and, let me tell you, if I slept a wink that night I don't remember, I was so nervous. But I went out and played, I guess, as good a round as I ever played in my life. I can remember every shot to this day. I shot 71—this is at Oakland Hills—in front of maybe 500 people, a huge gallery for those days, and beat Jurado badly, I think by five or six shots.

So all of a sudden I start getting phone calls. See, in those days you could buy places in the championship. A lot of people nowadays don't know that. Let's say I finish fifth in the qualifying, as I did in '32, and some pro who finished sixth wanted to pay for my spot. That could be arranged, privately. The public didn't know anything about this, of course. Well, they tried to get me to sell my spot to Jurado. I received two calls from interested parties, shall we say. They offered the going rate, $150, a helluva lot of money during the Depression. I told them I wouldn't accept it.

Now, in those days when you traveled to the PGA championship you received three cents a mile from the association—travel expenses. But if you went over government property during the trip they could take that mileage off if they wanted to. So the PGA scrutinized my itinerary from Saginaw to St. Paul, where the championship was being played. It's 566 miles, total, but they reduced it to 542 because some of the rail lines went over government property.

Now, I no more than get into St. Paul and there's a big headline in the paper, "Young Michigan Star Sells His Place in Championship to Jurado." I don't know how the paper conjured that up, but I get a call to report to PGA headquarters and, I tell you, I would rather have been facing three devils than those officers. They jumped on me right away, wouldn't let me explain anything. They demanded I tell them who gave me the money. I told them who called, and that I refused. "What would I be doing in St. Paul if I sold my place?" I asked them. "You don't see my name withdrawn. I can't help it if Jurado's name is there as an alternate. No one gave me any money." I convinced them, but remained a little under a cloud. They changed the rules after that so an alternate was taken from the section where a player qualified. As it turned out, I didn't do well in the championship, probably because I was so shook up by all the controversy. But I never did well in national championships, regardless.

Tournament golf was another kind of game for me, but, as it happened, I eventually had something to do with how the tour came to be structured the way it is now. When Mr. Geist died, in 1938, someone around the club offered me a job in a brokerage firm, and I decided to get out of professional golf and try it to see what it was like in another world. But I didn't care for the selling of stocks and bonds, and after six months went to Maryland to run a golf club. From there I spent five years and three months in the Army. After my discharge, with the help of my brother, Sonny, I had an opportunity to buy the Atlantic City Country Club. So I was back in golf for good—I was never really out of it—and eventually I became an officer of the national PGA. Before I was elected to the national office

Leo Fraser

I was president of the Philadelphia section of the PGA for six years.

When the parent organization and the touring pros got into the battle for control of the tournament circuit, I was president of the national PGA, and I determined that an accommodation had to be reached amenable to both factions. What was it all about? To put it as simply as possible, starting in the 1950s there was a year-'round tournament circuit for very good purses, and most of the players played it full-time; they didn't have club jobs during the summer, like in the old days. The PGA was running the tour, and the tour players began to feel this wasn't right because the PGA's main concern was with the club professionals—which was only partially true. Starting in the '60's, the players felt the PGA was using money generated from television for things that didn't affect them. So they wanted to control the circuit, and the money that came out of it. The tour players threatened to create their own tour and split from the PGA completely, which wouldn't have been a good thing. It became very bitter, and was in the press a lot. The public didn't appear to be that interested, but it made all of us look bad as professionals.

To this day I can't understand the players' total dissatisfaction, because the tournament committee was made up of four tour pros and three PGA club pros or officers. So the players always had the majority. But there was the question of the PGA spending too much of their money, and what worried me more than anything was the fact that the PGA was running a monopoly. It wasn't on paper anywhere, but in fact it was arranged that the pros could not play in conflicting tournaments, which was not really a legal position. It was a kind of restraint of trade. If we were taken to court on it, we probably would have lost.

It came down to who knew best how to run the tour, and who were the ones really making it work. The tour pros were the best players in the game, and, as it is with the best athletes of any game, the tendency is to think that if you can play something very well, then you're entitled to make the decisions. But then, if I was in their position I wouldn't have accepted anything I didn't want. They were the show, the dancing girls, and they could call the shots. The final accommodation resulted in forming a new ten-man policy board, in 1970, which is still in existence, comprised of three outstanding amateurs, three PGA officers, and four player-directors. And engaging Joe Dey of the USGA as the tour commissioner.

I'm extremely proud of my involvement in the matter, as well as suggesting Joe Dey become commissioner. The final proof of the solution lies in the present results, the condition of the tour fifteen years later.

Leo Fraser

Leo Fraser owns and operates the Atlantic City Country Club, which is actually in Northfield, New Jersey. His sons, Doug and Jim, handle most of the day-to-day operations, and Leo's son-in-law, Don Siok, is the head professional. Leo is definitely a family man. He also has a golf and country club consultancy business.

Leo received the Richardson and Gold Tee awards from the Golf Writers Association of America and the Metropolitan Golf Association, largely for his work in bringing about a settlement of the issue between the PGA and the touring pros when he was president of the PGA of America from 1969 to 1970.

PATTY BERG

Photograph by Wide World Photos

Photograph by Al Barkow

"You're always learning new ideas, new methods. It keeps you young."

When I was a little child living in Minneapolis, about seven doors down from me lived a fellow by the name of Charles "Bud" Wilkinson. He was a guard on the University of Minnesota football team, and in his last year was the quarterback. So anything he did, I had to do. We had a football team called the 50th Street Tigers. Bud was the guard, coach, and captain, and I was the quarterback because I was the only one who could remember the signals. We had one—22—and when I yelled it out everyone ran whichever way they wanted. Well, Bud finally told me I had to quit because I was too slow and short and there wasn't any future in it for me.

So I went into speed skating, and did a lot of that. I skated in the national junior championships, intermediate division, and in the state championships; won some medals, too. Then there was a time when we were skating in some little town in Minnesota and, oh, it was cold. I remember coming to the finishing line going so fast I ended up in one of the drifts, and my dad came over and said, "Well, your mother and I are going to Florida tomorrow," and I told them to wait for me.

I was about twelve years old when I started swinging a club. I would swing away in the backyard, and my father was always wondering who was taking the divots—see, my sisters also played a little golf. Well, Dad caught me out there one day

157

knocking up the grass and said, "How would you like to get that clubhead in back of a golf ball?" I said I'd like that, and that's when it really began. We were members at the Interlachen Country Club, which was where Bobby Jones won one of his Grand Slam championships in 1930—the U.S. Open. I wasn't there for that. I was in 6B at John Brown's Elementary School at the time, running in a track meet—won the thirty-yard dash.

Anyway, I took my first lessons at Interlachen from Willie Kidd, the head professional, and Jim Pringle, his assistant. But then for about forty years I took lessons from Lester Bolstead, who was the golf professional at the University of Minnesota. He coached the men's golf team at the university. His team won the Big Ten championship one year, which was quite something to do in Minnesota. He was a real taskmaster with me. He would stand there and say, "Now, Patricia Jane, Patricia Jane"—he never called me Patty—"you've got to strive for perfection, you must conquer your flaws, you must use your legs." And every time he said my name he would clap his hands: "Patricia Jane," clap, "Patricia Jane," clap. But he is a great golf professional and a very knowledgeable man. He knows so much about anatomy, and uses that in his teaching.

I won the 1934 Minneapolis City Ladies Championship, which was the most memorable event in my golf career because I probably wouldn't have had a golf career if not for what happened. I played in my first City Ladies championship the year before, when I was fifteen, and shot 122. That qualified me for the last flight, and in my first match some lady beat me on just about every hole. After that defeat I walked back to the clubhouse and said to myself, "I'm going to spend the next 365 days trying to improve." For the next year, all I did was eat, sleep, and play golf. I thought if I could move up a flight or shoot better than 122, that would be an improvement. Well, 365 days later I was medalist and won the Minneapolis City Ladies' Championship.

It's very possible that if I didn't improve on my 122, or didn't move up a flight or so, I might not be in golf today. But I didn't think I'd win that tournament. When I did, I started to dream. I thought, maybe I'll be able to play the Minnesota

State Womens championship; maybe I'll be able to play in some of the tournaments in Florida, maybe even play in the Trans-Mississippi and the Women's Western Amateur and the United States Women's Amateur. I really started to dream that golf was my future, and that's exactly how it turned out.

That's a long time to spend on one endeavor, isn't it—365 days? But I'll tell you, it was worth every freckle on my face. What did I learn during that time? To hit the ball straighter by improving my tempo, timing, and rhythm. I got to know more about the swing, so I could correct myself during a round—you know, you're quarterback out there. And I spent a lot of time chipping and putting, because I knew I wasn't going to hit all the greens—no one does—especially when you were as small as I was.

Of course, we had a short golf season up in Minnesota. If we were lucky, we would start playing in the first part of May. But a lot of times we'd play through October and November. If I made any swing changes at all, it was in October and November, because by the time we could play in the spring there wasn't time for that; the tournaments started coming up. I'd hit balls into a canvas, indoors, and in 1935 my family starting going to Florida for a good bit of the winter. I spent a month in Florida the winter of '35, and that helped a lot in my winning the Minnesota State Womens Golf Championship and getting to the finals of the USGA Women's Amateur Championship. I would make up the schooling I missed, and when I made the U.S. Curtis Cup team in my last year of high school I was gone so much that my dad got a tutor for me.

My father had a grain company, H. L. Berg Company. He was a member of the Chicago Board of Trade, the Minneapolis Board of Trade, and the Winnipeg Board of Trade. He was a businessman golfer, and had a ten handicap. My brother was a fine player; he played in the city league and state championships. But he had scarlet fever when he was a boy that left him with a bad heart, and he died at forty-three.

I went two years to the University of Minnesota, but didn't play golf for the school. There was just a men's golf team. But after I won that city championship my father sent me to tournaments. I played in the Minnesota State, of course, then the Trans-Miss, which was my first major event. I qualified for the championship flight and got beat by Opal Hill in the second round. But I did win the driving contest. I won a beautiful mirror. Then, in 1935 I was runner-up to Glenna Vare in the Women's National Amateur. In 1937 I was runner-up in just about everything, and somebody wrote an article calling me the uncrowned champion. But in 1938 I turned it all around and won ten out of thirteen tournaments.

I played amateur golf for part of 1939. Then, while I was on my way to defend one of my championships and having a wonderful year, I had an emergency appendectomy and was in the hospital for almost a month with a private nurse. I was finished for the season, so in September I took a trip for the University of Minnesota to raise funds. What I did was play in exhibitions that we wouldn't charge anything for, but at night we'd have dinners and raise money for the Student Union Building. We went out into the Dakotas and Montana and California, about eight or nine states, contacting alumni. That's when I played Pebble Beach for the first time, and met Bing Crosby and Richard Arlen. And Helen Langfeld, who has done so much for women's golf. She put on a lot of golf tournaments, including one for the LPGA, and does to this day at age eighty-five. A lot of the girls on the tour today played in Helen Langfeld's junior tournaments in California.

After I got back from that trip I went to college for another year, then in 1940 I turned pro. I went with the Wilson Sporting Goods Company. They offered me a job, and it was a very good arrangement. My father went to Chicago and discussed it with Mr. Icely, the president of Wilson. You know, at that time you didn't have any managers, so your father was your manager, or at least helped you. My father was the greatest.

I wasn't the first woman pro, though. There were several before me, including Helen Hicks and Bessie Finn. Bessie became the pro at the Breakers in Palm Beach, where she succeeded her dad. She taught, but I think did mostly administrative work. Then there was Helen Dettweiler, Opal Hill, Hope Seignious. When I first turned pro, I think there were something like three tournaments—the Western Open, the Titleholders, and maybe the Asheville Invitational. Sometimes some other tournament would come along. The total prize money was about $500, and we had a field sometimes of only five players, plus outstanding women amateur golfers.

So we gave a lot of clinics for Wilson. I was used to doing the clinics, and learned how to do it during the eight years I played amateur golf. My father had me play around the state of Minnesota giving little clinics and exhibitions on weekends for different charities. A pro would give the instruction, while I hit the balls. Of course, I listened to how the pro made his presentation and picked up the technique that way.

What tour there was we did by train, or bus, or car, and in 1941 I had a terrible accident going from Corsicana, Texas, to Memphis. This was actually to play an exhibition for British War Relief. I was on the passenger side of the car, Helen Dettweiler was driving. Somebody hit us and I went into the dashboard and broke my left knee in three places. And, of course, my face hit the windshield—no seat belts in those days. Well, I was laid up for eighteen months and when they took the cast off I couldn't get the leg bent because of the adhesions. The knee started to turn blue, so they gave me gas and ether and hit it, or manipulated it. They did that twice, and I fell once, so I ended up with about seventy-five percent use of the leg in terms of bending it.

When I got out of the hospital, I went down to Mobile, Alabama, and took a training program with a prize fighter named Tommy Littleton, who had a gym down there. I rode a bicycle and did two hours of gym work a day with Tommy Littleton, and I got so I could hit golf balls, then so I could pick them up, and then finally so I could play. The first thing I did after that was play an exhibition at George S. May's Tam O'Shanter Country Club in Chicago. He had a nice luncheon for me, and I played and shot 78 from the men's tees. The course was playing long because it had rained a lot, so I thought I was back.

The doctors think now that maybe my hip was displaced a little from that accident and I didn't know it, and I walked for thirty-nine years with it that way. The doctors now ask me if I ever felt the displacement, or the pain, and I said I didn't. But I guess after a while you don't feel pain. Of course, in 1980

I had a total hip operation, I have an artificial left hip now. And in 1971 I had a battle with cancer. I had a massive tumor close to the kidney. But I'm fine now.

I joined the Marine Corps during World War II, and was an officer. I went to Camp LeJeune for officer's training, then to Philadelphia and worked in public relations and recruiting. I went in the service in 1943 and came out in 1945.

In 1946 we had an organization called the Women's Professional Golf Association. Later, Babe Zaharias and her husband, George, Fred Corcoran, and myself reorganized it into the Ladies Professional Golf Association, which is the LPGA of today. In January 1948 we met at the Venetian Hotel in Miami. We wanted to get more tournaments to play, and that was Fred Corcoran's job. He had been the PGA tour manager and knew everybody in the game. But the first thing we did was change the name from Womens to Ladies Professional Golf Association. Fred thought it would be better to be Ladies than Women.

Then Wilson Sporting Goods gave us money for six years, not for prize money but for administrative purposes and to pay Fred Corcoran and his expenses. He was paid quite a bit of money for that time, but he did a good job. Then other manufacturers put in some money, and, well, it just grew and grew. It was so hard to envision then that women would be playing for $9 million in purses, as they are now.

The Babe—Zaharias—was a tremendous asset in the early days of the ladies tour. She starred in the 1932 Olympics and people wanted to come out and see her play golf. She was a household name. She gave them a show, too—a great competitor, a great player, and fun. I remember the time we played the British Walker Cup team in England. In the morning matches Babe and myself lost to Davenport and a fellow named Beck; Betsy Rawls and Peggy Bush lost, too. But Peggy Kirk and Betty Jameson tied their match, so we're behind two points to a half-point. We're sitting around the table at lunch, with all the little American flags on it, and I said, "All of those who expect to win their singles, follow me." Babe says, "Come on, follow Napoleon." Anyway, we went out and all won our singles matches and beat them, six to two. Babe played Leonard Crawley, the golf writer. Leonard had this big mustache, and before they teed off Babe said to him, "If I beat you, do I get to cut your mustache off?" Leonard said, "You sure do." So after Babe beat him that afternoon she was running around the parking lot with a scissors, trying to catch Crawley. She never did.

People have said that the Babe was a little crude once in a while, but I didn't see that in her. No, I saw a wonderful athlete and someone with a lot of class. I remember when she was suffering from cancer so badly, she'd tell everybody it wasn't so bad, we're all going to get better. She knew she didn't have a chance, but she went around to hospitals telling patients they were going to get better, and so was she. You think that's a lady with class? Yes, sir. She gave everybody hope.

I guess a woman athlete in my younger days had to deal with the tomboy image a little more than nowadays, but I never got ragged for being an athlete. I had a tremendous amount of support from everybody. I never had any problem with that, whatsoever. And the men pros always welcomed us with open arms when we played a tournament or gave a clinic at their clubs. In fact, I would get a lot of good instruction from some of the men. Johnny Revolta had a magnificent short game, and I took a lot of lessons from him whenever I was around Chicago during the summer, or out in California. Sam Snead helped me a lot. I think he's a marvelous teacher. He has a keen eye, and I always liked the way he rolled in with his left foot; that movement he did with his feet and ankles was terrific. But I'm not tall—only five feet two—so I had to swing like Gene Sarazen, who was a terrific competitor and player. I watched him a lot.

But if there is one thing I would tell all golfers about technique, it would be that the grip has a tendency to change even during the course of a round and you have to keep checking it day in and day out. The grip is the foundation of the swing. Well, there's another thing. You must work constantly on timing and tempo. You know, some days you just cannot do anything with your tempo—it gets too fast sometimes. Besides, I tend to do everything quickly because that's my nature. So if I got too fast and didn't complete my backswing, I'd just swing the club with my left hand—practice swing—then, without stopping, put my right hand on the club. That's how I'd get my tempo back. You see players on the tour doing this all the time, trying to get their tempo back; it's the best way I know to do it.

I guess there's one more thing I've learned about this game. I remember Bob Jones saying that no one could ever conquer golf, because it has so much to do with the nervous system. The big thing about this is you stand up there and you're hitting it just super and you start hitting it harder and harder, and pretty soon you're beyond your hitting capacity. You end up losing your timing and tempo, and have to start all over again. But there's always something to learn about this game. A lot of professionals, after playing a lot of years, decide to change their swing, make it more upright or flatter or something. You're always learning new ideas, new methods. It keeps you young.

In the beginning of my career, it was ninety-nine percent clinics and one percent tournaments for me, then it turned around to where it was eighty-five–fifteen in favor of tournaments. Now I'm back to where it's 100 percent clinics or golf shows, due to my hip problem. I can't play on the tour anymore, but I still give a lot of golf shows. Last year I gave over forty.

Patty Berg

Patty Berg has won forty-one "official" tournaments as a professional, and some forty "unofficial" ones prior to 1950. She won some forty-five events as an amateur. Patty won the first United States Women's Open, in 1946, taking the qualifying medal, then defeating Betty Jameson five and four in the final match. Patty was three times the leading money winner on the LPGA tour, three times a winner of the Vare Trophy for lowest scoring average.

She has won numerous awards over her distinguished career, including the 1975 Ben Hogan Award of the Golf Writers Association of America for her comeback from cancer, and the USGA's Bobby Jones Award. In 1976 she became the first woman to receive the Humanitarian Sports Award from the United Cerebral Palsy Foundation. Fittingly enough, in 1978 an award was founded in her name by the LPGA, the Patty Berg Award for a person's outstanding contributions to women's golf. She is one of the four original inductees into the LPGA Hall of Fame.

Patty now lives in Fort Myers, Florida, with her stepmother, Vera, who at age eighty-four made her fifth hole in one.

JIM FERRIER

Photograph by Al Barkow

"I suppose I was always an outsider, but that's a marvelous experience. It steels you. . . ."

My father's family came from Carnoustie, in Scotland. They had a little old pub there which was kind of an unofficial clubhouse. They named the street it was on Ferrier Street. But I was the first golf pro in my family, and it was something my father had to think about before he accepted it. You know, the old caste system was still in existence then. You see, my father was an accountant. He worked in Shanghai for American Tobacco, got married to an Australian girl there, then took the position of secretary and general manager of the Manly Golf Club in Sydney. He was a member of the club, and all that stuff. So when I wrote my dad in 1940 that I had accepted a nice position with the Wilson Sporting Goods Company, I didn't hear from him for several months. Of course, when I won the PGA championship in 1947 he was very happy.

My dad was a good golfer, a plus-three handicap. He taught me how to play; started me out when I was four and a half. I was born in Sydney, and we lived across the street from the clubhouse, so when I came back from grammar school, boy, I was over there every day. That's when I learned to putt, and play, for money. There were three guys used to play every afternoon at Manly: the superintendent's son, a guy that had a little public putting green on the beach at Manly—made a hell of a living off that—and the assistant pro. Those guys were gamblers supreme. They used to putt for a shilling or two a hole, and occasionally play seven holes for a pound, which was like the national deficit to me—it was big, big money. As a schoolboy I used to watch them, and finally I saved up four shillings from my allowance and asked if I could join them for sixpence or a shilling a hole. They said I better stay at home, but I got into the game and that's how I opened my first bank account. After I'd won about £4 or £5 I deposited it in the Government Savings Bank. I guess I was fourteen. My dad didn't mind where I got the money, because I was out playing golf. All that paid off on the American tour. A shilling a hole was good money, so your stroke sure tightened up.

When I was almost sixteen I quit school and went to work. I was playing pretty good golf, was club champion at fifteen, a plus-1 handicapper, and then in 1931 I almost won the Australian National Open. If I hadn't taken six on the last hole I would have won, when I was sixteen. With that, and all the other stuff, I thought if I got all tangled up in the educational system it would be tough on my game. My dad's bosom friend was the fire commissioner in Sydney, and he gave me a job in his office. It was just piddling around, tapping the girls on the bum once in a while. Plenty of time to play golf. I did that two or three years, went into the insurance business briefly, then starting writing about golf for the Australian *Women's Weekly*. Kind of funny, writing golf for the *Women's Weekly*. But then the publisher, Frank Packer, bought the *Daily Telegraph* and I was the golf writer there for two or three years. After that I went to work for the Sydney *Morning Herald*. I didn't write all that well, but good enough to get by, and after the boys in the office worked on it, well, you know . . .

Eventually, they started to syndicate my stuff to papers in Brisbane, Melbourne, all the big cities. I wrote a lot of stuff on the tournaments and how I played, but never how *to* play, because that would jeopardize my amateur standing. Anyway, by 1939 I had won everything in Australia and thought I'd like to come over to the United States. I wasn't the first Australian to do that. Joe Kirkwood was the first, then me, then Norman Von Nida. Kirkwood came over in 1920. He would come back to Australia to do exhibitions and bring Walter Hagen and Gene Sarazen, and they always played their first one at Manly

Golf Club. Kirkwood had caddied there for my dad. Well, I would get to play with them. That had something to do with my wanting to come over to the U.S.

Then, in 1934 an American team made a tour of Australia, played a lot of matches and exhibitions—Paul Runyan, Harry Cooper, Denny Shute, Craig Wood, and someone else. I played with Cooper. He was the straightest hitter I ever saw, but a funny guy to play with. He'd hit two beautiful shots and be twelve feet from the hole, but it seemed like even before he hit the putt he'd be saying how the s.o.b. hit a spike mark and that cost him a birdie. All this while the ball's still running! Funny guy. Anyway, I looked at these guys—famous, won the British Open, the PGA—and felt I could give a good performance against them. I wanted to come to the States because if you wanted to play golf, the tour here was it. Still is. I sold the idea that I'd write columns from there. I could throw in a few bucks of my own, and that would pay for the trip. It was meant to be for six months, but it ended up a lifetime.

So me and my wife, Norma, come over in January 1940; twenty-one days by boat. Soon as we got here I bought an old Packard car for $400 and took off across the country to catch up with the tour. My first tournament was in Thomasville, Georgia. Then we did the ones in Florida, and in the spring I played in the Masters. I was invited because of my amateur record in Australia. That was in 1940.

Before coming over I had sent in my entry for the 1940 U.S. Amateur championship, and now I get a letter from the USGA rejecting it. They gave no reason, so I queried them on it and they said I was making my living from golf by writing about it, which made me a professional. Well, I called up the president of the USGA and said, "How about Bobby Jones? He's an amateur and he wrote for the *American Golfer* for many years." The president said that was different, and I told him if he could explain to me how it was different I would be glad to listen. But they were adamant and rejected my entry. As soon as they did that, sometime in May or June, I just turned pro and started in. I was twenty-five.

I chased the tour from 1940 to 1961, with a few breaks in between. Remember the boy in the iron lung, Fred Snite, Jr., in Chicago? He said to me the war was coming, so why didn't

Jim Ferrier

I work at Elmhurst Country Club; he had just bought it. Things were unsettled in golf then, 1941, so I spent a couple of summers at Elmhurst. I could play all I wanted, but there weren't many tournaments. Then a member at Elmhurst who was in the defense contracting business was building the big bomber plant in south Chicago, a mile square, it was famous, it was where they built the B-29 bombers. He said to me, "Look, what are you going to do? There's no tour. Why don't you work for me in the winter? I'll put you on the job. You're sharp enough." So I started down there at the bomber plant. I didn't know anything about snow, and had never driven on it, and I was picking up a couple of guys every day on the way to the plant. One time I couldn't get the car started because the snow had blown under the hood. So from then on we had the *Chicago Tribune* covering the engine. But one time we forgot about it and the car caught fire. That was a *cold* winter. The building—the roof was on, but no sides. Oh Jesus, we had funny experiences in those days.

Then I was drafted into the Army. In those days they could draft non-citizens, and if you didn't want to serve, you could never become a citizen. Well, we wanted to become citizens, because we figured we were going to live here and play golf here. It was our new home, the United States. We liked it, everything was fun, and joining the army to become a citizen was a cinch. Norma got her citizenship through me joining up. I was assigned to the artillery, but it was just like with Hogan and Dutch Harrison and all the other boys. When they found out who they were, they were put in special services and taught golf.

I was stationed in Camp Robertson, California, then was transferred to the Presidio in San Francisco. I remember I had a couple of Italian prisoners of war who shagged the balls for my lessons. They liked me because they weren't banging around in the garbage. They were at the country club, having fun. I gave a colonel a lesson one day—he was an all-American football player later, a real big guy. Well, I'd been hitting some balls before he came and the Italians were picking them up. When the lesson started, the colonel was hitting them all over the place. It was a hot day, and one of the Italians came back with the balls, dumped them out in from of the colonel, and said to him, "Why don't you hit them like him?" pointing at me.

I think there was a certain amount of resentment in Australia for my having left. And once in a while there was some from the American pros at me being a foreigner. But I was cured of all that in 1936 in the British Amateur at St. Andrews. I played a Scotsman in the finals, and a Scot hadn't won the title in twenty-eight years. So that fixed me. Oh, they were happy when I blew a shot, and dead cold when I hit a good one. That can get to you. The Scotsman beat me on the last green. I'd had that kind of stuff in Australia, too, playing in the different states, when I'd play the local champion as the outsider. I suppose I was always an outsider, but that's a marvelous experience. It steels you against things that could otherwise bother you.

For example, in 1947 in the U.S. Open in St. Louis, I had seventy-five putts in the last two rounds and finished tied for fifth. The next week is the PGA championship in Detroit—two majors in a row. So I went up there and Norma says I'm not going to hit balls, I'm just going to work on my putting. I had a wonderful wife in the way she could look at my game. I taught her how to play, and she became very adept. She got down to a three handicap once. Well, she was like a video. She could look at me and could tell when my pace was quicker or the movements were different, and that was all I needed. Anyway, in Detroit we spent an entire day and a half on the putting green. We never went out, and I'll tell you how well I putted. In the final match, against Chick Harbert, I beat him two and one, and the only time my putter hit a second putt was on the last green, the thirty-fifth hole. It was a foot from the hole and Chick said I'd better knock it in, because it was for the victory. The rest of the day I had been putting so close he was just giving me the second ones.

But what I started out to say was here was another time when I was the outsider. Chick was from Detroit, the local boy, and there were some funny things going on that week. A lot of people thought Clayton Heafner should have beaten Harbert in the semi-final, but a couple of balls that were out of bounds were found a foot inside the fence. Chick didn't want it—nobody wants it that way—but there were these guys kicking the ball out of the bunkers, and all.

I knew this was going on, so I'm driving out to the club, trying to figure out how in hell I'm going to cope with this thing. You cope with a lot of things, but you can't cope with people 250 yards away. Well, there were a couple of cops at the course drinking Cokes and I said to them, "Would you guys like to make fifty bucks apiece today?" They asked how, and I said, "Very simple, I want one of you on the left side of the fairway, one of you on the right on every hole. When my ball comes to rest I just want one of you standing close to it, maybe four feet away. I don't want anybody to touch it. I don't care what they do to his ball, but I don't want mine stepped on, kicked in a bunker or under a tree." The two cops were happy, and I was superior happy. To me that was the best $100 I've ever spent.

As I say, you learn to cope. A little later in that year I won the St. Paul Open, and Bobby Locke comes up to me there and says, "Boy, why don't you and I play together in the next International Four-Ball tournament? The way you putt, and the way I putt and play, we could win that." I said fine. I went home to Australia, he went back to South Africa, and we were to meet at the Los Angeles Open the following January. When I get to Los Angeles I read a piece in the paper that Locke was going to play in the Four-Ball with Lloyd Mangrum. I thought there was a misprint or something, but when I ask Locke about it at the club, he said, "Yes, I've decided to play with Mangrum, who is a much better player than you are, and I'll have a much better chance with him."

Classic Locke. I knew him from '36 in England, when he was an amateur. He couldn't putt then. He learned to putt during the war, in Cairo, when he was in the South African army. Some guy, an Englishman, I think, showed him how, on sand greens. Gave him that hook stroke. He would never tell me who it was. I guess he figured I might find the guy and learn something from him. Anyway, I have to find a partner for the Four-Ball, which is in March. I'm scrounging around, and in Phoenix I see this guy hitting thousands of practice balls. It's Cary Middlecoff, who had just turned pro. I asked him who he was playing with in the Four-Ball, and he said he couldn't even get an invitation. I said, "Well, you've got one now." Well, we beat Mangrum and Locke in the final, on the thirty-seventh green. A helluva match. On the extra hole Doc Middlecoff hooked one into the palms and Locke missed his second shot badly, so it was Lloyd and I. Lloyd put one about six feet behind the hole coming downhill, I put mine in there fifteen feet or so, coming across the hill. I pop mine in, Lloyd misses, and we win. So we're walking back to the clubhouse and Locke says to Mangrum, "Look, don't you realize I'm the world's finest putter? Why didn't you ask my opinion on the line of that putt? You'd have holed it if I told you where to putt." Mangrum looked up and said, "You sonofabitch, I've put up with you for a week now. Never again!" That was a real twosome. They didn't speak much all week.

After the war I played the tour full-time, ten months out of the year. We never had a real home, just sort of a base in Los Angeles. It was a lot of golf, but I was in pretty good shape and you had to make a living. I had a salary from Wilson's. I started off with them for $75 a week, then I could spend some money when I was representing them. So I picked up another $25 or $30 a week. I'd go out with a representative and meet some guy he was trying to sell clubs to. That would pay for my lunch. Of course, the writing broke off during the war, because there was nothing around. I wrote again in '45 and '46, but then they realized I wasn't coming back, so that was over. But we managed.

The traveling was interesting. I remember we drove into Charlotte one night, Ky Laffoon and his wife and me and Norma. There were no motels then, and the hotels were full, so we went looking for guest homes. You could get a beautiful room in a guest home for $2.50, $3 a night. Well, we went into this one, a beautiful Southern mansion, big pillars, beautiful rooms. The manager, a woman, was showing us the two front rooms when we hear this awful racket from the other room. It's Ky chasing bloody cockroaches in the bathroom. He had a newspaper and he's swatting them. He said, "That's all right, I got them." Then he said to the manager, "I want a dollar off if we're going to have cockroaches around here."

Another time we stopped in Effingham, Illinois, on the

way to Chicago, and found this guest room for $2.50. You went up some steps into the bathtub. It was delightful. Well, we're sound asleep when we get this enormous noise. It turned out the room was about six feet from a railroad track, and this train came by, five o'clock in the morning, the steam out of its wheels pouring right through our window. Boy, it scared the hell out of us.

Oh yes, and there was a time we're asleep in a motel room in El Paso. Beautiful room, but walls Kleenex thin. We're woken up by a door slamming in the next room. "C'mon, honey," we hear the guy say, and there's the clicking of high heels. They get into the shower, which is right at the foot of our bed, and they're having at it, you know. Norma's upset and I said, "Well, honey, he's only having a little fun." But it kept us awake for an hour and a half. You know, he's giving her the tour.

There was always travel, although I only played in the British Open once. In 1936, at Liverpool, when Alf Padgham won it. Money was a big thing, and it was a long trip. In '36 I went by boat, of course, stopped in Ceylon, Malta, went through the Suez Canal. Jesus, I was on that boat for several weeks. I stayed over there for a while, won the Gold Vase and some other tournaments. Then an Australian friend of mine there who ran the Royal Automobile Club, Major Radcliff, said to me, "Don't get on that damn boat to go back. Give me your ticket." He had connections all over the world, used to be an aide to the Prince of Wales, and he arranged for me to sail on the *Normandie* to New York. I had four days in New York, stayed at the Waldorf-Astoria, then he had me fly across the U.S. to California. My first long flight, on a DC-3. Landed in Burbank, where I now live, and played a round at the Wilshire Country Club. That was arranged through the Australian ambassador, who was a member there. Now I'm a member. Then I got on the *Monterrey* for home and met Gene Sarazen and Helen Hicks. They were going over for some exhibitions, and I ended up playing with them. Quite a journey. Golf is a tremendous game. It opens all the right doors. If you can play golf, you can get in anywhere. Make friends, go anywhere.

You see how lucky I was. I came along in the Hagen-Sarazen-Jones era, played with Snead and Hogan, and ran into the

Jim Ferrier

Palmers and Nicklauses. A great span. Yeah, I had a good career. I won twenty-four tournaments, including the PGA and two Canadian Opens. Had I been a little better tee-shot player, I'd have won as many more, but my knee bothered me and I had to cope with it. I'd injured it playing soccer when I was a kid. Ran into a fellow and broke off a piece of bone. When I walked it would click. About a year later I had it operated on by an old German doctor who wouldn't join the Australian Medical Association because he was interned during the First World War. They said he was the only one who would definitely have a ninty-five-percent chance of doing it right—you didn't have many good doctors in Australia at the time—and he did a good job. The knee was always a little weak and it would get sore and I'd have to use a heating pad and stuff, but I could play. I dipped into the ball. Nelson had a dip, but his was more graceful than mine. I used to swing kind of different. I'd have a hook swing one week, a cut swing the next.

A lot of things, when they happened, were serious. Like that train waking us up. Scared the hell out of us. But when you look back, it's wonderful to have all that stuff, to remember it.

Jim Ferrier lives in Burbank, California. He plays golf regularly at the Wilshire Country Club. His first wife, Norma, who was as well known on the tour as Jim, died a few years ago. Jim has remarried.

GEORGE FAZIO

Photograph by Wide World Photos

Photograph by Al Barkow

"You should do six or eight or twenty things in a lifetime."

I never thought I'd do anything in golf, really, because I was so small and skinny as a kid. And sort of unhealthy. At least, my mother thought I was. All mothers do. She said I better go up there to the golf course and get some fresh air, so I went when I was around seven years of age. To the Plymouth Golf Club in Norristown, Pennsylvania. My brother Sal took me. He played a little golf, but I was the only one in the family to get into it, and I remember my father being criticized for letting me play this stupid game, as they said. He didn't mind, he was a very kind man. But the problem I had was my mother and father were immigrants and they only spoke Italian. Oh, my father spoke some broken English, but he made an x for his name. So I couldn't talk to my parents about anything. They didn't know golf, they didn't know a lot of things, and I had to go into the outside world.

Well, from the time I was nine until I was about twelve you just couldn't get me off the golf course. I got there at daybreak and always went home in the dark. I was one of these whacky kids that, when he likes something, he can't get enough of it. Of course, the Depression came and they had a thing called Continuation School, where you get out of school when you're fourteen and go once a week on Monday. If you had a job and your parents vouched for you, you went to Continuation School. So I started working at the Valley Forge Club, shining clubs, gripping them, and going through the wooden-shaft deal—you know, sanding them down and so forth. I did a lot of that in the winter, and I caddied in the summer.

When I got older I tried to get assistant-pro jobs, but I had no chance. I don't know why. It was in the heart of the Depression—'31, '32, '33—I was born in 1912, and there were other people in front of me who had been playing tournaments. I played in only one when I was still a caddie, an assistant-pro thing. I thought I was going to be in the caddie yard forever. I caddied until I was twenty-two years of age. The way I got to play, I would caddie for someone and play with him. There were certain people who had that privilege, and I was one of them.

Finally, I built a driving range. Bud Lewis, myself, and Jack Gately. We built it ourselves with a horse and scoop, in Jeffersonville. Now I could play and practice, because it had been so hard to find a place to hit a golf ball. Then we went out and built two more driving ranges, and they were very successful. We would take in $200 a day selling those little buckets of balls. The bank presidents in Philadelphia weren't taking in $200 a day. Then I started buying land.

I did get a couple of assistant-pro jobs after a while, at a little nine-hole course outside Philadelphia, and then at another one. But then I went over and got the job at Pine Valley Golf Club. John Arthur Brown ran the club. He was like a czar, and at that time, when the pros came to play there, they had to change their shoes in the car because—or so I was told—Walter Hagen and a few others had been over there and got to drinking and broke up some furniture. So pros were not allowed in the clubhouse. I asked for the job, and we were coming real close and I said to Mr. Brown that I would take it under one condition, that I could go in the clubhouse and so could all my pro friends. I told him that if ever I did anything wrong he could just shake his finger at me and I'd pack my bags and leave, because I had enough confidence in my behavior. I told him my mother and father taught me as good social manners as anyone in this club, all the English with their manners—the English think they're the only ones with good manners. He said, "Those are big words, but can you handle all that?" I said I sure could. It took some guts to say all that. Brown was a tough guy. But if you stood up to him, he liked you. They paid me $15,000 a year, and I had the shop, But I was only there as club pro for about two years. I played out of there the rest of the time.

I took that job in 1940, then the war came along, and after that I became the head pro at Hillcrest Country Club in Los Angeles. Well, Stan Kertes had been the pro there and he wanted his job back. There was something about the Smith Act where a man could get his job back if he demanded it, and Kertes did. I told the members no problem, they had a year to work it out, and in the meantime I'd go out and play the tour for a while, or go home, or do something else. I'd played a few tournaments on the tour in 1938 and '39, and won the California Open when I started working out there. Well, a member of Hillcrest named Lew Rosensteil heard about this deal at the club and that's how I went to work for Schenley, which was his company. He told me to see a man in New York named MacDonald. I knew what Lew wanted, what he was doing, so I went to New York all by myself, with no lawyers, and got the best contract ever written in sports up to that time. That's what Freddie Corcoran said, anyhow. He was Snead's business manager.

The deal was Jimmy Demaret and I would get $25,000 a year and all the whiskey we wanted to promote a rum drink— Rum Ron Rico, I think it was called—out on the tour. They gave us enough to throw parties every week, and we threw some good ones, especially since it was right after the war and there wasn't much whiskey around. At first they wanted Sam Snead instead of Demaret, but I told them, "What is Sam Snead going to do with me? He won't go into a bar. He won't drink." Then they mentioned Craig Wood, but I held out for Jimmy and we got $25,000 plus expenses. The leading money winner on the tour was making only around $18,000, so we were leading money winners before we started. Demaret, being the kind of person he was, took that very lightly.

You know, people think Demaret would have won more

tournaments if he'd been serious, but I'll tell you what: if you got Jimmy mad enough to say, "I'll beat him," if you backed him in a corner, he'd beat Nicklaus, Hogan, Palmer, anybody. I saw him beat Hogan in a playoff. Everybody says he was a coward, that he didn't want to be up there. No, I think he was just lazy. If Jimmy concentrated and wanted to go, he could be a tiger. But he didn't want to be a tiger, he wanted to be a pussy-cat. He wanted to have some fun. I liked his style, because he did both, played and had fun. I really miss him.

So with that Schenley deal I went out and started playing regularly, and pretty good. I won the Canadian Open in 1946, the next year tied for the Crosby tournament with Ed Furgol—they didn't have a playoff because of the weather—and in 1950 got into a playoff for the U.S. Open with Hogan and Mangrum. I also did well in some other tournaments. But that year, 1946, was the only time I played the tour full-time. I got tired of it. What are you going to do, hit golf balls the rest of your life? I'm not saying it's wrong, but for me it was boring. I don't think anybody should take more than five years to do anything. You should do six or eight or twenty things in a lifetime. Of course, I played tournaments here and there. I kept my game up. You know, I worked hard at it as a young kid, although even then I didn't do a lot of practice. I did what a lot of people do in various endeavors, they give it a lot of thought and work it out in their mind. You know, monkey see, monkey do.

The best golf lessons I know of . . . Well, tell it this way. There was this newspaper writer in Birmingham, Alabama, who needed a story. We were playing a tournament there. Out on the putting green he has his pad in his hand and he goes over to Lloyd Mangrum and says, "Mr. Mangrum, I'm a reporter and I have to write something for the local newspaper about what you think of the game of golf, the golf swing, everything." Now, Mangrum acted tough, he talked out of the side of his mouth—they used to call him Riverboat because he loved to play cards and was always hustling something—and he kind of snarled at this reporter. So the fellow says, "I know, Mr. Mangrum, that you don't like this sort of thing, but I have a family and kids I have to support." So Mangrum says, "Well, in that case, okay." So the guy gets his pad all ready, looking very happy, and he says, "Okay, Mr. Mangrum, I'm ready." And Lloyd says, "Monkey see, monkey do," and he keeps putting. "Okay, Mr. Mangrum, fine. Go ahead." Mangrum says, "That's it. That's how you learn to play golf. Monkey see, monkey do." The reporter shook his head. Mangrum wouldn't give him any more.

I'm there through all this, of course, so I tell the reporter to go over to Jimmy Demaret. "Get him," I say. "Jim loves to talk, and he's a name player." So he goes through the whole thing again with Jimmy. Demaret asks him if he's ready, then he says, "If you can't see it, you can't hit it." "Fine, Mr. Demaret, go on." And Demaret says, "That's it," and he walks off.

What Lloyd was saying is you learn to play golf by imitating others. Of course, you want the others to have good swings. Like, the pros of my time always wanted to play with me in practice rounds before tournaments, and in tournaments, because they wanted to get some of my rhythm. When I was young I studied Ed Dudley's swing, which was one of the most beautiful you ever saw, but I didn't copy his swing, because it wasn't that good. But he was the person I psychologically went with. He played shots. Every shot was a hook or slice or blockout. He was always working the ball some way or another, working against something. What Demaret was saying was that you have to keep your eye on the ball through the whole swing. If you do that, everything else pretty much falls into place naturally. It's just a matter of hand-eye coordination.

Anyway, after Demaret walks off, the reporter shakes his head and comes over to me and asks if I can give him any more than that, and I said, "Oh, I can give you a lot of nonsense, but you watch all sports—kicking, boxing, whatever—and it is more through than to." I didn't get into it with the reporter, but what I mean is . . . well, I've talked to a lot of athletes about it and Joe Louis once told me that when he got to the point of contact he wanted to hit the floor with his fist. Joe envisioned getting his punch down to the floor, not hitting the guy. Same in golf. Knowing you have to follow through completely is the only way to get enough clubhead speed. If you're thinking hit *to* it, that stops the club and you don't get enough out of the shot. Most people work *to* the ball, not *through* it. That's the reason I opened my left side the way I did, in order to get through the ball. If I had repeated and repeated it by practicing more often, then naturally I would have done more in tournaments. But then I wouldn't have done the other things. I would rather be a Da Vinci-type person than a Michelangelo, because Da Vinci was more versatile.

I felt I could play up with the best players, and showed it a few times, although playing with Nelson was tough. He had a natural instinct, you know, the way he danced on the ball; just like poetry in motion. Nelson hit it so straight and had the best flight of the golf ball I've ever seen. Snead's ball would drill in, but Nelson's would rise up and drop nearly straight down. He was the only man I ever played with that I felt, Boy, I wish it would get dark. With everybody else I felt I might be able to outluck them, they might get a bad bounce or I might hit a lucky shot or something—even Hogan. Like in that playoff for the '50 Open. I was first up on the first tee, and when I went to put it down I was shaking. When Ben went I was looking at him tee it up and he was shaking, too, so I said, "This is not too bad." Mangrum liked to play the cool cat, but he was shaking, too.

Actually, I was too keyed up for that playoff. I usually drove even with Hogan for length, and that day I was ten and fifteen yards ahead of him. But I'd forget I was keyed up and knock the approach shots over the greens—taking too much club. I was just blind about everything. They would hit five-iron, I'd hit six and knock it over. But Hogan was only one shot ahead of Lloyd and me going to fourteen. Then I put one out of bounds, and so did Lloyd.

But you talk about playing with Ben Hogan. In the 1948 U.S. Open he won at Riviera, we're paired in the third round. We get to the third hole and I drive in the rough to the right and that ball went forever. Hogan and the other guy in our group—Mangrum, I think—drive up the left side and can play their next shot right at the pin, which is on the far right. They get on with five-irons, and I have an eight-iron in my hand because I have only one shot in town. I have to play over the bunker, because if I play to the opening I can't put it on the green. I had an odd angle. So I hit the eight-iron, and it goes in the hole for a two. Of course, there was a huge gallery, and I was the hometown boy at the time, being back as pro at Hillcrest, and there is this tremendous roar. I couldn't see the ball go in, but I could tell it did by the sound of the crowd. People were roaring and roaring forever, you know.

So after the round, going up to the clubhouse, I hand Ben my scorecard and he looked at it, turned it over, and kept walking up that hill. He didn't sign it. Now Joe Dey [of the USGA] comes over to me and says, "George, you better sign your card or you'll be disqualified." I said, "Oh no, not me. You see Mr. Hogan and get *him* to sign it, or *he* gets disqualified." I had signed it, because I knew what I did. Hogan didn't, and he wanted to verify, because he didn't remember I made the two. I said to him, "You s.o.b., I hit my career shot and you don't even remember it." I told them I wouldn't go out for the last round until Hogan signed my card, and he finally did. He said to me, "George, I didn't remember." I said, "Thanks a lot."

Now, Hogan is the most perfect gentleman on the golf course that I ever played with. I mean, he's not going to do anything *for* you, but he's not going to do anything against you. You play your game, he plays his. There's nobody better than that to play with, and I've always admired Hogan for that. He just had tunnel vision. He concentrated so hard on one thing, the outside influence was not there. You know, Sam Snead, if a pretty girl gave him a smile, he might lose his composure, his concentration. But not Ben Hogan.

When I tied for the Open in '50 I was the club pro at Woodmont in Washington, D.C., for four months and played a few afternoons a week. But I was also in the scrap-metal business at the same time. Which I enjoyed no end, because I don't like to throw things away. I was also in the real-estate business, and for fourteen years I had a Ford agency. Then I got into golf architecture. The first course I built was Atlantis, in Tuckertown, New Jersey, but I didn't start out as the architect. Some people—Tom White, Bill Gordon—asked me to consult with them and be part of a land-development deal. It was about 1,200 acres. I liked the land, but everybody, including myself, didn't like the layout of the course that someone had done. So one night after four or five drinks they kept saying to me, "*You* do it." I said I didn't want to, I didn't want to be bothered, it was hard for me to do because I'd never done it. They said, "Yeah, you can be critical, but doing it is different."

Well, I got half bombed and at about nine o'clock at night I drove back to Flowertown Golf Club and on the dance floor there I spread out the gray velox paper, got down on my knees, and drew out the topo of the course. It took me six or seven hours to chart it, because I didn't know how wide fairways were supposed to be and stuff like that. I had to recall all my knowledge of golf courses I'd played. And I'll tell you, my knees were killing me when I got through. That dance floor was *hard*.

George Fazio

George Fazio has left an indelible mark on the landscape of this country and other lands around the world with his golf courses. Among the best known of his designs are Butler National, outside Chicago, home of the Western Open; the Jupiter Hills Club in Jupiter, Florida; and Cypress Creek course of the Champions Golf Club in Houston, site of a U.S. Open. George brought his nephew, Tom Fazio, into the golf-architecture business, and Tom is taking after his uncle in the quality of his work.

George was retired for a time, but when we spoke he was completing construction of a new course in Fort Pierce, Florida. He lives in Jupiter, Florida.

IVAN GANTZ

Photograph by Patricia McHale

Photograph by Al Barkow

" . . . and, man, I raised that putter up and knocked myself in the head with it."

There have been a lot of stories about my temper, over the years. Not that many of them are true, but I don't mind. Mr. Barnum once told me, in Baltimore, he said, "Let me tell you, kid, as long as they keep talking about you, it makes no difference what they say." Billy Casper and several others have stood right beside me and said, "Remember the time at Oakmont when you dove into the sand trap on the seventeenth hole?" Well, I never did that. Then there's the one about how I always stomped on my driver and one time I couldn't get it off my shoe because the spikes got so deep, and I was walking along as if I had a ski on my foot. Well, that's Tommy Bolt's story. But he was the one. He had brand-new spikes on his shoes and he stomps on his driver, and it did stick. And, man, it wouldn't come off. He had to step on it with his other foot to get it off. It was a beautiful Tommy Armour driver, really a beauty. I had made it myself in the MacGregor plant in Cincinnati.

Then they tell the one about me hitting myself in the head with my putter after missing a short putt, and me falling to the ground knocked out cold. Actually, that happened a few times, hitting myself in the head. I was playing on the tour once in Houston, at Memorial Park, and missed a short putt on the last green that would've given me a 68, and, man, I raised that putter up and knocked myself in the head with it. I made a pretty good chunk in there, but I didn't fall down and I wasn't knocked cold. I've also hit myself in the jaw many times.

You see, when I began playing golf I didn't understand what was good and what was bad. I got into golf as a caddie at the Elk Ridge Club in Baltimore. Jimmy Roach, the pro, had a beautiful swing and as a kid I copied it right off. I was a good athlete, I guess. I could run, and ride a bicycle. I won fourteen 100-mile bike races as a kid, and rode to Philadelphia once in seven hours and thirty minutes—103 miles. So the first round of golf I played I shot 94, and of course I was mad because I didn't play better; I was getting mad already. I thought this golf game was the greatest thing in the world, and I worked at it, and I got better, but I never knew how good I hit it. A lot of people thought I hit it very good, but I thought I should hit it better because I pictured myself hitting it like Jimmy Roach did. Perception and reality are quite different. I thought I should be able to hit every shot perfect, and then when I found out that I could sometimes not hit it perfectly and it would go closer to the hole than when I hit it good, that really burned me up. I couldn't understand that, and I would get *so* mad.

I got this from my mother. She had temper—oh, it was fierce. And she read a lot, and learned how to play the accordion in two hours. Well, I figured that if she coordinated so good, why not me? You inherit everything from your mother— some things from your father, but not too much—and a boy especially. That's the reason a girl loves her father, a boy his mother. Just think, if God made the earth and all that, that's the way it has to be. Because if you had a great calamity, the father and daughter or mother and son could repopulate the earth . . . if it came to that. So lots of times I had a high estimate of myself. I had a good memory and went through high school in a hurry—three years without any trouble, a polytechnic school. But my parents always told me how stupid I was, which was very unusual. A lot of their attitude about me being stupid was because of my interest in golf. If I had been a good woodcutter or bricklayer, they would have understood that, but golf didn't have any ultimation. It didn't seem to them that there would be a future in it.

Ivan Gantz

My father was a gardener, and he cut pulp wood in the winter. I had an older brother and sister who worked in a cotton mill. We rented a house for $6 a month, and my father got $10 or $11 a week as a gardener, but when he cut pulp wood he'd make as much as $100 a week, because he was better than average. He wasn't very big, but he was a strong man. He didn't have much of a temper, but, as I say, my mother did. She was small but strong, and worked in the fields with my father. She could outwork a lot of men. She wasn't so beautiful, but she was formed exceptionally well and . . . she was better than average.

We were poor, but I was pretty good at football, so the Gilman Country School gave me a scholarship. This was a prep school, and I went through the eight grades in five years.

When I was fourteen I was pushing a greens mower at the Elk Ridge Club, and then I learned how to make clubs. Jimmy Roach helped me with that. Then other pros came over, and they showed me things about it. You know, the hickory shafts came in square, and we had to shave them down and make them round. And I would make wooden heads sometimes. When I got older I'd go down to MacGregor's in the winter and work—in Cincinnati. They gave me a place to sleep in the factory. I guess anything was legal in those days. Sure. I came from Baltimore on the train, through the mountains, and when I got there I knew a lot of people, such as Clarence Rickey, who was the president. He said, "Buzz, there's no reason why you should get a room unless you want to." They had showers and all, so I just stayed there. I got forty cents an hour. But I had a wonderful time.

I had no intention, at first, to be a pro. I'll tell you, I helped build the Five Farms Golf Club in Baltimore, and I qualified for the U.S. Amateur there. But they wouldn't let me play. They marked me off, saying I was a pro because I built golf courses, worked in pro shops, and caddied. I did work as an assistant greenskeeper, and in pro shops, and I caddied, but I did that only to learn the game. I just wanted to be a good golfer. I was going to try to emulate Bobby Jones. I was only sixteen or seventeen at the time, and not being allowed to play in that tournament affected my whole career. The USGA didn't do that to me. Some of the members at Five Farms complained because they'd seen me working around there. But the real reason was I played too good and wasn't from the amateur class at the time. I was from a poor background, and I made a lot of money beating a lot of those amateurs.

So I turned pro by accident. I went up to Beaver Brook, in Rome, New York, to work as an assistant greenskeeper. Some friends of mine up there, Augie Nordone and others, got me into the PGA. They were wonderful people. From Rome I went to Lancaster, Pennsylvania. As greenskeeper, not the pro. They offered the pro job to me, but I didn't want to take it from the guy who was there. I figured, fair play. I worked for Tommy Armour at Congressional Country Club for two seasons. I wasn't an assistant or a teaching pro. I was the general flunky. I was in the rack room, mostly.

I had head-pro jobs. I had one in Easton, on the eastern shore of Maryland. I enjoyed those jobs, they were fun in a lot of ways, but you have people who get jealous and all and they gave me a hard time and I'd say that if they could run the place better, go ahead, and I'd leave. Although I got fired once in a while. The last job I had was at Elwood, Indiana. I had that job for a few years. Wendell Willkie was from Elwood. That's the only thing the town ever had. No, the Ray Packing Company has a big tomato factory there, too.

The other thing is I had to know everything and I never could. I could hit the ball, but there were periods when I didn't know exactly how to hit the shot and I would just get mad and hit it anyhow. That's one of the reasons I never made it on the tour. The most I ever won on the tour was $1,900. I never really made anything. I'd get out there and get mad at myself and then have a letdown. Then someone would come along and tell me I was crazy for getting mad, that I was childish and all that stuff. I wondered about it, but I never thought I was being childish. I generally don't get angry at other people, only at myself. I think the Lord is wonderful and caused me to live this long, you know, so I never get angry that way. Just at myself, because I sense or feel that I have in me to get everything I want and I never knew how it worked. I worked at it, studied, met everybody I could—some of the best psychiatrists in the country—and they all said to me, "Ivan, you've gotta be crazy." And I'd say, "Well, that's good, there's nothing wrong with that."

What I mean by not knowing how it worked is how do you get things? A human doesn't understand. The brain is a function we really don't know a whole lot about. But we have a mind, and that mind is a system that tries to give us everything we want. So if you want something, like you want to hit a golf shot, immediately the mind tells the brain that you want it and the brain gets every muscle ready to do it. That has got to be the operation, because I've studied everything there is, including the Talmud, and just by thinking and spending a lot of sleepless nights. You see, they say concentration. But there is no such thing. Oh no! That's impossible. How can you concentrate? You don't know how, no living man knows how. There's no way. But if I *want*, I don't have to concentrate. If I want to hit a golf ball onto a green, and if I want it strong enough, I can do it. We say intuition is at work here, and I have worked a lot with that. But all you do is want. The Lord has been generous, he gave you the ability to get it. That's the answer to how to get it. Just *want* it! You don't have to figure out how, the system already knows how.

You see, in golf if you reason too much you can't play. Or you can't play as well as you could otherwise. Take a man who can hit the ball 150 yards with a five-iron. But he wants to hit the ball to a hole that's 165 yards away. If he wants it hard enough he'll hit that five-iron 165 yards. He couldn't do that, normally. Then he says, "Man, if I could get that feel," and now he starts searching for the feel and he loses it. You see, Adam and Eve ate from the tree of knowledge, not from the tree of good and evil. So man has used his knowledge to destroy himself ever since. It's great to have knowledge, and to reason and consider yourself and all that, but generally necessity is the mother of invention. If you want it, you get it.

I'll tell you this: temper and desperation are near about the same. There was this little woman no bigger than ninety pounds who had a husband weighed 180. She carried him a mile and a half because he had a heart attack. She loved him, and she carried him. When she rested a couple of days afterwards, she couldn't pick him up. Because there was no want or desperation. So when you get angry you can birdie some holes.

In that way anger, or temper, can be good, and that's why I never really tried to stop getting angry. It can be a wonderful thing. If I could have understood that earlier I could have driven myself to win anything. Yet it is also terrible, because it dominates you many times.

The last time I played the tour was in 1955. I wanted to play the tour, but a lot of things happened that interfered with it. I had a family and it was necessary to make the money. I was married twice, when I was twenty-three and when I was forty-eight. Had one child by the first wife, three by the second. And you wonder if you're good enough when you fail enough times. And I failed enough times. You kind of get the message. I knew, or felt I knew, I had the ability, because when I played with all those great players they didn't hit it any better than I did. But they putted and chipped it better. But, you see, putting is want. Like Bobby Locke. He *wanted* to get that ball in the hole. Physically, it's almost impossible to take that putter back and roll the ball over all that terrain and into that little hole from any distance. But want, that is something else.

I have wondered and wondered about it. I worked on it. I would sit for hours at night with these big sheets of foolscap and write what I thought I had, what I thought I'd like to have, what I thought I was working toward, what I would like to get in my golf game, what I wanted with people. I wanted to be liked, and I wondered if I ever was. Many times people tried to belittle me, and all. It came out of my own sense of smallness. I wasn't small, but I felt I was. I went through school better than they did, but I never thought of myself as being intelligent, and I still don't. I thought I could excel at golf, and I was good at it. But I defeated myself. I didn't want strong enough. So I punished myself by getting angry. But, you see, to keep yourself keyed up in an emotional state to get what you want, that's bordering on anger. But the anger, in the end, was hurtful to me. It gave me wonderful things a lot of times, but in the long run it was detrimental.

Ivan Gantz

Ivan Gantz continues to teach golf in the north during the summer and during the winter in West Palm Beach, Florida.

WALTER "CHINK" STEWART

Photograph by Al Barkow

"When I first got to playing, the clubs I used were made out of coathangers. . . . Yessir!"

I was born in Norfolk, Virginia, and grew up in a section where the blacks lived, near the Norfolk and Western Railroad. My nickname has nothing to do with the game of golf. No, when I was the age of nine they put on a play in my grammar school and wanted somebody who they could make up to look like a Chinee. So they did me up and, you know, the kids started calling me Chinaman. Then it became Chink, Chink Chinaman, and they finally shortened it to just call me Chink. About the same time some kids asked me to come on go to a golf course where they used caddies. I decided to go, because you could make some money over there. They would give you a quarter for nine holes; it was a nine-hole course.

The minute I got there it was so fascinating to me to see them hit that ball that I decided I was going to learn this game. I wanted so much to be good at it, good at caddying, good at anything that had to do with golf. I would go to school in the morning, and at 2:30 every afternoon I'd walk to the golf course—seven miles. When I first got to playing, the clubs I used were made out of coathangers, long wire ones. Yessir. You'd put about six or seven of them together and twist and turn them around until you had it. For balls we used little nuts that came off a tree. We'd knock the prongs off them and roll them in mud and oil so they wouldn't break so easy when they

195

were hit. After caddying for a time the members gave us some old sticks—real golf clubs. We'd take them out and do amazing things with them.

When I reached fourteen I got so good at the game I could chase balls for the pro while he was giving a lesson and tell from the distance whether the player was going to slice or hook by just looking at the swing. Well, as I got to know the game, I started offering suggestions on how to play to the people I was caddying for. It got so they were asking for me so much until the pro got curious and wondered why they weren't asking him for help. He found out I was helping people, so he called me in. See, I had made some suggestions to a lady and afterwards she told the pro that she just had the best game she ever played and "that caddie was wonderful." At the time I don't know this is going on, understand. So the pro said to me, "Let me tell you something, boy, I want you to stop teaching the members." Well, next day I'm caddying for this doctor I caddied regularly for, and it was only natural for me to ask how he was hitting it, and when he said not so good and I should suggest something to him, I did. He said, "My God, that's somehting," and after the round he tells the pro how I helped him, showing him what it was an' all. So the pro sends for me again.

Now, this will kill you. The pro says to me, "Imagine the kind of spot I'm in. I'm a man in my fifties, got two kids going to school, and you got my job in jeopardy giving those suggestions." I give a lot of thought to what he said and I say to him I'll give it up, to satisfy him. But he thinks about that and figures the members are going to ask what happened to me, and he couldn't say I was run off for teaching because it would go hard on him. So he called me in again and said, "Look, I'm going to give you a job on the inside, cleaning clubs, and I'll teach you to be a clubmaker and repairman." After school and on Saturdays, Sundays, and holidays. So I quit caddying. I was paid $8 a week, which was a lot of money. And, of course, I got some tips and I would still give some suggestions, only I'd tell the people not to get that around because I didn't want to get into any more trouble. This was at the Norfolk Country Club, which was the only private club in town.

Walter "Chink" Stewart

There was a public course, but blacks couldn't play it. I was fortunate, though, by working in the golf shop, to be able to play the golf course. Not any time I wanted to, but on days when it rained, for instance. All the members would come in and I'd dry their clubs off, put linseed oil on the shafts to keep them from warping, and afterwards if it cleared up I could play maybe six or eight holes. Then sometimes me and my friends would come down six o'clock in the morning, at the first sunlight, and get in as many holes as we could before eight o'clock, when the course opened and we had to be at work. We didn't play much after work, though, it put too much on us the next morning. You see, if those clubs had been used, they had to be cleaned and ready in their pen for the next day.

Now, the other black boys that worked at other courses were golfers, too, so we'd always have our little group and play at the different courses—where they worked, where we worked. Then there were times when we were kids we'd play where we weren't allowed to, and some guys would drive by in a car and shoot at us. Yeah. We'd get down on our stomachs and when they went away we'd get up and finish the hole. These guys were hired to shoot at us. Night watchmen. This was on all the golf courses down around Virginia. 'Course, it was our fault, because we were told not to play. So we took our chances.

I hardly ever got to play tournaments. There was a black tour, but who had the money to go to the tournaments? I didn't. You had to go for at least a week to play just one of them. Some of the other black boys working at other clubs, the members would give them a little money to go play in tournaments, but down where I was in Virginia it was entirely different. I was kind of isolated. The first real big tournament I ever played in was the Joe Louis Open in Detroit in 1946. That was a tournament for blacks, but white pros were allowed to enter, and they did and they often won. Funny thing, of course, because they wouldn't let us play in their tournaments. But Teddy Rhodes won it often, and Bill Bishop from Philadelphia. And Bill Spiller and Zeke Hartsfield. Only one time I went up to Detroit, and I remember the lady in the registration booth saying my entry fee had already been paid. Well, *I* hadn't paid, so I talked to Clyde Martin, who was Joe's golf teacher, and he told me Joe paid my entry fee. He paid for all the black pros. He was that type of man. And after the tournament was over he chartered a plane and flew a lot of the pros up to Canada for a tournament there. I couldn't go. I had to get back to my job in Virginia.

Most of the black golfers of my time had what you might call peculiar swings, sort of unorthodox styles. Like Howard Wheeler played cross-handed. That's because they were always trying to hit the ball hard. See, we didn't always have whole sets of clubs and many times just had to use a club that wasn't enough to get us to where we had to go and so we hit the hell out of it. Well, you're going to make some odd swings that way. And, besides, there was no one around to show us the right way.

Howard Wheeler was the best black player, then there was Teddy Rhodes, who came after him, then Charlie Sifford. But I knew a dozen other boys who were just as great but didn't have the money to play. Wheeler made his living hustling at golf. I don't mean he hustled like someone who was faking his handicap, or like that. He just played guys for money, giving strokes or playing them even and beating them. For instance, Ray Mangrum, Lloyd's brother, played the best-ball of Howard and Teddy and they beat that man so bad and for so much money until Lloyd told Ray that if he played those guys for money again he'd disown him as a brother. And a lot of people say Ray was a better player than Lloyd, who won the U.S. Open and all.

So I was an assistant pro when I was sixteen. I never did get a head-pro job, because back then there was never any opening. None whatsoever. In those days, being an assistant to a white pro, he always felt like his job was intact, safe, because there was no chance of me relieving him. Now, if he got a real intelligent young white boy in, it would've been different. Then I worked at the Navy golf course in Norfolk for a long time. I played a little bit at the country club I worked at, although not when I wanted to, but at the Navy course it was different. Most of the time I played only by sneaking out. Most of the officers didn't say anything, but it was always a sneaking kind of thing. One time an admiral saw me on the course and stopped me and asked me who gave me permission to play, I said my golf pro, and he said, "Well, I'm telling you you can't play anymore. I don't want to catch you out here playing." So I told the pro to get someone else, because I was leaving. He said not to leave, that he would take it up with the golf chairman. But he was just a lieutenant, so who was he to buck the admiral? I said I didn't want no hassle, I could always get a job.

What happened then was a new admiral came in who outranked the other admiral, and one day he said, "Chink, will you take my son out and help him with his game?" I said I was sorry but I couldn't go on the course, and I explained the situation to him and he said I could go out as much as I wanted so long as it didn't interfere with my duties, and that I should help his son. And if the other admiral says anything, he should just give him a call. So I'm showing off now. This little golf course is situated right near these homes and I'm playing this hole and the first admiral comes out and chews me up and down, and asks who gave me permission to be out there and all. I call out this other admiral's name and tell the first admiral he should contact him. So he goes in and calls and comes out and says, all nice now, "Everything is all right, you go right ahead."

I had been working at the Navy course for thirteen years when World War II broke out, and when it did they gave me a guarantee. If I volunteered for the service, they would send me up to Bainbridge for my training and get orders to send me right back to the golf course in Norfolk. And that's what happened. Frankly, I wanted to go overseas, but they wouldn't let me. I got my same salary, plus my Navy pay. In the meantime the head pro got into the real-estate business and would only come in to give a few lessons in the morning. So they wanted me to be in charge. But around this time Sam Snead, Paul Runyan, Lew Worsham, and a lot of other top pros were stationed at Norfolk, and I said there was no way in the world I was going to be any boss over Sam Snead, Paul Runyan, and all those men. Who the hell was I to be boss over them! But it didn't work that way in the service. The man in charge of the course told me that all those men had to do was teach the officers. And they gave plenty of lessons. The officers would take three a day if they wanted. So all I did was give those lessons out. I'd say, "Mr. Runyan, you take it." He was the greatest of them as a teacher. He just had a way of getting it across. I didn't give any lessons myself, other than if I had to play with someone. Then I'd give some suggestions as we went around.

In the years before the war, even through the Depression, I worked in golf—caddying, working in the shops as an assistant. Never did anything else. I was never a member of the PGA, though. Every time I put my application in, they turned it down because I was black. Then, when it was offered to me, I told them it was too late, I was over the hill. Same with Howard Wheeler. There was one golf course in Washington, D.C., where blacks could play. Langston. Another public course there was East Potomac Park, but you'd go over there and they'd send you back to Langston. "Go play over there," they said. Oh, and we could play at Cobbs Creek in Philadelphia. All that began to change in the 1950s.

What happened in Baltimore was there were certain days when blacks could play here at Carroll Park or Mount Pleasant. Tuesday would be black man's day, and I'd go out there with some friends and we'd be the only foursome on the whole golf course all day long. One foursome. Well, the white pros were not making any money on the black man's day, so they got on our side. We raised money, raised money, raised money, and finally took the thing to court. We had Thurgood Marshall as our lawyer, who is now on the Supreme Court, and when we walked in there the judge said he respected this man's ability as a great, great lawyer and he wasn't going to go through a whole lot of riff, raff, and roll. He said, "As of now, every public golf course in Baltimore is open to everybody at any time."

Some time after, the mayor of Baltimore city walked right in here to Carroll Park and asked me if there were any problems. I said, "What do you mean, problems? More whites are playing. We blacks are better players and they want the experience of playing with us. Sit around and watch," I told him. So here comes one of the white boys up to me and he says, "Man, don't you know what time it is? Look how long we been waiting for you. Hell, we started to go off without you." That was a big thing. It was coincidental that that happened. They didn't know the mayor was there.

Actually, when I first came over to Baltimore it was to get away from golf. I got tired of it. But a good friend of mine in golf said I had to be in the game and he was going to find me a job in it. So I hung around and got me a job at Fort Holabird. Then the Korean War broke out and I came over here to Carroll Park. The job as head pro was open and people asked me to put my application in for it. I said no, Clyde Martin was here in Baltimore before me, so he should have it. But Clyde didn't want it, and I sent in my application, as did a few others. And there came up a hassle about it. They questioned my ability to hold the job, and I was enjoying it all because I didn't want the job in the first place. Anyway, fourteen of my friends, all coloreds, sent in recommendations for me. So did some Jewish members of the country club where I worked as a caddie once in a while just to be around the game. So there came a showdown, the black politicians trying to get me the job, and they decided to let me go down before the Parks Department board and answer some questions. They told me to not say anything that would harm me, and I said, "since I didn't want the job anyway, what could I say to harm me?"

Well, when I got down there I told them that I didn't have to prove myself after all I had done in golf, and if I got the course I was going to do the job as I saw fit—close up the shop and go play golf if I wanted to—and if they didn't like it they could take the job and ram it, thank you, ladies and gentlemen. And I turned and walked away, seeing all these politicians looking confused. I go over to Carroll Park to play nine holes, and here comes this big Cadillac with a police escort and I'm wondering what in hell is going on. So this politician jumps out of the car and says to me, "Let me congratulate you, you have the job." I may be the first black man to ever have a head-professional job in golf.

It was always hard for me, being black, but I'd do it again just for the love of the game. I never went into golf with the idea of making a lot of money, I just enjoyed being around the course. I've had some of the best times in the world. Oh, man, when you get around guys like Sam Snead and Paul Runyan, the way I did at the Navy course in Norfolk. I liked to tease

Sam, tell him it was easy out there on the tour, that he had no competition. But I used to learn a lot from them about playing. Paul Runyan was a great putter, and he used to tell us how to putt. But we'd go out there and see him in action and he didn't putt no damn way the way he said he did. We got on our knees to see from all angles and he never showed the stroke of the ball that he said he did. The lesson I learned from that day to this is you can't teach a man to putt. You must learn that for yourself.

I guess I was just fortunate. I had a gift for golf. I never had a lesson, a real lesson, where someone would stand there and watch me hit balls. I would get little tips here and there, of course. I used to caddie for a little old pro and he used to play chip shots with loose wrists. I'd see him stub the club in the ground and never get to the ball. I said to him one day, "You don't do that right." My theory was to be firmer with the wrists. So he said, "Let's see you do it," and I knocked it up there close. He didn't know it all. Just because he was a pro and had a pro job, that didn't mean he knew everything.

Well, it's like everything else. You got good doctors, you got bad ones.

Walter "Chink" Stewart

Walter "Chink" Stewart is the head golf professional at the Carroll Park Golf Course in Baltimore, Maryland.

ERRIE BALL

Photograph by Al Barkow

"I tried so hard that I got scared I would win."

It's something you can't explain, the feeling of playing in a major championship. I'll never forget, I was playing well at Tam O'Shanter one year. I opened up with 66–68 and the third day I was coming into the club and the minute I hit the gate I could feel this pressure, this electricity, whatever it is. I said to myself, Boy, you're really in it now. Well, I shot a 70, then I blew it to a 77, and instead of winning the $50,000 first prize I finished up winning about $500. It's something you can't explain, a funny thing. You haven't picked up a club yet, but you still feel it. It's entirely different from the tour—you get settled on the tour.

Then there was the time when I played the first Masters, in 1934, which I felt even then was going to be something pretty big. I played with Charlie Yates the last day and we were about even starting out—he was then the British Amateur champ. On the first two holes, which are now the tenth and eleventh, I made two good fours and it looked like I would do well. Then I get to the short hole, which is now the twelfth, and I hit a beautiful six-iron about ten feet from the hole. Now, in those days I used to put my putter in front of the ball, then behind, and this time it got stuck. I couldn't move it. I said to myself, I've got to make a pass at it, so I went bang, hit it hard, and it lipped the cup and jiggled off into the bunker—

the green was very fast. It looked like I was going to get a two, and I finished with a six. Well, I finished the round with 80-odd, I forget, and it ruined my putting for quite some time. I got the yips, and everything else.

It just hit me there, all of a sudden. Just like that. I'd been a good putter up until then. I wasn't going to win the tournament, but I was going to finish pretty well up. Just like that, and it stayed with me for about eight years. There were a lot of tournaments I could have won easily but for that putting. . . . And, of course, someone would say, "Boy, if he could only putt," and that was the worst thing I could have heard.

I must be about the fourth or fifth generation of golfers in my family. My great-grand-uncle was John Ball, who won the British Amateur eight times, the first time in 1888. He once held both the British Open and Amateur titles in one year. No one did that again until Bob Jones, forty years later. I only recall seeing him once, with my dad. John Ball owned a hotel just across from the golf course at Hoylake. He was a very shy man. Very shy, and was never a pro.

That's where it all started, at Hoylake, near Liverpool on the River Mersey. My father and my uncles were all pros. My father started in golf when the feathery ball was still out. I served my apprenticeship in England, for five years under my dad at the Lancaster Golf Club. One of my jobs as a young boy was to repaint golf balls. I always hated that damn job. You had to take the old paint off with lye, and put the new paint in the middle of your hand and roll the ball around in it and work the thumb to smooth it over. You had to be careful not to fill up the mesh, or dimples—in those days they weren't really dimples, but mesh-markings—because if the paint blobbed in there the ball wouldn't fly. So there was quite a knack to it. We'd do about four dozen balls a day, and sell each one for sixpence or a shilling.

I also had to sandpaper the clubs, the hickory shafts, and it took time for each one. You'd sandpaper it once very smooth, put it under water to bring the grain up, then sandpaper it again. After that it didn't make any difference how much water got on them, because the pores were closed. Then you'd put on pitch to harden the wood, then varnish it with linseed oil you rubbed on with a rag. It would be as smooth as glass. I notice today they're trying to imitate the old wooden shafts, but the grain is not aligned. In our day the grain had to be right dead-center so it was like a pointer or arrowhead going right down the center of the shaft. Now they've got it to the sides, and everything. Oh, if my old man ever saw that, he'd have thrown it right out the window. Having the grain down the center was for esthetic purposes, but it was also for strength. Also, the fact that it was almost a straight line gave you a better visual image for playing shots. Otherwise, it would be like putting a jacket on crooked.

It was drudgery, all the work in the shop. I think my father was paying me five shillings a week, and I was living at home, but if the work wasn't done I couldn't play. And I couldn't wait to get on the golf course. But in the winter it got dark around four o'clock in the afternoon, so that's when the golf professionals made up all their inventory. We'd get there at nine o'clock and work through. So when it was light again, in summer, we didn't have to work as hard except for reshafting and splicing of clubs. A lot of clubs were spliced, and the heads would fly off according to the weather. When it got dry, you know, the wood would shrink, and off would come the head, and we'd put them back together with glue. But in summer it stays light until 10:30 or eleven o'clock, so it was nothing to play two rounds of golf beginning at six o'clock at night. As kids you do that. I played four rounds of golf in a day sometimes, when I was a boy, carrying my own bag.

Of course, you only had six clubs in those days. You learned to play with a driver, a spoon, a mid-iron, which is equivalent to a two-iron, a mashie-niblick, which is like a seven-iron, a niblick, and a putter. You learned to do a lot of things with each club. You could play bunker shots, sometimes, with your driver. That's why in those days there were better shotmakers. You had to be. Now we have an entirely different game. Today it's computer golf, as I call it. Everything is perfect and spelled out; yardage on sprinkler heads, and stuff like that.

My Uncle Frank came to America and was a pro at the East Lake club in Atlanta, where Bob Jones was a member. In the meantime I met Jones in England in 1930 when he was making his Grand Slam; I was the youngest competitor in the British Open that year—I was twenty. Well, talking to Jones there, and my uncle being the pro at his club, Bob said to me, "You have a good opportunity, and I like the way you swing." So in 1930 I came over to the States as an assistant to my uncle at East Lake.

When I first came over they hadn't gotten into steel shafts yet, and Monday morning in Atlanta we'd have a lot of broken shafts. Some were broken accidentally, some were from those hot Georgians throwing them. We spent all Monday reshafting clubs. It was a tough day, but the shafts cost us fifty cents and we'd charge $3, so that was a pretty good profit. At least in those days it sounded like an awful lot. I had to string Jones' putter a few times, too. He had a temper, you know. Poof! and the shaft would split down at the head. I'd put in a new shaft and he'd go out and putt with it, but if he had an important match we'd have to put the old shaft back. The old shaft had a lot of torque in it. That's how delicate his stroke was. He was a beautiful putter.

The first golf lesson I ever gave was in Atlanta. I didn't give any in England, because they thought I was too young. Since I'd been there all my young life, they always thought of me as a little boy, even when I got up to nineteen years old. So my first lesson was in Atlanta, a lady whose name I've forgotten. I didn't have any particular idea of what I wanted to do with her, so I fell into the trick of using the left side, because everyone was beginning to get more left-side-conscious then. But the time it was scariest was in North Carolina. Bob Jones was a little off his game and was hitting wood shots to the first green of this course, Highland, and he said, "Errie, come on down and see what I'm doing wrong." Well, his swing, even when he was just half hitting them, was beautiful, but I thought I had to say something. I couldn't act like a damn dummy. So I stood behind him and to the side of him, and I finally said, "Bob, you're letting go with your left hand." He had control of it in the fingers, but he'd let go of it otherwise. He said, "But, Errie, I've always done that, because I like to feel the clubhead." See, the clubhead would kind of tug on his wrists and he'd kind of open up the hand. When he regripped, the clubhead would fall into perfect position coming down.

Well, I told him that was all I could see, and he said I was very observant. His tempo was off, is all. That's usually what it is with anyone who can swing a club. Tempo. That was a scary lesson.

I never played with Jones during the height of his career, but I played with him quite a lot in North Carolina right after he made his Slam. And I watched him play in the first Masters, but by then he wasn't nearly the player he had been. He retired in 1930 and the first Masters was in 1934, and it was surprising what a difference that four-year period made in his game.

For a kid, I was an especially good player. They said I was, anyway, and in 1931, my first full year in America, I won the Southeastern PGA championship, which in those days was a fairly big tournament. I beat Henry Picard, Tony Manero, Toney Penna. And I remember Johnny Bulla who was too young to play in the tournament, congratulating me and asking me what I had done to win. He was looking for technique. I was only a young kid, and I ended up more or less talking down to him and trying to encourage him.

My father helped me with my game, when I was five years of age. My father had a fine swing, so I copied him, and then I was fortunate to play a lot with Jones in North Carolina, and to be able to play with the other big players of those years. So I had good instruction as a youngster.

Winning the tournament in 1931 was awfully good for me, because it gave me a lot of publicity, a lot of write-ups—this young kid coming from England and beating the American pros. You know, there hadn't been any English players who had done that in a long while, certainly not at my age. Winning that tournament set me up. It could have been difficult, otherwise, but doors opened up for me. I had a lot of friends, like Charlie Yates, who was a U.S. Amateur champion, and, of course, Jones, who wrote beautiful letters of recommendation for me. Having a real British accent also helped a lot in those days. I believe my prize for winning that tournament was $150, but it was worth far more to me in terms of opportunities.

Errie Ball

I got my first head-pro job at twenty-one, at the Mobile Country Club in Alabama, and in 1936 I took a freighter from there to go over and play in the British Open. It was the first time I'd been back home since coming away. It was a four-passenger ship of the Waterman Steamship Line, and it took me two weeks and cost me $80. The Open that year was at Hoylake, right at home, and I played pretty well. I think I finished tied for eighth. On the *Anconia*, a big ship, coming back, I met my wife. When I got back I qualified for the PGA championship, played at Pinehurst. I won my first match, then Bobby Cruickshank beat me on the nineteenth hole of the second round. But from that match I got the pro job at Farmington Country Club in Virginia. My wife was from Richmond, Virginia, Cruickshank was then pro at the Country Club of Virginia, in Richmond, so that combination and Bobby having a hard time beating me gave me a boost. He knew the Farmington job was open and suggested I apply for it. And Bob Jones called there for me. So I was there until the start of World War II.

I had had about 100 hours in the air as a flight instructor while at Farmington, and I knew the war was coming on, so I tried to get into something. I was an American citizen for seven years at that time, but you had to be a citizen eight years to get a commission, so I ended up teaching aerology and navigation at the University of Virginia for about a year and a half. Then the Navy drafted me. The Navy was a lot of fun for me. I was stationed at the Board of Trade Building in downtown Chicago. I was a Seaman Third Class, and the Lieutenant Commander was Harry Kipke, an all-American football player from Michigan. He found out I was a golf pro, and he was a pretty good player himself, so we played a good bit. Through him I got on the staff of Admiral Hardison, a dead-ringer for Chick Evans and a pretty good golfer—74, 75 shooter—who was stationed at the Glenview Naval Air Station. After the war I stayed in the Chicago area. I became head pro at the Oak Park Country Club and was there for quite a lot of summers.

I played the tour from 1936 until the start of the war— the winter tour—and then for a few years after, but I'd have to say I was primarily a teaching pro. I was not too good a merchandiser, but I always had people in there who could do that. That part of the profession I didn't care for much at all.

Teaching methods have improved since I began, but only because of the videotapes we have now. Otherwise, I don't think teaching itself has improved much over the past 100 years. You read some of those old books and they're just as good as today's. Take Percy Boomer's book. There's one of the greatest ever written, because Boomer dwells with the mental part of it, and mostly on feel. How you should take the mechanics or mathematics out of the game, stop thinking and go to feel and tempo. The science of the swing is very small, but developing muscle memory, that's what it is. As Boomer says, it's like the boxer who's out on his feet but is still boxing from memory. You should be able to do that with the golf swing, even though you're sometimes befuddled or something's upset you. You should still be able to retain that feel. Boomer's fundamentals were very simple and up to date, and that book [*On Learning Golf*] must go back forty years.

Feel, that's what I teach. For instance, the other day . . . it just shows you how it all comes back . . . I had a man on the lesson tee, a pretty good player, but all he could do was use the upper part of his body—an arms-and-shoulders swing. I told him he wasn't using his legs, so he tried it but couldn't do it, and when he did, it was all wrong. I told him the best way to get it was to put his feet very close together and think he's swinging in a waist-high barrel. Right away he felt his feet and legs and hips working. It worked. God, he was all over me; I was the greatest pro he'd ever seen. Well, it's as old as the hills. My father told me that a long time ago. It sounds simple, put your feet close together, but it's like a drill. It makes you aware of your feet and legs and hips working. I'm teaching him feel, and that's the only way you can teach. It's hard, but that's what you do. I don't think you can teach a set way of playing. I think you have to have the correct grip and address positions, but that's all fundamentals.

I think I've been very successful in the golf business, but I'm disappointed I didn't become a more successful player. I would have liked to have been much better. I may have been a little too small, so my timing had to be absolutely perfect, although I could hit it up with most of them when I was younger. I came close in several big tournaments and I won a lot of sectional events—the Illinois PGA and Open, the Arizona Open. I played in all the big tournaments, but I was just one of those who missed.

The putting became a factor, and it all started at that Masters in 1934. Then I hit the time I thought I was going to do well, and was doing well, playing a lot of good rounds and finishing well up on the tour in 1938 and '39. But the war came and broke up the game in the prime of my life, you might say.

Then I got scared that I might win one, you know. Funny thing. I tried so hard that I got scared I would win. I think Nelson and Snead and those felt it, too. How did they overcome it? I think Nelson had, like Percy Boomer said, this instinct of the fighter who is knocked out but keeps swinging. Hogan blocked out everything so he didn't know anybody was around, so I know he was feeling his swing. He knew exactly what he was doing. And Snead had that natural swing, so he could go. You could easily see the players with faulty swings, and how that would be magnified under pressure. It must have done it for me, too. I must have had some faults in it somewhere. Something happened.

I don't know. I think it's a matter of you wanting it so bad, but I didn't quite do it. A lot of people won that I thought I could beat any day. But they came back with a title and here I was either runner-up or finishing out of the money or missing the cut. All the people who I thought were great always thought my swing was probably as good as anybody's. They would say, "You've got this damn swing, why don't you do something with it?" But I never got the best out of it. It wasn't that I was too busy trying to make a living. It just didn't work.

Errie Ball

Errie Ball's given name is Samuel Henry, but he has gone by the nickname of Errie, pronounced Erie, all his life. He signs all his official documents as Samuel H., but says if someone were to call him Sam he wouldn't even turn around. However, when he's played badly he does consider going by the name of Sam.

During the summer months Errie is Golf Professional Emeritus at the Butler National Golf Club, outside Chicago, and during the winter he is Golf Director at the Stuart Yacht and Country Club, Stuart, Florida.

BETSY RAWLS

The players in the 1954 Triangle Round Robin, sponsored by the Triangle Conduit & Pipe Co., and played at the Cascades course of the Homestead, in Hot Springs, Virginia. From left to right, top row: Betty Jameson, Jackie Pung, Betty McKinnon, Betty Hicks, Marilynn Smith; middle row: Patty Berg, Beverly Hanson, Louise Suggs, Babe Zaharias, Betty Dodd; bottom row: Fay Crocker, Marlene Hagge, Mary Lena Faulk, Betty Bush, Alice Bauer, Marlene Stewart Streit, Betsy Rawls.

Photograph by Al Barkow

"You don't have the responsibilities people have in the real world."

My father was the only one in my family who played golf, and he taught me the basics. Then I started taking lessons from Harvey Penick at the Austin Country Club when I was in college at the University of Texas. For my first lesson Harvey charged me $3. Even then that wasn't a lot, but Harvey never charged a lot, so it wasn't because he knew me or anything like that. Anyway, I stayed out there with him for about an hour and a half. The next time I went out to him, when I got ready to pay he said, "No, I'm just telling you things I told you last week," and he never let me pay him again. I got a lot of mileage out of that first $3. I took lessons from Harvey for twenty years. He's the only teacher I ever had, and I owe a great deal of my success as a player to him, just as Ben Crenshaw, Tom Kite, and a lot of others do.

It didn't take me too long to become a good player, and one reason, I think, is because I started a little later than most—at seventeen. I think you can do it easier at that age than at twelve or thirteen, because you're more mature and stronger. Also, I always thought well on the course. I was a good student. Phi Beta Kappa. I studied a lot, and that helped my concentration. Maybe it helps to have a very controlled, logical sort of mind to play golf. I studied physics in college, and my father was an engineer. Maybe there's something to

215

that. Of course, you also have to just play a lot when you're young. You have to pay those dues. When I was in college it was hard to play much, because I had a lot of math. In summer, though, I played just about every day, round and round and round.

There is always the problem of women athletes being taken as tomboys, as being too masculine. But when I started out I can't remember there being any kind of stigma attached to women athletes in Texas, at least not to women golfers. You see, golfers weren't that way, much. Most of them I ran into were at country clubs and from the upper classes, so to speak, and knew how to behave. So that didn't seem much of a problem. Eventually I was given a membership at Austin Country Club, but at the start I played golf. I played with the boys except in tournaments, carried my own bag, did a little gambling—skin games, you know—and held my own. It was fun.

Maybe we weren't socially conscious back then. Of course, women golfers are different in that they wear skirts—*we* did, anyhow—and golf is not that physical a game; you don't have to be very muscular or big. If you watched women's basketball you'd get a much different impression of women athletes. A lot of women golfers are small and feminine-looking. So we never really fought that battle. We were always conscious of needing to dress properly and look and act ladylike, and we always did.

The feminist movement never really touched the women's tour, we were all just totally unaware of it. I think that's because we were so involved in playing golf and winning tournaments. We weren't interested in furthering women's rights. We felt we had everything, and nothing to prove. We had a golden opportunity to go out there and make money if we played well. We were treated well, and had nothing to gain from the women's movement, so consequently we pretty much ignored it.

I didn't pattern my swing after anyone in particular, because for quite some time after I started I never saw a real good player, man or woman. The first good player I ever saw was Byron Nelson, in an exhibition in Fort Worth. I was absolutely amazed. I had no idea golf could be played that way, that people could hit the ball so far. I was so green. At the first tournament I entered, the Women's Texas Open, at the Colonial Country Club—imagine playing your first tournament at Colonial? Good Lord!—I didn't know anything. I didn't know people had shag bags and warmed up before they played. I came from a little town in Texas. Arlington was pretty small then, and I had never even *seen* a golf tournament before. I just went out and played, and that was it.

Anyway, I qualified for the championship flight and won my first match. But I lost my second match, to Dot Kiltie. She was runner-up once in the Women's U.S. Amateur. Then I lost in the first round of the consolation matches. I did pretty well for my first tournament ever, but I was *so* mad that I lost. I just hated losing. After that is when I really started working on it. I gathered together some practice balls and went at it. Once you play in a tournament, you get hooked on that.

I played amateur golf for only about two and a half years, because I turned pro in 1950. Wilson Sporting Goods asked me to join their staff. They had Patty Berg and Babe Zaharias, and needed someone else to do clinics and play exhibitions. I considered the offer carefully and decided that golf would be more interesting than physics. I played professional golf for almost twenty-five years, and was in on the beginnings of the Ladies Professional Golf Association. The LPGA got started in 1950, and Wilson hired Freddie Corcoran to be tournament director. Wilson needed places for Patty and Babe to play. Eventually, MacGregor and Spalding, the other two major equipment manufacturers at the time, joined Wilson to help pay Freddie's salary. Fred booked tournaments, but that's all he really did; none of the promotional stunts he was known for when he ran the men's tour. We handled the day-to-day operation of our tour, did it all, and it was a kind of interesting situation. One of us kept the books and wrote out the checks, someone else did all the correspondence. I look back and can remember making rulings on other players in a tournament I was competing in. In this day and time, good gracious, you'd probably get sued for something like that.

We didn't have any staff, because we couldn't afford to hire people. That was the situation for a long time. I mean, the average purse in our tournaments was $3,000, perhaps $4,000— total. Five thousand was a good tournament in the early 1950s.

Can you imagine that? But, you know, it didn't seem like a small amount. It was fine for us. We were happy to get that much, and didn't mind that the men pros were getting so much more for their tournaments. You see, we didn't compare ourselves to men pros, or expect as much.

How do I account for that feeling? I guess the men are more spectacular. They hit the ball farther, score better, are just better players because of their strength. It's simply a matter of strength. I think that's the only way they differ. Then, again, we could have our moments. One year six of us women pros were in England and played the British Walker Cup team, the country's best men amateurs. We beat them, and, oh, it was a black day in England for them! We played doubles in the morning and were behind by one point, but in the afternoon singles every woman won her match. We had Babe, Patty Berg, myself, Betty Jameson, Peggy Kirk, and Betty Bush. Well, those men were just stricken. They just couldn't believe it. We played at Wentworth, the "Burma Road" course, and from the same tees as the men—about in the middle of the members' men's tees. It was the funniest thing. The press made a big thing about it.

On our circuit at home, in the early days, we drove almost everyplace. We didn't have as many tournaments as they have now, so we didn't play every week. I got my own car my second year on the tour, a Cadillac, which everyone drove because of its weight and room for clubs and baggage. We would travel two in a car, and caravan. Caravaning was following each other on the road, usually two cars. It was fun. I got to see the country. We drove across the United States at least twice a year, and did a lot of sightseeing. Driving through the Rockies, we'd stop and have picnics. I know if I were starting out now I would never see the country, because I would fly everyplace. I would see the golf course, the hotel, the airport, and that's it. So today's players miss a lot, I think, by not driving. Of course, it's impractical to drive now, but I'm glad we did it.

In the beginning a woman could get on the tour by just showing up. She would apply to join the LPGA and come out and play. She was either good enough to stay on tour or she wasn't. Money was the only limiting factor. If she ran out, she had to go get some more or not play. People didn't turn pro back then unless they were good players, because the only appeal was golf. Nowadays there are other things that appeal to players—the life, the exposure, the endorsements, being on television. In the early days you just made out from the purse money, and the only reason you did it was because you loved to play golf.

When I first turned pro, there were only fifteen people playing our tour regularly. Then it went to about twenty, and gradually built up. Now, almost every good amateur turns pro. And back then the galleries weren't that big. But we didn't worry about that too much. We thought of the tour as more of a competition than a show. We thought of it as playing a tournament and producing a winner. The first prize would usually be around $1,000. We all decided at one of our meetings how much the winner would get, and then break down the remaining money places. There was no particular formula for that. I must have made up a hundred formulas over the years. We just figured what percentage of the total purse we wanted to give first place—it was usually fifteen percent—then go from there. It was an unwieldy process sometimes, because there were people who felt strongly about certain issues. Anytime you talked about money there would be vehement discussions. But, to everyone's credit, I can't think of any wrong decisions that were made.

We had some tournament sponsors in the first years who were kind of patrons and saw us through. The first was Alvin Handmacher, who made Weathervane suits for women. The next big one was Sears, Roebuck. But most of the tournaments were sponsored by local organizations, the Lions Club or Chamber of Commerce. They could afford to put one on because the prize money was low and it was nice for the community.

We had some sponsors who reneged on the prize money. There was one in Oklahoma City, I remember, but it wasn't Waco Turner. He had plenty of money and we never had anything to worry about with Waco. He put on two or three tournaments for us. He built his own course in Burneyville, Oklahoma, out in the wilderness. The course was so new when we played there the first time, and so badly built. I remember Bob Hagge and some other guy who was on tour with us went out to cut the cups, and the greens were so hard they couldn't get them cut. They had to hammer them out. So they didn't change the cups for the rest of the week. That was when Waco was paying so much for every birdie and eagle you made, and I remember having a good week. I won the tournament and made two or three eagles, which were worth $500 apiece. I walked away with all kinds of money.

Then there was Tam O'Shanter in Chicago, George S. May's tournament. That was the biggest event on our tour, the biggest purse we played for. It was very exciting, because you got to see everybody in the whole world, the whole golf world at least. There was a tournament for men and women pros and men and women amateurs. Four tournaments at once. It was quite a phenomenon. It's hard to find a tournament to compare with Tam O'Shanter in excitement. Everybody in the game was there, the money was terrific, the clubhouse facilities were special, and there were the biggest crowds. People came out and had picnics in the rough. First time I ever saw that. And it was fun to see all the top men pros and amateurs, and foreign players. I watched Sam Snead and Ben Hogan and other great men players. But I didn't get much of lasting value from their swings that I could use in mine.

The strength of my game was the short game. I could really scramble well, manufacture shots, play out of difficult situations. I always got a kick out of that. Driving was my weakest part, and whenever I did drive well I won tournaments. But nobody is ever going to be better than Mickey Wright.

Mickey was much better than Babe Zaharias. No comparison. Babe was stronger, any maybe a better athlete—she was so well coordinated—but Mickey had a better golf swing, hit the ball better, could play rings around Babe. See, I think Babe got started in golf too late. She didn't really take it up until she was past thirty. If she had started as a kid, the way Mickey did, maybe nobody would ever have beaten her. She was just that good an athlete. And Babe loved to win. Or she hated to lose is the better way to put it. She was absolutely the worst loser I ever saw. She wasn't a bad sportsman, but if things didn't go her way she could show her displeasure. She didn't like it when people crossed her. I guess that's often the way with great athletes.

The sponsors made all the decisions about running their tournaments in the early days, and I must say they were greatly influenced by Babe Zaharias. And Babe was not above saying she would drop out of a tournament if this or that wasn't done. She knew how much they really needed her, and they did. She was the draw, really. For instance, back in '51 we were playing someplace and Babe was leading the tournament. Patty Berg was second. They were paired together for the last round, in the last group, and Babe started out horrendously. So Patty caught her and passed her. Then it started raining. They were near the clubhouse at the time and Babe marched in there and told the sponsors it was raining and she wanted the round canceled. And they did it. They rescheduled for the next day. It wasn't even close to being rained out, or the course being unplayable. Well, Patty was absolutely furious, just livid. But Patty beat Babe the next day anyway. Played rings around her.

But I loved Babe. She was good to play with, fun to be around. She was very witty and kept the gallery laughing all the time. Wisecracks all the way around. Very uninhibited. She was a little crude, and some things she said shocked me a little because I was just the opposite, but the gallery loved her. There will never be another like her.

Sometimes we resented Babe for the way she was in cases like that rain-out. I didn't admire her tactics then, but I never really got angry at her. She was just that way. The thing I objected to more was that we had no control over sponsors being influenced in that way, that they could do whatever they pretty much pleased. I think the sponsors treated us in such a high-handed way for two reasons: because we were women, and because we weren't that big a draw and needed them more than they needed us. They felt they were doing us a favor, and didn't look upon us as great athletes. It was just a matter of having a nice little tournament; fun having the girls come to town, I guess. I didn't have a big problem living with that sort of thing, though, mainly because there was nothing to compare it with. If we had been able to look into the future and see how tournaments would be run and what kind of control the organization would have, I'm sure we would have been appalled. But back then we didn't know any differently. We had our hand out, and couldn't be too demanding.

In those early years the local greens superintendent or pro would set the cups and tee markers, and as a result we played tough courses. We would never play a ladies' tee. It was generally from the middle or the back of the men's tees. They just couldn't stand it for the women to score well on their courses. We played some monstrous courses, much longer than they play now. And pin placements were tough. But nobody ever thought of complaining. There was nothing wrong with long courses; everybody had to play them. It was when we got so concerned with our public image and the scores in the newspapers that we became concerned with long courses. But back then it didn't matter if you shot a 75, so long as you won the tournament.

But I remember Patty Berg shooting 64 at the Richmond Country Club in California—a tough course. I was playing with her, and to this day it may be the best round of golf I've ever seen played. Now the players come close to shooting 64, but on courses that were nothing like those we played in the early years. Those courses averaged 6,400 yards. Then, again, I didn't want any shorter courses. Mickey and Babe had an advantage on them, and so did I, although Mickey would have won on any golf course, any length. Anyway, the cream really came to the top on a 6,400-yard course. You just had to have a good swing to play it, or you'd have a 90.

In the early days there was not much of a future for women pros in golf after tournament life. There were very few if any club jobs available. But I don't think the really good players ever thought that far ahead. Patty Berg, Louise Suggs, myself, we had contracts with Wilson and MacGregor and had clubs made with our names on them, so we didn't have to worry too much. But when you got past the first five, it was a problem. I don't know that any of them were prepared for living without tournament golf. When you're playing the tournament circuit you think you'll always play and there will never come a time when you will have to do something else, quit and go to work. People become addicted to it. It's a very protected kind of existence. You don't have the responsibilities people have in the real world. You go from place to place, and nowadays sponsors take care of all your needs—they meet you at airports, provide so many services. You don't have to make beds, do wash, and such mundane things. People hate to give that up, even players who aren't having a lot of success, and I'm afraid a lot of them don't prepare for life after tournament golf. I had a lot of success, and can't imagine anyone staying out there as long as I did without winning.

It was a shock for me to quit the tour. I had withdrawal symptoms. It was traumatic. But that was mainly in making the decision to quit. Once I did it, I got so involved in the work of a tournament director that it never bothered me at all.

Now it's much easier for women to get club-professional jobs. They are in great demand. More women golfers want to take lessons from women pros. I get a lot of offers to take a teaching job. Women pros are admired now. The women's movement probably has something to do with that, and being on television. Women pros are admired now.

I won fifty-five tournaments as a professional. I won ten of them in 1959, and won a little over $26,000. But I don't feel any resentment at the amount of money the girls are playing for now. That's not why I played, for the money. If it was a lot of money I was after, I probably would have done something else. I thoroughly enjoyed playing and got a lot of satisfaction out of it. I take pride in being a pioneer that helped make today's tour possible.

Betsy Rawls is a member of the LPGA Hall of Fame. She won a total of fifty-five tournaments, her last one in 1972. After serving six years as the LPGA's Tournament Director, she left the position to become executive director for the McDonald's Championship, an LPGA event played annually at the White Meadow Country Club in Malvern, Pennsylvania. Betsy lives in the neighborhood, which is just outside Philadelphia.

BILL SPILLER

Photograph by Al Barkow

"I stuck my neck out, and it destroyed my career."

I was born in 1913 in Tishomingo, Oklahoma, a little town. I lived with my grandmother in Tishomingo until I was nine, then I went to Tulsa, where my father was living, to go to elementary school and high school. They were all-black schools. Everything was separated in those days. Actually, my great-grandmother was a full-blooded Cherokee, and I've got a little bit of everything in me. Which is why I can't understand people getting hung up on race. Anyway, I was a star on the track and basketball teams in high school, then I went to Wiley College, an all-black school in Marshall, Texas. I studied education and sociology, to be a teacher. I ran in three national black championships while I was at Wiley. When I finished there I tried to get a job—I have a degree and a state permit certificate out of the State of Texas—but the best I could get was a rural school at $60 a month. I said I could do better than that in a pool hall. I could shoot pool. My mother was living in Los Angeles, so I went there. That was in 1938. I looked around for a job for eight months, and then the railroad station opened up. I had my application in there, and they gave me a job as a redcap. That's when I got stuck up in the golf game.

I'd played a little golf before. In 1931 my father was working at the Hillcrest Country Club in Bartlesville, Oklahoma, and he had me come up there to work. They sent me to the

225

locker room to shine shoes and bootleg whiskey. When I was there my father took me out to play five holes. I was a baseball player, and I said, "Shoot, I can hit a baseball over the center-field wall, so I know I can hit this golf ball nine miles." I swung eight times before I finally hit the ball, and it went ten feet. I said, "This is not for me." Oh, and I hit two golf balls on the campus at Wiley, with an iron. So I'd say I started in golf from scratch when I was twenty-nine years old. In December 1942.

The workers at the railroad station were always doing some kind of gambling. We played pool and cards, shot dice, bet the day's ballgames. One day one of the guys says to me, "You can beat me playing pool, but you can't beat me playing golf." Well, I had that attitude most people have who don't grow up in golf, I said I wasn't going to chase a little ball around, hit it, then go chase it again. But on Christmas Eve, 1942, this fella said he wished he had somebody to play golf with, and I said I'd go with him. He gave me a stroke a hole. In two weeks he was giving me two strokes on nine holes, and in a month I was playing even. That got me started.

We played at Sunset Fields, which is where I played my first tournament, the Southern California Open. I played in the five-to-seven Handicap Division and was tied at the end of the tournament with Bill Chase, a policeman. I beat him in the playoff. So I ended up winning the first tournament I ever played in. Won a $75 War Bond.

Then the L.A. Open came, at Wilshire Country Club. I thought I was a player and put in my entry to qualify. I missed, but I got a ticket to see the tournament and the first thing I said to myself when I saw those guys hit the ball was that I was sure glad I didn't qualify. I would have been embarrassed to tears out there. What would I be doing out there with my little old slice? I had never seen any players like that. I was carried away with Toney Penna's irons, the way he hit them. Johnny Bulla was one of my favorite drivers. And Byron Nelson. I bought a Byron Nelson book, and some other books, and would get under a tree and read something, then go practice it, read some more, practice it. By 1946 I had won all the black tournaments in southern California. That's when I met Teddy Rhodes.

Bill Spiller

Teddy came out to California with Joe Louis. Joe made him his pro. Teddy'd been a caddie in Nashville and around, so he'd been playing much longer than me, but I could beat him; he was long, but wild. But Joe gave Paul Mangrum $5 a lesson to teach Teddy. He must have given him 100 lessons. I'd pick Teddy up to take him to his lesson and stand over on the side and listen and learn what I could.

This was also at Sunset Fields, which was a public course. There never had been any restrictions on blacks at public courses in Los Angeles. There was resentment, though. Like one time I qualified for the first flight of the Los Angeles City championship and a newspaperman asked me what club I belonged to. I said I didn't belong to any, but played most of my golf at Sunset Fields. So he put in the paper that Bill Spiller of Sunset Fields qualified for the tournament. Next time I'm at Sunset this white guy walks up to me and says, "I see you put your name in as a Sunsetter. Well, you're not a Sunsetter, and you never will be." Actually, I didn't know what he was talking about, because I wasn't that much up on the game at the time. But I knew it wasn't what I was liking, the way he was talking to me. So I said, "Oh yes, I know that you won't allow colored people to belong here—to the men's club—but I'll tell you something. Two years ago I would have knocked you down and put my foot in your face for talking to me like that." Well, he got away from me. Then, in 1948, when I shot 68 at the Riviera Country Club in the L.A. Open, he was the first one to come up to shake my hand. Shows you how people change once you become a success. As long as you're hanging down there by yourself . . . That's the reason it's so hard for us.

Another time, years later, I was qualifying for the U.S. Open at the Bel-Air Country Club in Los Angeles. I'm in the locker room putting on my shoes and Fred Astaire walks in and gives me a stare as if to say, "What the hell are you doing here?" If eyes could kill, I would have died right there. But I looked right back at him, didn't bat an eye. He finally said, "Well, I guess maybe you're supposed to be here."

I had somewhat dedicated my life to do anything I could to help my people. I hated prejudice with a passion, because I

227

was brought up the wrong way, so to speak. I was slapped by a white man in a department store when I was twelve, because I wanted to bring something back that I bought. He wouldn't accept it and said I spoke out of turn. I knew if I told my father he would go down and probably get killed, so I strapped a gun on and carried it until I was a junior in college. I said, "The next guy who puts his hands on me is going to look down this barrel." It didn't set me off to the extent that I hated anybody, I just wanted what was coming to me. I went to school to get an education and was entitled to the good things in life just like anyone else.

I think the fact that I was a good athlete before had something to do with my getting pretty good at golf, even though I started pretty late. I'm an athlete all the way down. I also beat the gun on a lot of black players by working three and a half months at the Los Angeles Country Club, on the grill and waiting tables, so I could play there on Monday and Thursday mornings. I got experience playing country-club courses, which are different—longer, narrower, more sand traps and hazards.

There were white pros that helped us, and me. I'll tell you who was friendly with us, Sam Snead. I didn't expect that, he being a hillbilly. But, you see, he loved Joe Louis. Then there was a time I was teaching a gambler to play golf, a white man, and he took me to Phoenix to give him some lessons. How I got in the hotel, he went in and got the room and I would get on the floor in the back of the car and we would drive into the carport. Then I would go up into the room. He felt kind of concerned about that, but I told him not to worry about me. Anyway, one day I was down to the golf course giving him a lesson and started hitting balls myself, and here comes Lawson Little and Jimmy Demaret. "Bill Spiller, what are you doing over here?" they asked me. I think they thought I was going to start something, because this was after the time in Oakland, which I'll tell about. I said I was just giving some lessons to a friend, then Lawson said, "You sure do have a good golf swing," and I told him thank you but I can't get any punch into the ball. I wasn't getting any distance. He said I was trying to hit the ball like Byron Nelson, and he was right. I thought

228

Byron Nelson was the greatest golfer who ever lived. "You have to hit it like Hogan," Lawson said. "Byron has great big wrists and can take that short swing." He went on to give me a lesson, and I started hitting the ball longer. After that, whenever we ran into each other, Little would give me some pointers. But one day he told me, "You know, I like you and Teddy, and I'd do anything to help you get your game down, but I'll tell you one thing, I'm still from Tennessee." What he was saying was no mixing off the golf course.

That kind of thing happened other times, and it could shake you up. Like when I was trying to get a PGA membership. There was the issue of getting my application on the agenda at a national meeting. A California pro said he'd bring it up. He never did, but some guy from Mississippi did. He said, "I've had a black boy working for me for fifteen years, and he's good. I wouldn't vote for him to have a PGA card, but he's entitled to it."

When I was getting into golf we couldn't belong to white clubs, or even the men's clubs at public courses, because they were organized by whites. So we couldn't get an official handicap to make us eligible for USGA tournaments like the Publinx and National Amateur. We didn't bar white pros when they entered our tournaments, though. There was one white guy, Dave something, would finish second or third and pick up $300, $400 every week. The big names didn't play, except Al Besselink; he was maybe the biggest name. He won our national championship once. We had an association, the United Golf Association.

Before 1948 the only time we played against whites was in the Los Angeles Open, and at Tam O'Shanter in Chicago, which was a special occasion. George S. May was the promoter of that tournament, and he was a wonderful man. There was a tournament Byron Nelson won in Chicago, at Westward Ho. Blacks couldn't play, and Mr. May was out there and said to some black players that if they could qualify for his tournament they could play and win as much as they could. This was in the '40s. So in 1946 I won the Joe Louis Amateur, in Detroit, and was given $150 to play at Tam O'Shanter. I failed to qualify, and George May said he was sorry I missed but he would have his daughter take me to lunch in the clubhouse. She was a very attractive blonde girl. While we're having lunch a kid tapped me on the shoulder and asked for my autograph. I said, "Mine?" and he said, "You played in the tournament, didn't you? Well, I want your autograph." Then I noticed there were about twenty kids lined up. Shows you the difference in how generations react. Kids have no prejudice. That was a good lesson for me.

So we mostly played the black pro tour. I turned pro in '47 and that year played about fourteen tournaments. I didn't know there were so many good black players until I went east for the first time. I would tee it up against anybody, and it cost me $1,500 to find out they could play. Teddy was the best black player of my time—we called him Rags because he was a sharp dresser—and there was Howard Wheeler, Zeke Hartsfield. John Dendy, from Virginia, had a beautiful swing, and Chink Stewart. It was rough, the traveling, and you could just make expenses. If you won, you got $1,000, but second was only $350 or $250. And we had to buy our own equipment, until I spoke with Bob Rickey from MacGregor. When I was in Cincinnati once I went to the MacGregor factory to get me some woods made up. Bob Rickey was in the front office at the time and he asked me if anybody was giving me any clubs. I said no, so he told the guy to fit me up with what I wanted—irons, woods, bag, balls, shoes. Everything. He said, "You don't ever have to buy clubs anymore. Just send a letter and tell us what you want." Then the Wilson company started giving Teddy his equipment.

What happened in Oakland was, in the 1948 L.A. Open me and Teddy shot low enough to finish in the top sixty. According to the tour's system, that automatically qualified us to play in the next tournament, up in Richmond [outside Oakland]. So we go up there and play a couple of practice rounds with Paul O'Leary and Smiley Quick, and afterwards, in the bar, George Schneiter comes over and says he wants to talk to me. He was head of the Tournament Players Bureau at the time. He comes out with, "There are rules and regulations which govern all organizations and our organization is going by the rules." So I said, "Mr. Schneiter, I'm a college graduate. I understand English. If you want to say something to me, say it. I'll understand you." So he says something about having nothing against us fellows personally, but the PGA bylaws say so-and-so, and this was the first time I got to see the PGA bylaws. It said in there that membership was for Caucasians only. I said it doesn't say Caucasians had to qualify for the tournament. He said he was sorry, there was nothing he could do.

So I told Teddy, "Come on, let's get out of here, I know somebody who can help us." A man named Johnny Merrin, who I had run against in college, had a delicatessen in Berkeley. I told him I was coming by and had some talking for him; something I wanted him to do. When I explained what happened, that they weren't going to let us play, he called Ira Blue of ABC Sports. Blue put it on the air that night, on radio all over the country, and he blasted it. Then he contacted attorney John Rowell, from Redwood City, who'd handled a discrimination case in housing. He said he would take the case, no charge. Then I invited all the newspaper and radio men I could up to my hotel. I spent $150 on liquor, beer, and sandwiches so they'd be happy. We all deliberated and decided we'd hit them where it counted, in the pocketbook, and we announced we were filing a $250,000 suit against the PGA— me, Teddy, and Madison Gunter, a local black player. He qualified up there, but they wouldn't let him play.

So we went back to L.A. We never did play in Richmond. Six weeks later Rowell comes down on the train to meet us before going to court, and says that on the train he met the PGA attorney and they worked out a deal where the PGA promised it would not discriminate against blacks if we dropped the suit. Rowell said that would be okay. So we dropped the suit, but the PGA started calling its tournaments Invitationals instead of Opens so they could keep blacks out.

The action we took in Oakland didn't seem to do any good, because we didn't get to play the white tour for the next few years. But it did what I went out to do in the first place: make the public aware of the situation. I always said our salvation would be public opinion, because most people are primarily good people. I still believe that, because I've seen them do an about-face after they met me even though they didn't like me because I was a rebel.

Where it started to open up for us was at San Diego in 1953. What happened was, the San Diego tournament was a charity event and supposedly not under PGA auspices. They invited Joe Louis to play in it, as an amateur, and Joe said he would. Well, a week or so before that Teddy and I were playing in the Southern California Open over at Rancho Santa Fe and the pro invited us to try to qualify at San Diego. I qualified with 152 for thirty-six holes, playing them all in the rain. Teddy also qualified. Well, as the tournament was getting closer, there seemed to be no problem. I was assigned a locker and a caddie. Then the PGA came in and said we couldn't play, including Joe Louis. I remember Joe saying, "If you think I can't play, listen to Walter Winchell on Sunday night." Joe called Winchell and told him what was happening, and Winchell went on his radio show and said something about if Joe Louis could carry a gun in the U.S. Army he could carry a golf club in San Diego.

Well, Horton Smith was the big wheel at the PGA at the time, and he called a meeting there in San Diego with Joe, his friend Leonard Reed, and Euell Clark, a black and a good amateur player. That Horton Smith, he could talk a hole in your head, and he started this meeting without me. See, I was the guy doing all the rebelling and I think they didn't know how to talk to me because I wasn't a yes man. The fact that I was more educated may have had something to do with it, too. Also, I had right on my side. It wasn't just a bulldogger's situation.

Then Jimmy Demaret came out of the room and said to me, "Bill, you better come on in, they're having the meeting without you." See, Jimmy said to me earlier that week they should change things and that he was going to tell Horton Smith that we could bypass the states that weren't liberal instead of causing all this fuss, because, he said, "You fellas aren't going to Mississippi or Alabama anyway." I said he was right. I always appreciated Jimmy's attitude. So I go into the room and Horton Smith says, "You're Bill Spiller, aren't you?" I said I was and he asked if there was something I wanted to say. I said, "I know and you know that we're going to play in the tournaments. We all know it's coming. So if you like golf like you say you do, and I do, I think we should make an agreement so we can play without all this adverse publicity. And take this Caucasians-only clause out so we can have opportunities to get jobs as pros at clubs." I went on about how the PGA has a job-placement service and only PGA members are appointed to jobs and I would like to get one of those jobs. So Horton Smith says, "Yeah, we've got a job-placement service, but golf is social and semi-social and we have to be careful who we put on the job." So I said, "Mr. Smith, I heard a rumor that you made a statement that if you were as big as Joe Louis you would knock me down. Well, if I hated someone that much I wouldn't let size bother me." So someone said let's not turn this into personalities, and I said he should talk to me like a man, not a kid who doesn't know what he's talking about. Then I said I wanted to know why I wasn't entered in the pairings after I qualified for the tournament. Horton Smith said it was because I didn't have a PGA player's card. Then I said, "I don't know what you think I am. Everybody knows that I don't have a player's card. That's not good enough for me." So Smith says, "If you don't want to take my word for it, I'll just let the chips fall where they may." I said, "Okay, I'll see you in court. You stopped me the last time, but you won't this time." Leland Gibson, out of Kansas City, and Jackie Burke, another white pro, stopped me at the door and asked me to give them a chance to work it out, and I said, "Sure, but if you don't, I'll see you in court. You ran over me the last time, but you aren't going to do that this time." So I promised them I wouldn't bring the suit right away. And I never did.

What happened was, Joe Louis played in San Diego. Me and Teddy didn't, but the PGA added an amendment to its constitution where we would be what was called Approved Entries. We had no voting rights in the PGA, and the only tournaments we could play in were ones the sponsors invited us to. We got to play the next week in Phoenix, and the week after in Tucson. In all, we got into five tournaments in the West that year, and five in the East.

What was it like? In Phoenix and Tucson we stayed in a black neighborhood, at a friend's house. And I remember all the black waiters at the club were waiting for us to come in the dining room, but we never did. I had an argument with Joe and Teddy about using the dining room and locker room They said I was wrong to insist on it, and I had to promise them I wouldn't go in the clubhouse for a while, until things got better. In Tucson I asked the guys, "What if you want to use the restroom?" Teddy said, "Go in the halfway house." I said if they didn't want us in the clubhouse they didn't want us in the halfway house either, so we're back in the caddie shack. That's where we went, and it was filthy. I went over to the tournament director and asked him if he would go in there, and he said he wouldn't if there was a gun on him But, I never did use the clubhouse there, even when a white man I knew, a gambler who was a member, asked me in to have a drink. I said I would pass, because we didn't want to get into a fight with the PGA. So he invited me to his hotel to have a drink. But I couldn't go in the hotel, either.

Then there was a time at the L.A. Open when they paired Ted Rhodes, myself, and another black pro. When I came out on the first tee I told the starter, "You know, something puzzles me. How come we all three got paired together, all blacks?" He said, "You know how it is, we got some Texas guys to deal with." I said, "I thought this was the L.A. Open, not the Texas Open. If they don't want to play with us, tell 'em to go to hell back to Texas." Well, the starter's microphone was on all the time and, boy, the crowd heard all that, went wild, clapping and whistling. We could hardly get off the tee. They didn't do those kind of pairings anymore. Even at Tam O'Shanter they put us in the basement locker room at first, so I asked Mr. May why that was so and he said we just had to go slowly or we wouldn't have it at all. But we were put upstairs after that.

The best I ever did on the white tour was fourteenth in the Labatts tournament in Canada. I got a small check. I was four under par at Fort Wayne and finished four strokes out of the money. I won most of the tournaments on the black tour, but you just can't go out and play against the best in the world with so little experience.

The straw that broke the PGA's back and opened it up

once and for all was in 1960, when Stanley Mosk got into it. I was caddying out at Hillcrest Country Club, figuring maybe I could find someone to sponsor me. One day I was caddying for Mr. Harry Braverman, and he asked me why I wasn't out playing on the tour because he'd seen some of the scores I shot. I told him the situation, and he said I should write a letter explaining it and he would speak with his friend Stanley Mosk, who was the Attorney General of California. So I did, and Stanley Mosk put eight lawyers on the case and told the PGA it could not play any tournaments on public courses in California if everybody couldn't play in them. The PGA said it'd play on private courses, and Mosk told them they couldn't do that either, and he wrote letters to the Attorney Generals of most of the states telling them what he was doing. Finally, the PGA just caved in and dropped its Caucasians-only clause. That was late in 1961.

After the clause was broken I said to the younger black players, "It's open now, it's up to you fellows to keep it open. I have a family, and can't go out and play." Also, I was thirty-six. After San Diego, Charlie Sifford started playing the tour, but he was the only one for a while. Teddy played a little, but he was older, too, and then he got sick.

I stuck my neck out, and it destroyed my career. I couldn't get a job in a pro shop. I gave golf lessons at a driving range in Long Beach for three years, but I never actually worked in a pro shop. They said, if you work five years in a pro shop you get a PGA membership. But who was going to give me a job? I was the one who spoke up.

But I was disciplined. Golf teaches you that. The time I got slapped in the face was my first experience with discrimination, and I lived and worked with it from then on. But my mother didn't teach me to hate people. I remember asking her as a kid, during the Depression when there were lots of hoboes around and they'd come to our house, why she gave them something to eat. I said, "If the white man is so evil, why do you give them food?" She said her mother taught her never to turn a hungry person down, black or white. She lived by that rule, and I must say I have, too. I remember when I was playing golf I had two white boys who caddied for me—brothers.

Their mother and father were separated and they didn't have any clothes or shoes, so I took them over to my house and gave them a lot of clothes.

I think the situation equals out. You meet good people and you meet bad. Usually the good will overdo the bad. For instance, Calvin Peete made a statement over national television when asked if he had any problems playing on the tour in the white man's world. He said no, that Bill Spiller, Ted Rhodes, Maggie Hathaway, a lady here in Los Angeles, and a few others did the groundwork for him. Meantime I'm home one night and a man calls me from San Diego and says he remembers playing with me when I first started playing, and that when he saw me hit a ball he bet I would be a player someday. He called me three times to tell me what Calvin said about me on television. So it's rewarding. It may not be monetary, but it has a lot to do with the things you represent.

Bill Spiller

Bill Spiller lives in Los Angeles and plays golf occasionally at a public course. One of his sons is an attorney in the Public Defender's Office, City of Los Angeles, and another works in a bank. He has a daughter living in San Francisco. Bill never did become a member of the PGA.

JOE DEY

At the 1938 U.S. Amateur Championship, from left to right: Ed Dudley, Reynolds Smith, Clarence Buddington Kelland, Joseph C. Dey, Jr., and Grantland Rice.

Photograph by Al Barkow

"Fact is, I always stood for the game."

How did I get involved in this game of golf? Well, I was crazy about sports and, while going to high school in New Orleans, covered sports part-time for the *Times-Picayune*. Then I went on to college at the University of Pennsylvania, in Philadelphia, and, when I left there, went to work in the sports department of the Philadelphia *Public Ledger*. At the same time I got involved with a good friend of mine named Frank McCracken, who was publishing a magazine called the *Philadelphia Golfer & Sportsman*. I became a partner in that enterprise, and that really got me interested in golf—greatly interested.

When the golf writer for the *Evening Bulletin* retired, I put in to fill the vacancy. My boss at the *Ledger*, who was sort of an uncle to me, said he would give me more money if I stayed on with him, but I told him I wasn't interested in money, I just wanted to write golf. I wrote other sports—I covered the Philadelphia Phillies, wrote about squash and Penn U sports—but golf was my specialty, particularly in 1930 at Merion Golf Club, when Bob Jones completed his Grand Slam.

When I think back about Jones and that tournament, he was so smooth and dominant. It was as if there was no way to stop him, which of course was the case. I don't think any of his matches that week went past the fourteenth hole, and yet he three-putted thirteen times. I still have the notes on that. I saw every single shot he played, because my job was to report every one of them. I had a pad of paper and a relay of caddies. I'd write the text of how Jones played each hole and give it to one of the kids to leg back to the press room, where a telegrapher sent it in to the *Bulletin* office. That tells something of how golf journalism worked in those days. There's another anecdote along that line that didn't involve me directly, but which I've always enjoyed.

Maurice McCarthy, who was the Metropolitan Amateur champion at the time, got into a match with George Von Elm that became the longest match ever played in the championship—they went twenty-eight holes, ten extra. McCarthy won it with a three, and I can still see that little run-up shot from in front of the green that did it. But the amusing thing is, Allan Gould, who was the sports editor of the Associated Press, asked Cy Peterman, who was on our *Bulletin* staff, to signal from the back of the first green when the the match was over, and who won. Allan could see him from the press tent. It was to be the right hand raised if McCarthy won, the left if Von Elm did. Well, the match ended and old Cy held up his left hand and AP sent the flash around the world that Von Elm won the longest match in history—which, of course, was dead wrong. Cy got his signals mixed up.

In any case, from my having covered golf in the Philadelphia area, some members of the United States Golf Association's executive committee asked me if I would take the job as executive secretary of the USGA. I would oversee the administration of the organization from its New York headquarters. This was in 1934. A man named Tom McMahon had held this job since 1922, when the office of executive secretary was established, and Tom kind of ran it out of his hip pocket. Also, he was getting a little old—he seemed ancient to me, but I suspect he was only around sixty. The USGA wanted someone younger who would be a little more organized, and thought I was up to it. The decision to take the job was difficult for me only because at this time I was thinking seriously of joining the ministry of the Presbyterian Church. But I decided that everybody, in effect, inescapably, is a minister of whatever he believes in, and I certainly believed in the efficacy of sport, and especially golf. Perhaps my father being an avid sportsman had something to do with it. He didn't play golf, but was a very good football player in college.

So on December 10, 1934, I went to work for the USGA. My staff consisted of two secretaries, and all of us worked in a small office on 42nd Street in New York City. I remember that after a month or so a friend asked me how the job was going, and I said there was nothing to it, that I didn't have much to do. Well, as soon as the golf season started, things began popping. But I must say, a lot of the busyness that developed was my doing. Until then, when questions came in to the USGA office about rules, or amateur status, or having to do with course maintenance, it was the practice to rubber-stamp them: "Referred to the Chairman of the Rules Committee," "Referred to the Chairman of the Greens Committee," and so on. My office had been only a referral agency, sending the inquiries along to the chairmen, who were really businessmen who played golf as a hobby and made a contribution to the game as USGA committeemen. Well, I didn't see the job at all like that. My concept of the office was that the men who headed up the various USGA committees didn't have the time to handle all the multitudinous details. So I began drafting the replies to all the queries, and that kept me very, very busy.

You see, it was an expanding time in golf. I started in the middle of the Depression, but as the country's economy improved, the game of golf grew. Then, too, if you have someone interested in every aspect of the work, as I was, the workload just proliferates.

Speaking of my reporting of the 1930 U.S. Open, I remember also that it was very hard to see the play, because there was no roping the way there is now, which keeps the galleries on the perimeter of the fairway. There was only roping around tees and greens. So the crowds raced down the fairway right beside the golfers, and it was hard not only for me but for most of the gallery to see much of the play. Something was finally done about that in 1954 for the U.S. Open, at Baltusrol Golf Club. Robert Trent Jones, the golf architect, suggested to me and the club's championship committee that the gallery be

241

kept along the sides of the fairways by rope barriers, and it was decided to try it. The club bought a bunch of thick metal stakes and plenty of rope, and put everything in place. But the system broke down on the sixth hole—I remember it well. It was Ben Hogan's gallery. This was the year after he won the Masters and the British and U.S. Opens. The crowd just burst through the rope barriers, and some of the committee members suggested we just go back to the old system. But myself and the chairman of the gallery committee were determined to make the new system work. What we did was have special crews going up and down the lines telling the people that play would be stopped if they did not stay behind the ropes. We made it clear that we meant that. And it worked.

Actually, Trent Jones got the idea for roping off the fairways from the Masters tournament, which in turn adapted it from St. Andrews, Scotland. You know, the Old Course there is only two holes wide, so no gallery is allowed within the course, only along the outer perimeter. I like to think that our decision to stand firm on the sixth hole at Baltusrol in 1954 revolutionized tournament golf, or at least the spectating of it, because that's how it is done everywhere now, and it is, of course, fully accepted. More people can see the play with less effort, and this may have had something to do with the steady increase of galleries at tournaments from that time on.

I didn't have any expertise in respect to the work of the Greens Section—that is, the improvement of the grass on golf courses—but it was a wonderful experience being part of it. The USGA began the Greens Section in 1920, and it was headed up by Dr. John Monteith, a pure scientist who did more than anybody I can think of to improve the condition of our golf courses. You know, there had been very little interest in grasses until then. The USGA had tried to get the Department of Agriculture interested, but it felt golf was too narrow an area. But you never know where something will go, or what will lead to what. For example, Dr. Monteith was called on during World War II by the Army Air Force to put turf grass alongside airstrips to keep the dust down. The dust was impairing the efficiency of aircraft engines. I remember seeing a report that said an aircraft's engine life was prolonged by as much as ninty percent because of those strips of turf grass.

And all our roadsides and home lawns have benefited from the work of the USGA's Greens Section. That was where the impetus came from to improve grasses in general.

The two areas of the USGA's work in which I could have the most direct involvement were the rules of golf and running the national championships. We always tried to make the rules of the game more understandable. I can remember when I was the only person to conduct whole clinics on the rules of golf. Now the USGA and PGA have six or eight of them a year, which is a good thing, because the rules have become very complicated over the years. The original rules of golf were very simple, you know, but you couldn't play by them now. I think they've become increasingly more complex, because more people think about the rules and are more careful about them than before. This may be the result of the rules clinics, but what's the sense of playing the game if you don't know where the goalposts are? And, also, I think the professional game has had a bearing on the increasing definitiveness of the rules, which is another way of saying complexity. When a lot of money is involved, much more care is taken with the rules.

Some players have never been much concerned about using the rule book to their advantage. Sam Snead was one such. But Jack Nicklaus has used it very well. And when I say "used" it, I don't mean that in the negative sense. He learns all his rights, and goes by them. If it helps his cause, that's what the rules are for. Why not?

Johnny Miller is another one who uses the rules very well. I remember at Pebble Beach, during a U.S. Open, on the tenth hole he had driven to the right over the side of the cliff into the lateral hazard. I happened along while he was at the spot where the ball went in, and asked what the problem was. He wanted to make sure he could drop his ball according to the lateral-hazard rule. I said he sure could. So he dropped the ball about three feet from the edge of the cliff. It rolled over the edge down into the hazard, and he dropped twice more, according to the rules, and the same thing happened. Now he was allowed to place the ball by hand. He could have dropped farther away from the hazard, but no nearer the hole, without the ball going down into the hazard, but then he would have taken a chance on getting a bad lie. By being able to place the ball by hand, he could put it on a nice little tuft of grass, which he did, and he then hit it onto the green. I said to John that he was pretty keen on the rules, and he said, "Yes, it doesn't seem right, but the rule says I don't have to go out there to drop my ball."

I think one of my proudest achievements with the USGA was being part of the unification of the USGA rules of golf with those of the Royal and Ancient—the British rules. We unified them except for the size of the ball, but that's a *de facto* change because the R&A has required the use of the bigger American ball in the British Open for quite a few years now, and it's been used even longer on the British pro tour. The unification of the rules was an interesting thing. There had been casual meetings between USGA and R&A officials over the years on the matter, but nothing had been done. Then, right after World War II ended, the R&A came out with a new code that was completely different from ours.

For example, Bernard Darwin, the golf writer, who was chairman of the R&A rules committee, floated the idea that you could replay an unplayable lie, out of bounds, or lost ball without a penalty, only a loss of distance. Well, Darwin was a great writer but not a terrific rules maker. Darwin's thinking was to simplify things so that if you came up with an unplayable lie or a lost ball, it wasn't your fault and you shouldn't be penalized. Just do the shot over again. But it *is* the golfer's fault if he hits into the woods and gets an unplayable lie, or can't find the ball, or hits it out of bounds. Well, Darwin's idea didn't get through.

Understand, it wasn't only my doing in all this. I worked as part of a committee that had to agree on changes, amendments, and so forth. I could suggest, but not request. Anyhow, it was arranged in 1951 to have a conference between the USGA and R&A on unifying the rules of golf. There had been a lot of communications between the two bodies by mail, and in informal personal meetings over a period of time, but now we decided to sit down together formally and put together a new, unified code. In 1951 we met first in London and had a couple of meetings in the House of Lords. That was quite impressive, of course, but once we got to talking about the rules of golf we forgot where we were. Then we went up to St. Andrews and wrote the final version.

Mind you, the codes were quite different in language and concepts before we got together. But the changes were made in principle, not according to national interests. There was more concern for the game than national pride. For example, there was the issue of the center-shafted putter, the "Schenectady putter," which had been outlawed in Great Britain since 1904, after Walter Travis used it to become the first American to win the British Amateur championship. One reason, purportedly, that Ben Hogan would never go over to play in the British Open was because he used a center-shafted putter and wasn't going to change for that event. The center-shafted putter was legal in the United States. The British were insistent on keeping it illegal—they were more traditional, and felt the shaft of a club should be attached at the heel of the head— and we were prepared to go along with them on that, even though we knew we'd catch the devil back home. But the British knew we would catch the devil and, after a little caucus at lunch one day, came back and said they would go our way. You might recall that Ben Hogan then did go to the British Open, in 1953, for the only time in his career and won it, at Carnoustie.

Then there was the question of the stymie. The R&A had one version of it, we had another, but that's really by the way. The stymie was so unpopular among golfers on both sides that we decided to drop it altogether. I thought the stymie should be retained in some form, and still do, and so did others on both sides of our conference table. But in this case the law was made by the people—which is the best kind of law, because an unpopular law is generally unenforceable and so pointless to have on the books.

Running the national championships was not nearly as easy, especially when the question of disqualification came up. The one ruling on this that stays with me most was when six fellows were disqualified during the 1940 U.S. Open, including Ed Oliver, who would have tied for the championship. That was a very sad moment, very sad. There was a background to that one. In qualifying rounds in the state of Washington for that Open—one day, thirty-six holes—two players began their second round about a half-hour before they were officially scheduled. The local committee disqualified them for playing without authority, and when the players appealed to the USGA the ruling was upheld. At the Open itself, on the last day, Saturday, there was a break between rounds—we were still playing two rounds on the last day. I was the starter, and was having lunch when the boy I had left on the tee to guard the box of official scorecards came running up to my table and told me that three golfers had taken their cards from the box and started their second round. I went black, because the thought of the disqualification incident in Washington came immediately to mind.

What happened was, Ed Oliver and his two playing partners, and then another threesome after them, started twenty-eight minutes ahead of their scheduled time in an effort to beat a storm that was brewing. And, indeed, the storm did materialize. Ed and the others were told to stop playing while I went to round up the committee to see if they would sustain the players' eligibility and allow their drives off the first tee to stand. And they did stop. Ed Oliver was the key figure in the incident, because he was in contention and, indeed, would have been in the playoff with Lawson Little and Gene Sarazen. However, while I was looking for the committee members, another USGA official, who shall go nameless, came along and saw these players standing on the first fairway and asked them what the problem was. They said they were waiting for a ruling. The official told them to continue play and the ruling would be decided when they finished their round. So Ed and the others went ahead, and there was nothing to do then but disqualify them. It should never have happened. The players shouldn't have gone off ahead of schedule, and the official shouldn't have told them to continue playing. It was a rather tragic consequence, and certainly for Ed Oliver.

Another disqualification incident was less complicated, but no more pleasant. Jackie Pung, the fine player from Hawaii, was playing with Betty Jameson in the final round of the 1957

U.S. Women's Open at Winged Foot. Betty put down a five on a hole where Jackie made a six. Jackie signed the card, and, even though her total score for the round was correct, the error on the individual hole wasn't and she was disqualified. It was a great pity, because Jackie had lost a playoff to Betsy Rawls for this championship in 1953, and this time had come from behind to beat Betsy by one stroke. I didn't like that one at all, but there's nothing to be done about such a ruling.

The system is as it is because someone must mark your score. If you keep your own, there will always be some lingering doubt of honesty. Besides, the committee needs someone else to refer to in case there is any need for testimony. But every player has the right to check the numbers put down by another player. You are the last resort for the correctness of your card. You have a chance to check it out and get back to the committee, and to the caddies for verification of what you actually did score. It's a very technical game—in fact, it tends to be too technical. I don't like that side of it, but where the possibility exists for mistakes or cheating you've got to shore up the rules.

One of the most dramatic U.S. Opens played while I was with the USGA was the one in 1964, when Ken Venturi almost collapsed during the final round from the terrific heat. He made it through to win, and afterwards we changed the format of the championship. Until then the final two rounds were played on the last day, but we then spread the championship out over four days. Many people have thought it was only the Venturi incident that prompted that change, but my thinking, and that of Hord Hardin—who was president of the USGA at the time and now runs the Masters—was that it was a matter of better management.

We were playing the Open on Thursday, Friday, and Saturday. But what would happen if you couldn't finish the second round on Friday, as occurred at Oakmont the year before Venturi won? You can't make up the pairings for Saturday's two rounds until the second round has been completed, because you have to see who is going to make the cut among those who must complete their second round Saturday morning. Then you make the pairings and try to get both rounds in. It just wasn't feasible to operate that way anymore. I was for ending the championship on Saturday anyway, by starting it on Wednesday—I suppose my old ministerial leanings came in there—but we finally adopted the present format of four days ending on Sunday.

People have also adduced that the change was the result of pressure from television, which wanted an entire weekend to broadcast. That never entered my mind. Of course, it may have come into the minds of others sitting at a meeting, but I never heard anyone say anything. And there was the business of Venturi. The thing here was how many athletes in how many sports are in contention for eight or nine hours in a row, as Ken was at Congressional, or any golfer would be? None. That's a tremendous burden. It really is, particularly when you have the kind of weather we had in Washington that week. But it's more than any athlete should have to bear, heat or no heat. It's a matter of sustaining concentration for that long, and the essence of golf is concentration. So improved management and fairness to the players were the two reasons for the change in the Open format.

One of my favorite U.S. Opens was the one Ben Hogan won in 1951 at Oakland Hills in Detroit, a very tough course that he called "The Monster." What I remember very well about that championship is that Ben Hogan proved to be far more talkative while playing than he has been given credit for. I refereed his last two rounds. In the morning round Ben went out in 32 on that brutal course, then came back in 39 and was mad as hops. He said he was going to burn it up in the afternoon, and, sure enough, he went out in 35 and came back in 32. But my point is he chatted a lot during the round. Very early during the last round Ben asked me why we were holding a future Open at a particular course, and I gave him a reason, which he said was not good, or words to that effect. Then at the seventh, when he was really beginning to roll and the people were beginning to flock to watch him, after he hit his tee shot, with a three-wood, the crowd began running after him and he said to me, "You know, golf spectators certainly put up with an awful lot. They park their cars a mile away and come out here and get pushed around by the marshals and police just to see us play." I said that was true, but did he consider that they greatly admired his skill? He looked at the club he was carrying and said, "You know, I guess it does take some skill to hit a little ball with this thing." Now, I think that's good conversation, and right in the middle of the winning of the U.S. Open! Then he pitched his second shot on that hole close to the cup, and when the people started cheering, Ben said, to no one in particular, "Wait till I make the putt." And he made it.

I wish the USGA was better understood by the golfing public. It's what I tried to do when I was with the association. Many people think it's a club strictly for country-club golfers, when in fact it is the regulatory body for all golfers. I tried to make that point when I started up the *USGA Journal.* I used it to explain how and why we made our rules and rules decisions. I wanted to drive out the notion that the USGA is a kind of monolithic organization that felt it didn't need to explain, only rule. I also tried to make it clear that the people who did much of the work did it only for their love of the game. For example, there was an instance at one of our championships when a couple of officials were out on a green measuring to see which ball was furthest from the cup. One was Eugene Grace, the other was Ike Grainger. While they were out measuring I heard a spectator ask his companion what they were doing, and getting the response, "Oh, they're measuring the putts to see who's away. They have to do something to earn their salary." They couldn't have known that at the time Ike was president of the Chemical Bank and Eugene's father was president of Bethlehem Steel, and that both were volunteering their time. This is something I was always trying to get across about the USGA.

I think some people, over the years, perceived that through my work at the USGA I was primarily interested in amateur golf—I suppose because most of the USGA events are for amateurs. But I was interested in the pros as well, and particularly with the U.S. Open. Fact is, I always stood for *the game.* Which is one reason why I became the commissioner of the PGA tour. The USGA work was very constructive and interesting, but when the pros began fighting among themselves I felt they were disrupting part of the game, an important part of it. It seemed to me that if anybody could stabilize their situation, it would be good for golf. It was that simple. But it was not a one-man show by any means. Paul Austin was chairman of the policy board, and George Love and John Murchison were the independent directors. They were strong, very good fellows.

Strangely enough, while I was not aware of the perception of me as an upholder of amateurism, a number of the pros seemed to want me in the post of commissioner for what amateur sport is supposed to stand for. I suppose they saw me as honest, conscientous, moral, or at least so-called. I can't really say. You seldom see yourself as other people do.

Joe Dey

Joseph C. Dey, Jr.—Joe Dey—was executive secretary of the United States Golf Association from 1934 through 1968. He then became the first commissioner of the PGA tour, a post he held until 1973. Nominally retired, he still consults for the USGA on the rules of golf and writes opinions on questions pertaining to the rules. He is also writing a history of the USGA. He is one of only two Americans ever to be played-in as Captain of the Royal and Ancient Golf Club of St. Andrews, Scotland. (The other was Francis Ouimet.) Dey has received many other awards honoring his distinguished service to the game of golf.

Joe, who has never been better than a fifteen-handicap golfer, lives in Locust Valley, New York, and plays golf far more often than he did when he was busy administering golf at its highest levels.

JACK BURKE, JR.

Jack Burke, Sr., winner of the 1941 PGA of America Seniors Championship.

Photograph by Al Barkow

"...in this world, everything with its head down gets eaten."

I never did sit down for dinner when I was growing up that there weren't four golf pros around the table . . . and maybe two or three golf-ball salesmen. Because when my dad came to Texas there was nobody for him to talk golf with. I mean, there were just guys who worked on oil rigs, and only two courses in town. My dad may have been—and not just because he's my dad—one of the greatest golf instructors that ever lived. He taught the likes of Babe Zaharias and Johnny Dawson and Craig Wood. Henry Picard used to come down for lessons. That's why we always had so many people for dinner. But my dad had a great interest in people, in their achievements, whether they were in golf or working at a filling station. He was a great conversationalist and never forgot anything. He read all the time and enjoyed people with good minds. I can hear him to this day saying that we will not have peace on this earth until all the leaders are women, because women will not send their children to war. He was a great religious man. I don't care how much of a hangover you had, at seven o'clock Sunday morning you were at Mass. And on the first row, not in the back of the church. He never missed, and everybody was in there with him. Row one, and dressed. You weren't coming in there in any jeans; you have your best suit on. He could be a pretty tough dude in his way, and when you come out of a ship like that, well, that's pretty good discipline for golf.

Look at the people golf attracts, people who can concentrate for long periods of time, lawyers and doctors. Writers. James Michener likes golf, and he can spend seven years writing a book. Well, I mean you have to buy a book someone spent seven years on. I've got to find out what it was that took him so long. I read everything Michener writes, and it takes me seven years to read each one.

My dad was born and raised in Philadelphia, but he was the only one in his family to get into golf. His father was a hod-carrier. Dad started out caddying, of course, and, like with so many caddies, he got to play better and better, and next thing you know he thought he'd get into the thing. Dad finished tied for second in the 1920 U.S. Open, and won maybe twenty-five or thirty events, but he was a golf teacher first. He could make clubs, too, and liked to design them. He designed a lot of clubs for MacGregor in the early days, and invented the all-weather grip, that rubber grip with a heavy cord of cotton running through it. That was when the grips went from leather to rubber. In fact, he had the patent on it. Picard, Craig Wood, Ben Hogan, and Jimmy Demaret were the partners he put into the company we had here in Houston; Burke Par, it was called. He got the idea for it when a tire on his car blew out one day. He saw how the cord was wrapped up in those tires. He used to lose the club at the top of his backswing and always blamed the leather grips, so he wanted something better to hold on to, and saw the answer in that blown-out rubber tire. He made a grip he could use in any kind of weather, and all he had to do was scrub it down with soap and water and he had something he could hold on to. Picard was the first to use it on the tour, then Hogan did and it became very popular. When Dad died, the company sort of went down and the patents ran out and everybody started making the rubber-cord grip.

From Philadelphia, Dad went out to the Town and Country Club in St. Paul, Minnesota, as the pro, and he taught in the wintertime at a club in Fort Worth. I was born in Fort Worth, but we moved to Houston when I was real small. Dad met my mother in Fort Worth, and when they got married he had a choice of two jobs, up in Wheaton, Illinois, or at the River Oaks Club in Houston. My mother told him they could raise kids cheaper in Texas than in Illinois, so he took the River Oaks job.

So I grew up at River Oaks; actually, I just grew up in golf. Every day of my life has been in golf. I was born with asthma, so I couldn't really play many other games, and I used to go out with my dad every day when school was out and hang around with the caddies, shoot dice and caddie, work in the shop, do whatever he wanted me to do. Then I'd play golf and we'd gamble. I was about eleven when I started doing all this, and I shot 69 when I was twelve, so I suppose I had some sort of gift for the game. I was always a good putter and, as a kid, got to where I could hit it far. I remember playing with Babe Zaharias, who was a pretty good hitter. She'd come over to the club and say, "C'mon, little Jack, let's go," and when I got to where I could hit it past Babe, I thought, Man, I'm on my way. I was about fourteen, then.

When I started bugging my dad for instruction, he was teaching twenty-four hours a day, so he would just tell me two things: on the backswing, point the club to what I was shooting at, and finish with the shaft of the club on the back of my neck—just bang it against your neck. Then he'd say, "Now get out of here and don't let me hear you again." What he told me to do developed the golf turn and then finished the swing. He didn't like anyone with a short swing, He used to tell me, "If you have a short swing, you have a short career." So I was never tentative going through, and I never tried to guide the club. Of course, that was Ernest Jones' and Alex Morrison's theory, too—all those old teachers taught the same way. You didn't see people stick the club up in the air. Dad used to say that was for holding an umbrella. My dad was a great believer that only the inside half of the ball belonged to you, that you didn't have any part of the outside half of it. So you always worked the club from the inside—not inside out, but to the inside part of the ball so you sort of sideswiped it. That creates the inside plane.

We talked golf every night over dinner, a lot of it on the swing, because all the pros were instructors, golf professors.

Jack Burke, Jr.

Even out on the tour. Everybody'd sit around in the lobby of the hotel where we were all staying, and I'd listen to these famous old professionals telling stories and talking golf swing. See, when I first went out on tour I just wanted to play well enough so I'd get a little reputation and my lesson book would be full back at my club. If I had a pupil I couldn't teach, I'd ask Ky Laffoon or Lloyd Mangrum or Clayton Heafner what I could do. Or I'd ask Craig Wood about a guy's swing. He knew just about everybody in Westchester County—this was when I was pro up in White Plains, New York—and he'd say, "Oh, I remember him, he stays on his left side too long." Then when I'd get back I'd help my pupil with that. If I got better as a player, that was icing on the cake, but being a better teacher was more important, because the pressure of being a pro at a club was that if you weren't a good teacher, you were going down the road.

I gave my first lesson when I was thirteen. I taught a man in Houston who was sick and took the whole summer off from his company—John P. Fusler was his name. I taught him every day and we played, just hacked around, and he gave me $350 at the end of the summer. I did the job because I had the time, I was just a kid. But I got results. He went from a 100-shooter to shooting 85. He thought I was the greatest teacher in the world, but all I was doing was relating everything I heard at the dinner table. Monkey see, monkey do . . . you know? I can still teach the same way. You learn other things, and create your own verbiage and presentation, but you still teach what you first learned. You're only dealing with timing and balance in this game.

I got my first actual pro job when I was twenty, at the Galveston Country Club. An old man by the name of A. J. Dow gave me the job. I told him I was young, but that I could do the best job he'd ever seen. And he knew my father. In fact, he called him, asking him to recommend someone, and my dad said, "I got a kid here thinks he's pro,"—talking about me—"you can interview him, but I'm not recommending him." Of course, he was just half kidding. That's how I got to know Sam Maceo, the guy in Galveston who helped Jimmy Demaret get on the tour. Sam used to bet the dice dealers at night that

Jack Burke, Jr.

I could beat them on the golf course. They played golf all day and gambled all night. Sam used to love me to come down to his nightclub so he could tell me how much we won that day. I loved gambling on the golf course, not on the horses. In golf I have some control over my bet.

I really didn't play much amateur golf as a kid, I just gambled a lot. That was the only way to make any money during the Depression. You shot dice, did anything to win money. I never played a round of golf that I wasn't gambling. The early professionals, that's all they were was gamblers. That's the way they were brought up, in the caddie yards. Mangrum and Heafner . . . why, hell, they were making more money in the practice rounds than the whole tournament purse was worth. Gambling. Ky Laffoon, Leonard Dodson, and Ben Hogan. Hogan loved to bet. He'd bet $50 nassaus with you. Oh sure. I played with him at the Masters many the time, and he'd always take Claude Harmon for his partner because in those days, the late '40s, Claude was maybe as good a player as there was. I used to take Middlecoff, because he could run the tables when he got hot. See, you couldn't be as good as they were if you didn't gamble. You've got to have some gamble in you. I'm not saying I'd go out and hustle people. I like to go out and play for stakes, and from that you become more perceptive.

I mean, if I'm playing up one fairway and I see Bob Rosburg or Ben Hogan on the next fairway over and they're short of the green, when I get to that hole I'm going to be a little leery of that second shot. I'll be thinking the shot may be longer than it looks, that the wind may be a little stronger than it seems. Because Bob Rosburg can really pick the right club, and you know Ben Hogan is not going to pick the wrong club. If you weren't looking over there, you're liable to pick the wrong club when you get there, and be short of the green just like they were. I was taught one time that in this world everything with its head down gets eaten! Pigs and cows get eaten, leopards don't. Leopards have their heads up. You never saw Hogan with his head down. Nicklaus never has his head down. They walk in a room and they're looking. Like good boxers. Losers have their heads down, winners have their heads up.

Jack Burke, Jr.

I modeled myself after Heafner and Mangrum and those kinds of guys. They were fierce competitors, bet their own money. Heafner was a tough guy, the kind of guy you wouldn't mind going on night patrol with, because you didn't think he'd leave you. Mangrum, too, and Ted Kroll was another one. An admirable man. Look at their war records. They were gamblers, and gamblers are the most perceptive people. They're looking for the edge, seeing if you're making mistakes out there. They know when your hands are on the club a certain way, or if you're standing too far away from the ball, you're not going to beat them. That makes them feel more confident of their chances. Mangrum and Heafner and those guys didn't tell me any of that, specifically, but I perceived it in them. I played every practice round I could on the tour with Leonard Dodson, Ky Laffoon, Dutch Harrison. All these guys who were hustlers. I knew that's where I was going to learn. I'd sit and watch them gamble at cards, watch them when the money was up. I'd watch Mangrum the way he set up. Like in chipping, Mangrum put the club in a very upright position and had the ball only three inches off his right foot. He'd never follow through. He'd sit the club up on its toe and stick it right in the ground. He got that from Runyan. See, we didn't play on courses in the kind of condition they're in nowadays. Now they've got turf that if one blade is out of place the whole membership threatens to quit. So you've got to realize that when you play off bare dirt you're not going to follow through, and that you're going to get that ball at any price. That's what Lloyd was doing with his chipping. He wasn't about to hit behind the ball, playing it off of that dirt. Not for the kind of bets he had going.

All these old pros I grew up with were experts at managing the golf ball. They could maneuver it, move the ball in all directions, and they prided themselves in that. I remember playing with Heafner in a Ryder Cup match at Pinehurst. I was having trouble, just couldn't get it going, and he came over and says, "You dumb little jackass, you, don't you ever try to play a *shot* in there? Don't you try to fade it in, or hook it in? Quit shooting straight?" That day I learned that you've got to go in with some kind of curve. Why? Because there's a wind blowing most of the time and you deal with it by curving the ball. You take baseball. They pay a relief pitcher who can curve the ball a lot more money than they do the one who just throws it up there straight. The bowler that can curve the ball makes more money, because he knocks down more pins. The good golf player can curve the ball at will, so that if he has a crosswind, for instance, he can hold the ball into it. The poor player just lets the wind take the ball away.

The people I learned my golf from had a lot of animal still left in them, a lot of instinct. Now, you take young kids today, they're very homogenized. They're looking for a system, one way of doing things. But the older players were looking for a lot of ways to do things. That's because they were all teachers and had to be versatile to teach so many people, every one different, with different strengths and flexibility and so on. They had thirty minutes to perform a miracle. That was the length of a lesson, and the guy wanted you to redo him in that time, so you had to come up with something.

I'll never forget what Hogan told me. He said, "You think this is a game of stick and ball? It isn't. It's a game of adjustments, a game of constant change and adjustment. It's a game of stick, ball, and field. What you don't know how to do is adjust anything. You don't know enough about the swing and how to make changes and adjustments." I learned from that. I learned from a lot of people. I learned from a Basilian priest when I was in high school. I went to a Catholic high school. He came in to teach us some math one day and started off saying we were all pretty stupid and probably wouldn't get much farther than this; he wrote a 50 and a 51 on the board and said, "Now look, if you make fifty, don't spend fifty-one." No one can teach better than that. If the United States government was in that class, we wouldn't be in the debt we're in.

I learned a lot of things from a lot of people. Like if you want to deal with Toney Penna or Craig Wood or Claude Harmon, you're going to have to dress right, you have to have pride in what you look like. That's the first thing. You can't go out there looking like a slob and think you're going to shoot low numbers. You just weren't going to deal around Toney and Demaret and these kinds of guys as a dingo. I mean, you had to shape up.

I had a definite advantage coming from my background in

golf. Jimmy Demaret helped me a lot when I was starting up. Jimmy was like my big brother. He was fourteen years older than me, and worked for my dad. My dad thought Jimmy was the best player that ever lived, and Jimmy probably was. He had so much natural ability. My dad taught Jimmy, even if Demaret had a style that was sort of unique, overall. He taught Jimmy to stay on the inside of the golf ball. Jimmy took me out on the tour for the first time, when I was twenty, and that helped get me get in some games with guys who were such tremendous players. I mean, Lloyd Mangrum is not going to play with every duck coming out on the circuit. So, because of Jimmy, and because everybody knew my dad, I got to play with Mangrum and Penna, guys like that. They didn't mind me falling in.

And I had so much to recall when things got hard and I needed to pull something out of the hat. You know, when it really gets down to blocking and tackling, if you have just one shot at something, one drive to hit, everybody will go back to what his daddy or his coach told him. I could always remember something my old man had told me, or Jimmy, or Heafner, or somebody like that.

I went to Rice University for a year. I wanted to get a business degree, but they made me take physical education because of my golf. But I didn't want to be a coach. I believe I could have been good in law. I think I could have handled law. But the war broke up my education. I went into the Marine Corps for four years, and when I came back my dad had died, so I didn't have any money to continue in college. I went to Craig Wood and he got me an assistant's job at the Hollywood Golf Club in Deal, New Jersey. I worked a year there for an old Scotsman named George Fotheringham. Craig told me if I could work for Fotheringham I'd be a success in life. If you ever work for a Scotsman, you never forget it. He was the most difficult man who ever lived in the world. He would disagree with Jesus Christ. Nothing that you did was right. He was tough, but he was good. I learned a lot by him.

Then Craig got me a job with Claude Harmon at Winged Foot, and that year, through Herman Barron, I got the job as head pro at the Metropolis Club in White Plains, New York, where Paul Runyan had been. I went from there to the golf circuit and played it for twenty straight years, winter and summer.

I'd played the winter tour while I was working at club jobs, but after I'd won a lot of tournaments and a lot of money I thought I'd just go ahead and try this thing full-time. That was in 1950. I was a bachelor, twenty-seven years old, and had saved quite a bit of money from my jobs. And it got to where the tour was really getting started. There was the Tam O'Shanter thing with a big purse, and the Masters had gotten big. I had always played the whole winter circuit, so now I just kept right on going.

What do you learn about yourself, and competing, after twenty-odd years on the tour? Well, to anticipate a result is not a good idea. You don't anticipate you're going to miss or make a putt, you concentrate on your stroke. A good player is going to pay attention to detail, to making good swings. You know, a good swing produces a good shot. But, still, you win with your head. You can produce good shots all day long, but that doesn't mean you're going to win. You see a guy with the best swing on the circuit, very picturesque, and the shots go perfect, but he never wins. You wonder why. What's wrong with him? Well, it's simple. He's either an envious person or a jealous person; he hates people. Or he's greedy, and when the money gets there he wants it, so the money bucket gets in his way. You have to get past that.

Put it this way. In the early days of man, the hunter came out of the trees to get the deer. Now, he has to be very well balanced. I wouldn't send a clumsy man after the deer, would you? If I was a tribe leader, I'd send a man who was very well tuned in, was relaxed, who won't step on branches to run the deer away. So, you see, in golf when a guy steps up and looks like a machine, he will not beat you. The guy that steps up there and has this waggle that looks natural and his timing looks natural and he goes all the way around the course looking the same, he's the guy who's going to beat you. When he gets on the putting surface he doesn't look like an octopus falling out of a tree. When he grabs the putter it almost looks like he has the driver in his hands. He doesn't look out of place anywhere. He's a very relaxed player.

Of course, there was gamesmanship out there that you had to deal with. But they were very natural about it. You take a look at who starts out walking real fast. Well, you know, good players like Mangrum, they're not going to change their timing. He'll slow down the fast walker, he'll walk twice as slow as he usually does. You see, a slow player is not only using his time, he's using your time. So you've got to go over and talk to him a little bit. Except maybe if it's Hogan. I remember we were playing at Augusta one year and we were a couple of holes behind. An official asked me to go over and talk to Ben, and I said, "*You* go over. Hell, Ben Hogan's *wife* doesn't talk to him too much." But I did tell him, "Ben, they're going to put two strokes on you." He said, "Let 'em come out here and do it, then." He wasn't going to change his timing for any group of officials or anybody. You've got to be wary of the guys who are on center stage. They use that as a big advantage. And the only thing that will get you to center stage is if you sink more putts than anybody else. If you want to get to center stage, don't worry about doing it with your mouth. Do it with your clubs, and especially your putter. Like when I had my streak of four wins in a row.

It was probably the best putting streak I've ever had. I got into an unbelievable air of confidence. I knew that with my putter I could hit any side of the hole from any distance at any time. It wasn't a question of whether I was going to putt good, but how good I was going to putt. I had gotten hold of a putter that belonged to Jay Hebert, a mallet where I had been using a blade, and something just clicked with it. It was an old putter made by Otey Crisman. Otey quit the circuit because he couldn't putt, and started making putters. You know, you always find the guys who are bad putters, they make putters. Guys who are good putters, they can putt with a shoehorn. So the streak was putting, mainly. I didn't play that well. I played a lot better tournaments that I got beat in because I didn't have the putter. Otherwise, there was no pressure building up during the streak. There was no pressure on us playing tournament golf. We didn't come up with a fiftieth of the pressure these kids are playing under today. We didn't have a tour qualifying school. Hell, we didn't have enough people to fill up the field every week; we had amateurs playing in our tournaments. There was no thought you had to get in the top ten, because there was no money. Twentieth place was $100. There was no pressure to qualify for the next tournament. All you had to do was go over and put $10 down at the next one and you were in.

I enjoyed most of it, playing the tour. I got tired of the travel, and I never really liked being a celebrity. The golf was a lot of fun, but going to the cocktail parties and stuff I could have done without. I wasn't a Demaret or Trevino or Rodriguez, who can play off people. They sort of use the people. They're so damned nervous they talk to everybody, because that keeps them up, you know. They're doing it for themselves. Absolutely. It relaxes them. But it didn't relax me. I'm more relaxed talking to my caddie. That's why I used to like having a character-type caddie. Like in L.A. I'd have a guy named Jingles. He was a Jewish guy from Brooklyn, and how he ever got to caddying on the tour in L.A. I'll never know. Those were the days when I was sort of the fair-haired boy out there, and Jingles would get back in the crowd and get all the girls' phone numbers. He'd come up to me and say, "Boy, they're out here today. Good Lord, are they out here today." He'd have ten phone numbers before the day was out.

That's when I was still a bachelor. I got married in 1952 and played the tour eighteen years more. My wife came with me most of the time. We had our first child in 1953, then another one, and they used to get in the back of the Cadillac and away we'd go. My wife was from Buffalo, and I'd take everybody up east for the summer while I played, then we'd come back to Houston and I'd go traveling in and out on my own. Oh, it was pitiful. My wife worrying that someone's going to break into the house and she all alone with the kids—we had five all told—and me singing happy-birthday songs from the Holiday Inn. Once you get a family started, it's very difficult to deal with that circuit. That's why I think Nicklaus is the most fabulous golfer in the world. I mean, he did all the things he did and still dropped five kids on the ground. I did the same, and had my streak and won my two majors and all. It was difficult, but I was driven.

Jack Burke, Jr.

See, I was supposed to be the greatest thing since sliced bread. I was the most promising player coming up for the first twenty years of my life. I always had a good swing, but they were waiting for when it was going to happen. Man, that's a lot of pressure to play under, when your father was a good player and a famous teacher. Arnold's father was a pro, but not the player my dad was, and Nicklaus' father wasn't a player. I felt the pressure of having to succeed. I had to prove it to my dad that I could play. You're always trying to prove yourself to somebody who cares about you.

Jack Burke, Jr.

Jack Burke, Jr., won fifteen tournaments as a touring professional, including the 1956 Masters and PGA Championship. He was the PGA Player-of-the-Year in 1956. Jack won the Vardon Trophy in 1952, given for having the lowest stroke-average for a full season. He played on five U.S. Ryder Cup teams, and captained two of them.

Jack lives in Houston. His home base is the famed Champions Golf Club, where the 1969 U.S. Open was played, and which he founded with the late Jimmy Demaret. The Champions is not unlike Jackie's family dinner table when he was growing up. People in the game are always welcome; it's a place to hang their hat when in town, and have a place to play and talk golf.

POSTSCRIPT

One morning in early 1984 I read in a newspaper that Jimmy Demaret had died, and my immediate reaction was embarrassingly selfish. "Damn," I said, "now I won't be able to get him for my book"—this book. However, very soon after, almost spontaneously . . . yes, spontaneously . . . I felt saddened for the proper reasons: because Jimmy was a good guy, and was a friend—we had worked closely together for four years on the television series "Shell's Wonderful World of Golf." Jimmy would have been a terrific "chapter" in this book, of course, not only because he was one of the most notable pioneers of the modern pro tour, but because he was also an entertaining conversationalist.

Naturally, there are many other people no longer with us who should be in this book. A few are mentioned rather frequently in the preceding "chapters," such as Bobby Jones, and Ky Laffoon. Because they are, and not as the result of any memory-jogging group sessions—each interview was conducted individually—they obviously had an impact on many of their contemporaries. Thus, it seems to me I should expand on a few of them to some extent. By doing so, perhaps I can further enrich this collection of thoughts and reminiscences, and at the same time give the material developed in the "chapters" a certain perspective.

Postscript

As noted, I came to know Jimmy Demaret rather well during our time together on the Shell show. In that period I frequently traveled to Houston to have Jimmy record new language I had written to fit the picture we had spliced together up in New York. The recording was done out on one of the two courses at Jimmy's club, the Champions. Then we repaired to the bar in the men's locker room, where Jimmy would set up the beers and hold forth, telling stories and listening to them—he was a good listener for a celebrity. Jimmy was in a congenial mood wherever he was, but was especially so around his locker room, which he expressly designed to be like a comfortable den in a private home. It was a setting that prompted personal reminiscence, such as the time he recalled his caddie days in Houston forty years earlier, and recited the name of every street he crossed as he walked the couple of miles to the course. He did it rapidly and unerringly, with relish and in a spirit of fun and warm nostalgia. He may have been the first three-time winner of the Masters, the winner of over twenty other events on the pro tour, and a man of means through his various business enterprises, but his caddie days were good times, too . . . just different from the good times that would follow.

Another time I asked Jimmy how and why he began wearing the colorful clothes that were his trademark. In this he had more than a little to do with changing golf's wardrobe. He said he had gotten his taste for color from his father, a house painter—"the Michelangelo of house painters." In the days before paints were pre-mixed in the factory or on vibrators in the local hardware store, Demaret's father experimented around the house and dabbed the walls with his various color concoctions.

When Demaret first got into golf he wore the same type of clothing as everyone else—brown or gray slacks, brown or black shoes, white dress shirt and tie, sometimes a fedora hat. The clothing was not only very conservative in color and style, the materials also tended to be heavy, and, in hot weather, locker rooms "kind of stank," as Jimmy put it. One day when he was in New York City he visited a shop where movie stars had their clothes made. There he saw bolts and bolts of lightweight materials in many bright shades. Jimmy asked if he

268

could get some golf shirts and slacks made up from such goods. He was told the stuff was for ladies' garments, but Jimmy said he didn't care, he'd like to play golf in it. Shirts and slacks were made up for him, and a sartorial revolution in golf got under way. Not only did golfers come to wear more sprightly-looking clothes, the clothing was also lighter and had more give, which made swinging a golf club a little easier.

It was often said of Demaret that if he had taken his golf game more seriously he would have won every major championship in the game at least once, and many more tour events. Jimmy's good friend George Fazio, and business partner and "little brother," Jackie Burke, alluded to that in their "chapters" of this book. What was Jimmy's word on such speculation? Would he have won more if he had not lived his life as he did—the many late-night parties, at which he often sang in a Texas vibrato tenor that was not at all bad, his love of practical jokes, his interest in clothes and fishing and hunting, and relative lack of interest in visiting the practice tee? Jimmy said if he had passed all that up he probably wouldn't have won anything. In a word, Demaret was true to his nature and let the chips fall as they might. All in all, they fell pretty well.

It seems like everyone in this book had at least one Ky Laffoon story. Some got into the narratives, but I felt I had to leave others out or Ky would have gotten in the way of the narrator's own story. Thanks be to Postscripts. Jim Ferrier told of Ky's celebrated—or is the cerebrated?—temper. "Ky was very tough on Ky," said Ferrier. "He wanted to hit every shot perfectly. We were playing the eighteenth hole at Royal Melbourne, and after he hit a beautiful drive right down the center he hit his approach with an iron kind of skinny—skulled it. It went low, bounced way short of the green, but ran up about ten feet from the hole. Everybody in the gallery applauded, but Ky was distraught. He'd hit a couple of other skinny ones earlier, so he takes the club and *bing*, breaks it. Right in the middle of the fairway. Nobody could figure out what was wrong."

In 1978 I spent some time with Ky Laffoon, researching an article I would write on him for *Golf* magazine. I had seen Ky once before, in the mid-1940s, when he was playing a practice round at Tam O'Shanter Country Club, outside of Chicago, where I was a caddie. When I heard Ky was on the premises I rushed out to see him, as I did when any pro stopped by at Tam, but the experience of Laffoon was different. I caught up with him on the fifteenth tee, where he sliced his drive over the fence onto Caldwell Avenue. For one thing, the cussing that followed was spectacular. It wasn't that the words were unique, it was his juxtaposing of them—I won't go into further detail on that. There was also the red-faced vehemence with which he cursed. Finally, there was the shaft of his driver, which he was bending so it looked every bit like a bow primed to fling an arrow. The thing is, when his tantrum was over, Ky's driver shaft remained in that bowed condition, which led me to believe it was permanently warped from repeated outbursts of anger. But that was not quite the case, as I learned when I visited with Ky some thirty years later in Springfield, Missouri.

At this point I would like to reprint, in amended form, the article I did write about Ky for *Golf* magazine's 1978 Yearbook issue. My thanks to *Golf* for permission to do so.

One day back in the 1930s Ben Hogan was having a nap in the back seat of a car being driven by Ky Laffoon. The two were on their way to the next stop on the pro tour. When Hogan awoke from his sleep he was startled. The car was moving at highway speed, but he saw no one at the wheel. What's more, sparks and smoke were rising up just outside his window. Ben thought the car was on fire and about to go out of control. What was going on?

It was this. Laffoon was bent low and, while holding the bottom of the steering wheel with his right hand, with his left hand was holding his wedge out the slightly open door of the auto. Ky was grinding down the flange of the club by running it along the concrete pavement as the car sped along. Route 66 may have been "America's Main Street," but it was also Ky Laffoon's workbench grinding stone.

That is a Laffoon anecdote Ky himself tells. It is one of many about an original, a character from an era we will never see again in American golf. That's American golf. To be sure, the gentlemen on the east coast who imported the game to this country and first organized it were Americans. Yet, in manners and social cast of mind they were more in the way of Old World genteel. Some of that has been retained—USGA officials wearing dark coats and ties in summer heat, the ambience of the Masters tournament, where mention of prize money is as crude as a tailor dunning his liege lord. A touch of that is not so awful, and far be it from me to say it is not American, but the game in this country might ever have been a sedate lawn party if not for the likes of a Ky Laffoon, who gave it a meatier texture and coloration marked by yeasty language, a flair for innovation, individual enterprise, and an urge for movement that defines another aspect of the "American character."

A fair share of Laffoon's America was moistened by tobacco juice. Ky chewed, and those who chew spit. For good luck Ky often immersed the head of his driver in chew goo before firing away, and after bad holes was apt to drench the bottom of the cup with it—after he removed his ball. (Sam Snead said Ky could hit the cup from twenty feet—"Pfft, right in there. From six to eight feet he never missed.") Laffoon recalled a yellow Cadillac he drove that was flecked like a bird's egg with residue of his plug. He told of being stopped once for speeding along Chicago's Outer Drive. The cop didn't write a ticket, after recognizing the famous golfer at the wheel, but he did ask Ky to refrain from spitting out the window of his moving vehicle. It seems another motorcycle policeman on the chase ran off the road when a flying gob caught him in the eye. Ky could exaggerate, a little.

In 1915, at age seven, Ky Laffoon moved with his family from a failed farm in Zine, Arkansas, to Miami, Oklahoma, where the agriculture did not improve. The Laffoons were "Arkies who became Okies," making their passage from one disaster to the next with all their possessions in a covered wagon pulled by a brace of mules. When he hit Oklahoma, Ky didn't know a cow chip from a chip shot, but not many years later he was a sweet-swinging golf professional matching shots with the finest golfers of his day.

"My first pro job," Ky recalled, "was at the Miami Golf Club. I was around nineteen. My assistant was my cousin, Leonard Ott. I paid Leonard a dollar a day, but he had more

271

money than I did at the end of the year. He got his meals and a room over the shop. Didn't cost him a penny to live.

"*The next year I got the pro job at a club in Joplin and played in my first tournament, in Hot Springs, Arkansas, 350 miles away. It took me two days to get there in an old Ford that couldn't do much going uphill. They had a driving contest before the tournament. Jimmy Thomson and Johnny Rogers, the longest hitters in the game, were there, but I stepped under the ropes and hit a baby-dimple ball 300 yards with a hickory-shafted driver and won me a thousand hamburgers.*"

A thousand hamburgers?

"*Hamburgers cost a nickel apiece in those days, and I always figured money by how many I could buy with what I had.*"

How ya gonna keep 'im down on the farm after he's seen Hot Springs and hit it past the stars? No way, as we say today. Hot Springs was young Ky's appetizer, California would be his main course. He borrowed $50 from his father and "lit out" for Hollywood to become a movie idol. With his noble nose, sturdy chin, and high cheekbones, Laffoon was a curiously handsome fellow, a bit in the way of a 1920s Marlon Brando with raven-black hair smacked flat with pomade and parted down the middle. Nevertheless, "I only got honorable mention from the studios. Truth is, I was too scared to be a movie star. I just wanted to get out and see what else was happening in the world. I played in a tournament out there—finished out of the money. The Depression was beginning to set in about then, so I got a job as a roughneck in the oil fields. Talk about work! After that I decided if I ever got a good job I'd take care of it."

When he made a reputation as a golfer, and some friends in Hollywood, Ky received some movie offers. But by that time golf was his game. A natural athlete with a strong, sinewy body, Laffoon did not rely only on given gifts of strength and coordination. He was a thoughtful student of the game— teacher-student. "I never learned from anyone," he said, "because there was nobody around who knew much. There were all kinds of theories. Some broke their hands right at the takeaway, Runyan dragged them back from the ball, and so

272

on. I made my own swing, with everything working in one piece. Didn't break my wrists until about waist-high.

"And I always believed in holding the club real firm. The biggest problem most golfers have is losing the club at the top of the swing. They have to regrip it coming down, and then the thing can go anywhere. That was Hogan's trouble as a young player. Another thing, I took the club straight back and brought it down on the inside. Had a loop in my swing, but when it was going good I had a nice six-foot hook."

In 1934 Laffoon had his best competitive year. He won the Park Hill Open, in Denver, with 266, the lowest seventy-two-hole score on a regulation course recorded up to that time. In the '34 Western Open, Ky shot all six rounds in the 60s (there was a thirty-six-hole playoff), even though he lost to Harry Cooper. He won the Eastern Open by eight shots with a 65–67 finish, had the lowest stroke-average for the year, and was second-leading money winner on the tour, behind Paul Runyan. As further evidence of how good a golf swing Ky made for himself, in 1934 he was runner-up in the Canadian Open and fourteen years later tied for second in that event. And in 1950, at age forty-one, Ky tied Skip Alexander for the Empire State Open, only to lose the playoff. Yes sir, Ky Laffoon could play some. He won twelve events on the pro tour, all told. But he never won big, most likely because of that aspect of his personality that has rendered him one of the more memorable "characters" in the annals of American golf. His temperament.

True, there was also the matter of poor timing. He came along when the nation was busted and the tour barely survived. "In 1934 they didn't have enough money to put on a tournament in Phoenix and had a pro-am instead," Ky recalled. "My partner was Barry Goldwater, a young lawyer at the time. Up in Indianapolis the sponsor ran off with the cash and none of us got paid until the PGA made it good some time later. That was quite a little Depression we had going. The times made you think. We were eating breakfast in L.A. one day and Byron Nelson wanted some potatoes like I had on my plate. When he found out they cost an extra quarter he decided to go without."

It was an era when Byron Nelson, after winning the U.S.

273

Open, could be signed for only $900 by the MacGregor Company to play its golf equipment. Therefore, in the middle of 1935, while at the top of his game, Laffoon took a job as head pro at the Northmoor Country Club, outside Chicago. "They gave me everything I wanted. I had two brothers to take care of, so I took it. Sometimes I was giving lessons ten hours a day."

Still, Ben Hogan, Byron Nelson, Sam Snead, and others scraped through the Hard Times and fulfilled their playing talent. Laffoon's failure in this, if failure it was, had deeper reasons. "I was leading a tournament in Alabama once," Ky recalled, "but withdrew to go hunting. There was some good shooting down there. Hogan stuck it out, and won the thing."

Another time Hogan and Ky went to a movie, Of Mice and Men, *John Steinbeck's tale of itinerant farmhands during the Depression. One of them, a demented giant who caressed small animals to death, intrigued Laffoon. He was reminded of being a child left alone on the farm in Arkansas, and passing the time sticking chickens head-first on a picket fence and laughing himself into a heap watching the fowls' "bums" do frantic shimmies.*

Hogan would have none of Steinbeck. "He walked out after a short while," Ky recalled. "Waited in the lobby for two hours. He said he couldn't stand all that." In short, Ben Hogan allowed no substantive distractions from his legendary concentration on golfing excellence, while Ky Laffoon opted to "see what else was happening in the world."

Regrets? Ky answered. "Hogan went fishing and hunting maybe once each in his life. Now he has nothing to do but go to the factory, and hit golf balls over at his club. Me and my cousin visited Ben a couple of years ago, and he said he couldn't understand what we did with our time. Well, hell, there's a million things to do. I hunt, fish, drink, eat, play golf, play cards, got three dogs and a lot of friends to talk to. But you've got to get your interests when you're young, so when you get to be sixty-five you know what to do with your time."

Laffoon was a Rabelaisian rouser. "I got terrible cramps in Las Vegas once. The doctor said I shouldn't eat so much. I said I was a golfer and needed food for energy. He said if I didn't eat so much I wouldn't need so much energy. I didn't think the man was much of a doctor."

Almost from the moment he hit the pro circuit Laffoon was taken to be at least part Cherokee Indian. He said there isn't a drop of "injun" in him. "I was playing up in Boston one summer and was real red from the sun. 'Laffoon' sounds Indian and, what with the color of my skin at the time and being from Oklahoma and having high cheekbones and going by the name of Ky, my middle name—my first name is George, which don't sound like much—some sportswriter asked me if I was an Indian. I figured that would make a good story and I said, 'Sure.' He wrote it up, Porky Oliver started calling me Chief, and it stuck."

So the Oklahoma farm boy wanted some fun along the way. Fair enough. But the way was through a game that can swipe the smile from a tank full of laughing gas. Here was where Ky Laffoon lost it, most of all. Ky was a stormer, a man of Vesuvian rages when the game didn't go well. Such was his reputation for temper that the story of his grinding his wedge on Route 66 was transformed over the years into one of golf's grand old chestnuts—the one about having tied his putter to the rear bumper of his car and dragging it 1,000 miles across the Southwestern desert to make the blade pay for having betrayed him.

For a time Laffoon used a driver with a shaft curved like a bow, a weird-looking instrument some believed was a carefully calculated innovation in club design. It was not that calculated. "Hogan gave me the club in St. Paul," Laffoon explained, "but it had a hook face. We had some pretty poor clubs to play with in my time. Anyway, I got to hooking the ball too much with the club and got burned up and banged that driver hard a few times. That bowed the shaft, but straightened the face just right. I beat the hook right out of it, and played some pretty good golf with it until it finally snapped.

"Yeah, I was always a hothead. Guess it ran in the family, because my brother Bill was always walking out on me, getting mad at me for getting mad at golf. One time he was caddying for me in California and at the sixteenth hole he had

275

enough—dropped the bag and walked in. Walter Hagen carried my bag for one hole, and Dick Arlen, the movie actor, carried it the other.

"That driving contest I told you about in Hot Springs? In the tournament, the South Central Open, I threw a club up in a tree and it stuck. I threw two more up there to get it down, and they all stayed up there. Then it rained and the three shafts got warped something awful.

"But mostly it was putting, especially on those U.S. Open greens. They were the only real fast ones we played on all year, and I couldn't get used to them. Scared me to hell and gone. What got me was, how can a twenty-one-year old who can see the line miss an eight-foot putt? It's unnatural. I had a horror of eight-foot putts. I must've spent $50,000 batting the ball around the cup after missing short ones. You know, backhanding them. Walter Hagen said to me, 'Ky, I can't understand anybody taking so much time on an eight-foot putt, missing it, then back-handing it to miss even more.'

"Yeah, I could get hot. But I wasn't the only one. There was Ivan Gantz. And Lefty Stackhouse. I remember Lefty sitting cross-legged in front of a fire he had going with every wooden-shafted club in his bag. He turned them all into kindling. The guy who loaned him the sticks was standing over Lefty and chewing him out like you never heard before.

"I'll tell you, though, we could afford to be angry and lose our temper. It didn't cost enough to stay cool. If we played for a thousand instead of a hundred, we wouldn't have gotten so hot. Same with walking off yardages, the way they do now. We didn't because it wasn't worth the effort. When you play for peanuts, you got to salvage something for your time. Pride was another thing. I withdrew from a Western Open once, because they put the players' parking lot two holes from the clubhouse. That was a long walk. It made you feel like a bum. So I said to hell with it."

I'm giving you Ky Laffoon at some length because I don't think he should be missed and, as far I know, he has never been profiled elsewhere. Besides, while his behavior was in some respects, uh, unusual, in others he was quite representative of the professional golfers of his generation. For example, after our 1978 interview in Springfield we played nine holes of golf. Ky gave me some clubs to use from the trunk of his car, which reminded me of the famous Fibber McGee closet we had heard every week on the radio. If Ky's car could have been tipped on end, there would have been a great racket from everything falling out. Indeed, the whole car was something like a department store on wheels. The point is, the golf pros of Ky Laffoon's era were vagabonds, antsy movers wedded to their automobiles, in which they probably spent more time than they did on golf courses. Their cars were their homes away from home. It is difficult to break old habits, as Ky's car reflected. Here he was, seventy-one years old and living right there in Springfield, yet he had a metal rack across the back seat of his Cadillac that was crammed end to end with sport coats, slacks, and shirts. Why? "You never know when you might get into a scrap with your little lady." The trunk contained, among many, many things, four sets of golf clubs and two golf bags, numerous pairs of golf and street shoes—and some old socks—two handguns and a shotgun along with shells ("You never know when you might see some partridge along the road"), two bottles of scotch whisky, a vibrator ("Does wonders for your back"), heating cartridges for cold-weather warmers, a spotlight ("You plug it in the cigarette lighter to catch addresses at night"), a gross of chewing-tobacco packets, cans of sardines and a jar of peanut butter ("In case you get hungry. You never know"). I never got to the bottom of the trunk—we had to play golf.

For the nine holes Ky shot a 32—four under par—on a pretty fair layout. It was better than Ky had been playing. He no longer had the loose, fluid swing of his youth, if only because he had gained a lot of weight over the years and most of it seemed to have settled in his chest and shoulders—he was very thick through there. When I congratulated him on his play, he said, with a broad and happy smile, "Sure wanted to put a good round on you, Chief, for the press."

Which brings up another characteristic of the pros from Laffoon's time in the sun—their eye, ear, nose, and throat for making publicity, something for which the modern-day pro has little interest or, perhaps, flair. Gene Sarazen was another one who was always thinking of ways to get a mention in the

277

papers. They didn't do it only with their clubs. Ky letting the Indian-heritage story pass is one example. Sam Snead playing the country bumpkin is another. Sarazen once cried out for an eight-inch-diameter golf hole rather than the 4¼-inch hole that's been used forever. It was tried once in the '30s, in a tournament in Florida. The poor putters made a few more putts, but so did the good putters. It was a wash, artistically, but the idea caught the headlines.

The publicity-seeking of a Laffoon or Sarazen or Snead was essentially self-serving—Gene was putting badly, Ky figured if he got a lot of "print" he could get a good job—but that's the way of golfers, who are in a lonely game. In any case, the individual publicity-seeking also gave the game notice, which was important in the 1920s and 1930s, when golf was far from being a household name in Sportsworld.

Laffoon, by the way, took his own life a couple of years ago while suffering from cancer. He was a very strong and body-proud man. He said that when he was young he could rip a full deck of cards in half, cellophane and all, and that Tommy Armour would see him coming and bet anyone $50 that the next man in the room could rip the deck. "Yeah, but he never shared his winnings with me," said Ky. Ky Laffoon could live without someone else's money, but not with a body that was no longer his.

When I was editor-in-chief of *Golf* magazine from 1970 to 1972, I scheduled a superb, full-size Bernie Fuchs sketch of Bobby Jones for the cover of an issue featuring the Masters tournament. I was told by the circulation experts that whenever Jones was on the cover, newstand sales dropped. As a student of the game of golf, I was surprised to hear this. Jones was . . . gee, Bobby Jones, one of the greatest golfers of all time. I did have Jones on that cover, and the experts were right—the issue did not sell very well. I can't explain that, and would only suggest that Jones' fate in this respect may have been the result of the "What have you done lately?" syndrome. Then again, the issue may have sold poorly for any number of other reasons. In any case, it is very clear through the "chapters" of this book that Bobby Jones has not been forgotten by those of his era.

Postscript

The fondness with which Jones is remembered is interesting in that most of these people are professionals, and golf pros tend to be a chauvinistic lot. Those who don't make their living from the game—amateurs—are kept at a distance. What's more, this generation of professionals was more than a little class-conscious, since almost all of them came from a working-class background and were in a game largely dominated by a monied elite which was for the most part their employer. The distance they maintained between themselves and the amateur golfer who was a *country-club member* was not so much a matter of pride, but of deference. Yet, while Bobby Jones was of the country-club member set, there seemed to be an easygoing rapport between him and the professionals. So he must have had something special about him.

Naturally, the pros had to appreciate totally Jones' playing ability—any professional worth the title must acknowledge and accept great golf, even when it's played by an amateur. But Jones also appreciated the good golf of others. He understood how difficult it is to play the game consistently well, how hard one must work to get to a high level of performance, and he projected that understanding. It was a premise behind his Masters tournament, which Jones might have created only for amateurs. He wanted to give the best players a place to prove themselves, and to show themselves off.

In other, perhaps more practical, ways Jones helped those who had some talent or the promise of it. He wrote letters of recommendation for pros seeking jobs, or passed a good word when and where it counted about someone in need. He was a patron, but not in a patronizing way. He didn't help in the manner of a nabob throwing coins to the underlings. Jones loved a ripe joke, knew all the cuss words and used them, liked his "corn." In short, even though he was a "member," he was still one of the boys.

As I suggested in the Foreword, and as we have seen, the road to the "dance floor" was in good part carved through a forest of golf technique. Golfers have always been deeply immersed in method. It is in the nature of the golf swing, which is a rather complex series of related physical movements full of angles and planes and arcs. At least, that's the way most golf-

279

ers see it and work on it—as if they were erecting a bridge, constructing a building, doing custom carpentry. Indeed, golf seems to attract people with an engineering mentality, those who like to figure out how—and have a knack for making— things work. Gene Sarazen's father was a carpenter, and Gene worked at that trade for a time. Harry Cooper's father built golf courses without any formal training in the engineering aspects of such work. Bill Mehlhorn learned masonry and house-building with his father, a craftsman in those trades; Bill's brother was an engineer. Betsy Rawls' father was an engineer, and she took a college degree in physics.

The study of the golf swing by the people in this book may have been a bit more intense because of some significant changes in golf equipment in their era, particularly the coming of the steel shaft. Everyone was scratching around for a tip, a hint, a clue to the secret of the swing. A few drew from their experience in baseball, finding the swing of the bat comparable to golf. When the pros traveled the tournament circuit they picked each other's brains for ideas. There were also two men who were exclusively golf teachers that seem to have had a strong impact on swing theory. They were Ernest Jones and Alex Morrison, about whom Leo Fraser and Henry Picard were especially eloquent.

Just how original Jones and Morrison were in their teaching is difficult to say. Anyone who has studied golf instruction at all deeply conceives eventually that everything was thought up within five minutes after the game was invented, and that all that has followed is but an echo. In any case, Jones and Morrison seemed original at the time. Intelligent men, with self-assured, forceful personalities, they built up quite a large following of student/devotees.

When I was at *Golf* magazine, I ran a series on the Ernest Jones system, written by Betty Hicks, one of Jones' most successful disciples. By then, 1970–71, Jones was inactive (he died in 1972) and otherwise out of fashion. But after the series came out, the pro at Merion Golf Club, Bill Kittleman, told me he had to take a refresher course on the Ernest Jones "Swing the Clubhead" method. Older members of Merion, who were taught there by Fred Austin, Jones' son-in-law, were reinspired.

Jones and Morrison were provocative in their heyday.

280

Postscript

Their instruction books sold well—Morrison's in particular—and are collectors' items today. They were also very busy on the lesson tee. At the same time, they were not very popular among the PGA professionals as a group. Jones, because his system was "too simple," according to Fred Austin. And "Ernest also was taking a lot of pupils away from other professionals."

Morrison's lack of favor among the PGA pros was probably due, in part, to the fact that he was never a member of the PGA. Nor was he a very accomplished player, although his brother Fred was one of the best in the first two decades of this century. Alex never held a regular club-pro job. He did most of his teaching in a studio in midtown Manhattan. Alex, who at this writing is living in Riverside, California, also traveled the vaudeville circuit for many years as a "golf act." He gave lectures on the swing, and demonstrated it by hitting cotton balls into the audience. Alex didn't do a tap dance and tell jokes in between backswings and downswings. I met Alex and took a lesson from him. He is a serious man. A professional comedian who worked with him broke up the golf stuff with a pratfall-and-gag routine.

Of the two, a golf-technique historian/detective would probably find that Alex Morrison's ideas, more that Jones', have trickled down to the current generation of golfers. In fact, they have even influenced the current "greatest golfer in the world." Consider. At this very moment there is a renascence in golf teaching of the "flat" swing-plane—or what Alex Morrison/Henry Picard would call simply the "correct" plane. Among others, Jack Nicklaus has made a basic change in his swing to approximate a "flatter" plane, and has written a whole book on it. Now, Jack's lifelong teacher has been Jack Grout, who was an assistant to, and a very good friend of, Henry Picard. Grout's teaching was influenced by Picard, who is a very persuasive man and also had the playing record to support his views. Thus, what Alex Morrison was teaching in the 1920s and '30s has touched Jack Nicklaus sixty years later. Indeed, Jack told me that when he first started out he learned the Morrison system.

Golf's historical continuity was delineated in a different way during my conversation with Gene Sarazen. Gene was recalling U.S. Opens he had lost because of one bad hole. One of them was at Winged Foot in 1929. On television Gene watched the 1984 Open being played at Winged Foot, and at one point his memory was jogged—sharply. "I was watching Greg Norman, and on that par-five where he hooked it badly into the trees, on the front nine? I was in the exact same spot in '29. I took a seven, and he got a four on it. Yeah, that's just where I was."

Every golfer makes his own way to the "dance floor," but at one time or another, even a half-century later, some of that path will be shared with others.

A.B

AL BARKOW is editor in chief of *Golf Illustrated* magazine. In the past twenty-five years he has written hundreds of articles covering all aspects of golf, was chief writer on the television series, "Shell's Wonderful World of Golf," and editor of *Golf* magazine. His books include, *Golf's Golden Grind, the History of the Tour,* and golf instruction written in collaboration with Billy Casper, Ken Venturi, and George Low. While attending Western Illinois University, Barkow played on the golf team that won a national small college (NAIA) championship. He has also qualified to play in a United States Amateur Championship. He lives in Montclair, New Jersey.